THE LIFE OF
DOROTHEA VON MONTAU,
A FOURTEENTH-CENTURY RECLUSE

Dorotheenbild von Jakob von Karweysze
(1492)

The oldest known depiction of Dorothea von Montau
a woodcut of Jacop Karweysze's 1492 print
Des Leben der zeligen frawen Dorothee
clewsenerynne yn der thumkyrchen czu Marienwerdir
des landes czu Prewszen

Courtesy of Paul Nieborowski's *Die Selige Dorothea von Preußen*
Breslau: Ostdeutsche Verlagsanstalt, 1933

THE LIFE OF
DOROTHEA VON MONTAU,
A FOURTEENTH-CENTURY RECLUSE

Johannes von Marienwerder

Translated by
Ute Stargardt

Studies in Women and Religion
Volume 39

The Edwin Mellen Press
Lewiston•Queenston•Lampeter

Library of Congress Cataloging-in-Publication Data

ISBN 0-7734-8568-6 (hard)

This is volume 39 in the continuing series
Studies in Women and Religion
Volume 39   ISBN 0-7734-8568-6
SWR Series ISBN 0-88946-549-5

A CIP catalog record for this book is available from the British Library.

The Edwin Mellen Press   The Edwin Mellen Press
        Box 450   Box 67
Lewiston, New York   Queenston, Ontario
    USA 14092-0450   CANADA L0S 1L0

The Edwin Mellen Press, Ltd.
Lampeter, Ceredigion, Wales
UNITED KINGDOM SA48 8LT

Printed in the United States of America

For Erna, Karin, Hertha, and Marie

Contents

Acknowledgments

I thank the Provost and the Faculty Personnel Committee of Alma College for numerous travel grants that helped finance my research on Dorothea von Montau in Berlin, Einsiedeln, Gdansk, Kwydzyn, Münster, and Vienna. Donna Adams, Terri Powers, and Barb Tripp were most helpful in preparing this manuscript. My special thanks go to the Black Franciscans of Kwydzyn and Canon Wojciech Kruk who allowed me to spend many hours in Marienwerder Cathedral and patiently answered my questions.

Introduction

During the last two decades, largely due to feminist scholarship, the literature of medieval feminine spirituality has attracted much critical attention. Nevertheless, a lot of work remains to be done in studying the many texts written by or about medieval holy women. Scholars like Elizabeth Alvida Petroff have commented on the need for translations and editions of primary sources to facilitate such efforts and familiarize larger audiences with the spiritual histories now accessible only to a small number of specialists.

One medieval holy woman who remains little known even among medieval scholars is Dorothea von Montau (1347-1394), even though the many *vitae* her confessor, the theologian and Dominican canon Johannes von Marienwerder (1343-1417), composed in service of her canonization as Prussia's first native saint make her one of the most meticulously documented women saints of the later Middle Ages.[1] Historian Richard Kieckhefer, who in 1984 introduced Dorothea to American readers in *Unquiet Souls*, proposes "a series of detailed studies of individual saints and small groups of saints ... in their particular context" to link their spirituality to their specific historical settings (195). This translation of Johannes von Marienwerder's last *vita* on Dorothea and the only one written in the vernacular is meant to help address concerns such as his and Petroff's.

---

[1] Richard Stachnik's "Zum Schrifttum über die heilige Dorothea von Montau," *Dorothea von Montau: eine preußische Heilige des 14. Jahrhunderts*, eds. Richard Stachnik & Anneliese Triller (Münster: Selbstverlag des Historischen Vereins für Ermland, 1976) 59-105 provides a bibliography of primary and secondary sources.

The Text

Johannes' middle high German *vita* is essentially a translation, amalgamation, and summary of earlier Latin works he had composed after Dorothea's death for a papal commission conducting a canonization inquiry.[2] Completed by 1404-05, its appearance coincided with the first of two such inquiries then in session in Marienwerder (Kwydzyn). Ostensibly composed as an *Erbauungsbuch* for the Teutonic Knights and Prussia's lay populace, its primary purpose was to galvanize popular support for Dorothea's canonization. To acquaint the laity with her saintliness, chapters of the work furnished mealtime readings for the Teutonic Knights, and on instruction of the Prussian bishops, copies were being distributed to parish priests throughout Prussia for use in sermons and other religious instruction of lay people. Chapter I invites readers and listeners to "lift your eyes and incline your ears" to hitherto unknown details of the life and piety of a woman whom many of them must have remembered from the time she lived among them. Judging by the number of witnesses who came forward to testify to Dorothea's holiness--more than 260 gave sworn depositions about her sanctity and miracles--Johannes' effort to engage public support was a resounding success.

In spite of extremely favorable prospects for a speedy, positive end to the proceedings, political developments prevented Dorothea's canonization at that time. The second inquiry held at the end of the fifteenth century in Rome ended in failure as well, again the result of political events.[3] But Johannes' vernacular

---

[2] Books I, II, and III of *Leben* come from the *Vita Dorotheae Montoviensis Magistri Johannis Marienwerder* and the *Vita venerabilis dominae Dorotheae*, which describes Dorothea's life in 237 chapters within the seven allegorical pictures of the Apocalypse. Book IV of *Leben* consists of brief excerpts from the *Septililium venerabilis dominae Dorotheae Montoviensis*, which groups Dorothea's visions around the fifty most important holy days of the Church calendar. For publication information on these sources, see note 27.

[3] As Donald Weinstein and Rudolph Bell point out, only eight canonizations took place in the fourteenth century and only that of Saint Birgitta of Sweden during the Schism (*Saints and Society* 69). Because, as he put it, "at this time of strife absolute clarity about a spirit to be raised to glory in the Church Triumphant cannot be established in the Roman *curia*," Pope Boniface IX made the unusual decision for Dorothea's canonization inquiry to be conducted in Marienwerder rather than

vita played an important part in these efforts, too. To engage lay support once more, the goldsmith Jacop Karweysze, either at the behest of the Teutonic Knights or on his own initiative, in 1492 printed Johannes' work under the title *Des Leben der zeligen frawen Dorothee clewsenerynne yn der thumkyrchen czu Marienwerdir des landes czu Prewszen* as the first book to be printed in Prussia.[4] When the Prussian historian Max Toeppen published this *vita* in 1863 in *Scriptores rerum Prussicarum*, only two texts had survived the upheavals of the intervening centuries. One, entitled *Leben der seligen vrouwen Dorothee,* is a heavily mutilated vellum manuscript consisting of thirty-eight leaves written in an early fifteenth-century hand. The second is the single surviving copy of Jacop Karweysze's print. Toeppen based his edition on the manuscript, but because only slightly more than fifty percent of Johannes' original text survive in the MS, he substituted the missing parts from the print and published it under Jacop Karweysze's title. In 1893 this work became accessible to contemporary readers when Dominikus Korioth translated it into modern German. The 1965 Minerva Publishers reprint of Toeppen's edition provides the text for this translation.

---

in Rome and by Prussian eccliastics rather than members of the college of cardinals. This choice virtually assured a positive outcome. But by the time the records reached Rome Pope Boniface was dead and his successor embroiled in the politics of the Schism. By 1410, finally, the Teutonic Knights in Prussia were too impoverished to pursue Dorothea's cause. Their decisive defeat at the battle of Tannenberg (Grunwald) that year had deprived them of much of their territory and had reduced them to vassals of the Polish crown. When in 1486 their High Master Martin Truchsess von Wetzhausen succeeded in having the inquiry reopened in Rome, civil wars in Italy involving Pope Alexander VI interfered. All efforts to secure Dorothea's canonization ceased in 1525 when Albrecht von Hohenzollern, the last High Master of the Teutonic Knights, embraced Lutheranism, dissolved the Prussian branch of the Order, and ruled Prussia as a personal fief bestowed on him by the Polish king.

For a detailed discussion of the political issues attending Dorothea's canonization, consult my article "The Political and Social Backgrounds of the Canonization of Dorothea von Montau."

[4] "printed and completed," as its codicil states, "in the town of Marienburg (Malbork) through me, Jacop Karweysze, goldsmith, Tuesday after St. Gregory's [March 12] in the year of Our Lord MCCCC and CXII, praise be to God." Max Toeppen points to the error in the number CXII, which should read XCII.

The Translation

Like many late-medieval literary works, Johannes' vernacular, popularized *apologia* of Dorothea's spirituality reflects fascinating transitions. It looks backward and forward simultaneously: backward to the idealized *formulae* of the traditional saint's life, forward to the realism of a modern-day autobiography replete with ghostwriter; backward to a passive listening audience, forward to an active reading one; backward to orthodox Catholic spirituality and medieval mystical traditions, forward to a highly individualized lay spirituality that would culminate in the Reformation. Jacop Karweysze's print mirrors yet another transition: the shift from individually-produced, handwritten manuscripts for private patrons to mass-produced commercial products readily available in the market place.

The transitional nature of the work is evident in its "translated" nature as well. An attempt at producing an important Church document in vernacular prose, it betrays its Latin roots in diction, sentence structure, and style at every turn, testifying to its author's and the Church's lack of experience in handling the vernacular as an effective medium of spiritual communication with the laity. To preserve this flavor of *Leben*, I have maintained Johannes' sentence structure whenever possible. Only when the sheer abundance of clauses, squinting modifiers, and unclear or missing pronoun references obliterate clarity of meaning did I restructure his sentences. I took slightly more liberties with his phrasing because his fondness for repetitious, formulaic expressions makes for tedious reading of a text of *Leben*'s scope. Even so, I did preserve his language whenever possible to convey a sense of the pedestrian nature of his style, which often provides stark contrast to the exciting events he relates. To aid ease of reading, I divided texts of lengthy chapters into paragraphs. Capitalization and punctuation conform to modern American usage.

The eastern European territories ruled by the Teutonic Knights during the Middle Ages have changed hands numerous times in subsequent centuries, mainly between Poland and Germany. Consequently, placenames such as *Gdansk* for the city of Danzig and *Vistula* for the river Weichsel familiar to English readers in their Polish forms will be given in Polish only. On the other hand, place names not readily translatable into English and unfamiliar to modern readers at first use in the text and in the index will be stated in their form then in use, usually German, followed by present usages in parentheses. There is no consistency as yet in the translation of medieval personal names into English. Because the German preposition *von*, which indicates place of origin attached to a person's Christian name, and Christian names like Dorothea, Johannes, or Nikolaus cause English speakers little difficulty in terms of recognition and pronunciation, German names will maintain their present-day German form, *Dorothea von Montau, Johannes von Marienwerder, Nikolaus von Hohenstein*, etc. The dates of saints' days mentioned in the text are provided in brackets. Translations of primary and secondary sources, unless otherwise indicated, are my own.

Dorothea von Montau: Life and Spiritual Career

Dorothea von Montau, the self-proclaimed patroness of Prussia, the Teutonic Knights, and the town and cathedral of Marienwerder, was born in the Prussian village of Montau (Montowy) in 1347. The seventh of nine children born to the prosperous peasants Agatha and Wilhelm Swarze, Dorothea was baptized within a week of her birth, on February 6, the feast day of her namesake and patron Saint Dorothy of Cappadocia.[5] Her father had emigrated to Prussia from the Low Countries, probably because of generous settlement conditions the Teutonic Knights offered to farmers experienced in draining swamps and marshes, building dams and dikes, and cultivating farmland gained through such agricultural

---

[5] Franz Hipler, "Christliche Lehre und Erziehung in Ermland und im preußischen Ordenstaate während des Mittelalters," dates Dorothea's birth between January 30 and February 6 because the peace treaty of 1249 between the Teutonic Knights and the newly-christianized indigenous population stipulated infant baptism within a week of birth, a rule all inhabitants of Prussia were obliged to observe.

innovations in their newly-conquered territories. Apparently, he was one of the original citizens of this new village in the Vistula delta established by Ludolf König (High Master of the Teutonic Knights 1341-47) as part of the Order's efforts to harness the power of this vitally important waterway (Rühle 7).[6]

Like Saint Birgitta of Sweden, one of her revered models, Dorothea initiated her spiritual career at age seven in response to an epiphany. Birgitta's initiation occurred under felicitous circumstances--she saw a lady in shining garments offering her a crown and then placing it on her head so forcefully that "she distinctly felt...[its] ring on her brow" (Jorgensen 32). Dorothea's occurred under the painful circumstances that were to characterize so much of her spiritual life. Her entire body had been scalded by boiling water. The burns were so severe and the pain so excruciating that her mother nursed her in a cradle. While the child was thus incapacitated, Jesus appeared to her, promising to make her a "new person." No sooner had she recovered than she initiated spiritual exercises under her mother's supervision, starting out with simple genuflections. Not content with those, she soon took up more rigorous devotions, which she practiced at night to keep them hidden from her family. Such self-castigations had been popularized by the Franciscans in imitation of Christ's sufferings. When they became incorporated into the observance of the stations of the cross, they became widely practiced by devout lay people.

All the *vitae* provide detailed descriptions of the excruciating injuries God and Dorothea herself inflicted on her body. But according to the vernacular account, Dorothea's most cruel trials grew out of her marriage at age seventeen to Adalbert, a Gdansk weaponsmith more than twice her age. It is difficult to see how her family could have remained unaware of her strenuous spiritual exercises, bloody self-castigations, and inordinate hunger for the body of Christ in the

---

[6] Hartmut Boockmann's *Der Deutsche Orden* (München: Beck, 1989), pp. 15-37 provides a brief but concise description of the Order's settlement strategies, focusing on the importance of the Vistula in its success in conquering Prussia. After gaining a foothold and establishing Thorn (Thorun), the Order was able to extend its hegemony through a series of forts located along the shores of the Vistula and its tributaries.

sacrament, all of which had already manifested themselves when she was a mere child. At her canonization inquiry, Johannes Reymann, Johannes' fellow canon and Dorothea's alternate confessor, elaborated on the conflicts Dorothea's zeal had caused even with her own mother, herself a devout woman who prayed for hours daily until her fingers were permanently deformed "by the beads of her paternoster string."[7] Instead, her relatives must have chosen to ignore Dorothea's penchant for religious rather than domestic life in expectation of enhancing family fortune and status. So, as Johannes puts it, "her oldest brother espoused her to an honorable, successful artisan, wealthy according to his station in life," and Dorothea, though she perceived marriage as a serious impediment to the life she craved, nevertheless complied, "an obedient servant of her superiors."[8]

But even if Dorothea had defied her family's decision or her relatives had been receptive to her own wishes, her opportunities for fulfilling her spiritual needs still would have been quite limited. During their rule, the Teutonic Knights suppressed the establishment of convents by papal sanction to prevent rival institutions from challenging their own spiritual overlordship in Prussia. Apart from the few Cistercian houses that had buttressed the Knights' initial colonization efforts in the twelfth century, there existed just a handful of other, mainly Benedictine houses. Moreover, even if convents had been available to accommodate Dorothea's particular needs, as the seventh child of a peasant, though wealthy, she probably still could not command a dowry sizeable enough to purchase the "freedom" of convent life. If she did, she still would not have profited from the spiritual guidance of the Dominicans so influential on late-

---

[7] What studies like Rudolph Bell's *Holy Anorexia* observe about divinely or self-inflicted injury or illness, that a woman's saintliness is validated by her heroic ability to put up with illness attributable to her own "austerities," applies fully to Dorothea. Paul Nieborowski's *Die Selige Dorothea von Preußen* prints all 260 witness testimonies.

[8] Adalbert's house at Langgasse 64 in the New Town has been restored after falling victim to the conflagration that devastated all but one of the houses in the medieval section of Gdansk during the Russian liberation at the end of World War II. Its location, size, and appearance signal the prestige a peasant girl's marriage to such a substantial citizen of an important Hanseatic town would bring to her family.

medieval feminine spirituality and so supportive of visionaries like Dorothea. In Prussia the Order's presence was so severely restricted that Dorothea, as Kieckhefer observes, never did come under its sway to the extent she might have had she lived elsewhere in German-speaking areas (33).[9] Because her prosperous, conservative relatives looked askance at the poor and frequently berated Dorothea's largesse in supporting vagrants, her joining such "extremist" groups as the Beguines or the flagellants was out of the question.[10]

Saint Birgitta's new order of Saint Savior might have provided an acceptable compromise, given the Swedish saint's veneration in Prussia since 1373 when her remains on their way from Rome to Vadstena were deposited at St. Mary's church in Gdansk during the winter and Winrich von Kniprode, High Master of the Teutonic Knights, paid homage to them and hosted Birgitta's daughter Catherine and son Birger at the Order's headquarter in Marienburg. But membership in this religious community also eluded Dorothea all her life. When Birgitta secured papal confirmation in 1370, Dorothea was already married. In 1392, when the first Birgittine nuns arrived from the Order's mother house of Vadstena to negotiate the foundation of a daughter house in Gdansk, Dorothea

---

[9] One of the few Dominican houses was Marienwerder cathedral, which also served the Order of the Teutonic Knights as their main church in Prussia. Many of the tensions and rivalries surrounding Dorothea's enclosure stem from this peculiar situation of the partially convergent, partially competing interests of the two organizations. When Johannes became Dorothea's confessor, she did at last link up with Dominican spirituality and is, in fact, always depicted in a Dominican habit sometimes adorned with the cross of the Teutonic Knights. However, Johannes served as her confessor only during the last three years of her life. For a discussion of Dorothea's familiarity with fourteenth-century Dominican and Beguine spirituality, see my article "The Beguines of Belgium, the Dominican Nuns of Germany, and Margery Kempe."

[10] Dorothea's affinity with Beguine spirituality dates to her and Adalbert's first journey to Finsterwald (Einsiedeln), Switzerland, in 1384. During their extended stay there (1385-1387), the couple decided to separate, he to return to Prussia, she to remain. She apparently had decided on living as a mendicant Beguine, for as they were waiting for a priest to draw up a letter of separation, Dorothea practiced their chant "Bread for the sake of Our Lord."

According to the depositions of witnesses at her canonization inquiry of 1404-05, Dorothea enjoyed a considerable reputation of sanctity among Beguines. Several appeared as witnesses on her behalf, claiming miraculous cures and in one instance release from "exorbitant fleshly desires" that caused her to sin "without discernment with anyone who propositioned her" (Series IV, Witness # 25).

had left the city and was awaiting official decision concerning her enclosure as Prussia's first anchoress.[11] By the time Konrad von Jungingen, High Master of the Teutonic Knights, chartered the convent in July of 1394, Dorothea had died after having spent the last year of her life enclosed in a cell at Marienwerder cathedral.[12]

***

In her discussion of characteristics particular to medieval feminine spirituality, Barbara Newman identifies marriage as purgatory on Earth as prominent in the *vitae* of holy women and Dorothea as the epitome of what she calls "the Griselda paradigm" in bearing her misfortune "with patience enough to win the martyr's crown in heaven" (115). Unlike her adored models Saint Birgitta and Saint Elisabeth of Hungary, Dorothea did not enjoy an affectionate, harmonious conjugal life. Instead, she "donned the shield of patience" to endure Adalbert's derision, scorn, and beatings in response to her indifferent, ineffective performance as wife, mother, and nurse. The German *vita* stresses her unquestioning obedience to all male authority figures as the most noteworthy

---

[11] Strictly speaking, Dorothea was not Prussia's first anchoress. That distinction belongs to Jutta von Sangershausen (d. 1260), mother of Anno von Sangershausen (High Master of the Teutonic Knights 1256-73), who lived as a recluse in the church of Kulmsee (Chelmza). But the hermetic life so popular in southwestern Germany and Switzerland never caught on in Prussia. As a result, during the hundred and thirty-three years that separate Jutta's enclosure from Dorothea's, this custom passed so thoroughly from popular consciousness that even Dorothea's mother was scandalized at her daughter's decision: "Oh, poor woman! Are you so burdened with sins that you can't gain forgiveness in the world and procure your livelihood except through priests and canons?" (Nieborowski quoting Johannes' *Vita Latina* 171). Portraits and panel paintings dating from the Counter Reformation, on the other hand, sometimes commemorate the two of them together in the company of Saint Rosalie [July 15], a popular twelfth-century Sicilian recluse.

[12] Dorothea chose May 2 [1393] as the day of her enclosure because on that day the Teutonic Knights commemorated the translation of the remains of St. Elisabeth of Hungary, a major benefactress of their Order.

According to Stachnik's "Die Klosterchronik von St. Brigitten in Danzig," the first nuns took their vows on December 8, 1396. But the daughter house of Marienbrunn could not actually start operating until the arrival of the monks on March 5, 1400. The Order of St. Savior survives in Gdansk to this day. In the 1970s and '80s St. Brigitta's Church in Gdansk provided the spiritual center for the Solidarity movement, a fact commemorated by plaques and monuments throughout the building.

manifestation of her patience. Not only did she accept her brother's authority in arranging a marriage advantageous to the family: married to Adalbert, she patiently tried to serve two husbands at once by rendering "unto Caesar what is his due and unto God what is due him. Thus she became a mother in the flesh, but in spirit she remained a virgin."

At the same time she was also the obedient daughter of her Gdansk confessor Nikolaus von Hohenstein, an allegiance she transferred to Johannes von Marienwerder and Johannes Reymann when she left Gdansk in 1391 to seek enclosure at Marienwerder cathedral. At God's behest she placed herself into their "authority" to be with them as though she "belonged" to them and "to consider them grander than yourself and yourself ... unfit to have contact with them." Dorothea's abject obedience to them, "I insist on not having a will of my own but will be ruled by yours," is probably surpassed only by Saint Elisabeth's to her confessor Conrad von Marburg but not surprising in view of God's admonitions. Mindful of his promise that "not only virgins and all those living chastely enter heaven but also all those married people who through proper faith and good works earn God's grace," Dorothea came to see patience and obedience as the major characteristics of her own "proper faith" and the only acceptable substitutes for spotless virginity.

As was true for many religious women who had been wives and mothers, Dorothea betrayed life-long *angst* over her past. According to Newman, "by the fourteenth century, the Magdalene's contested status had become a focal point for the anxieties of the newly devout: ... could sexually experienced women really achieve a status equivalent or even superior to the old idea of *virginitas intacta*?" (177). Mary Magdalene does not play a conspicuous role in *Leben*. But Dorothea's regret over her loss of maidenhood is extreme because for women like her virginity has "connotations of independence and self-sufficiency" (Petroff *Visionary Literature* 34), which Dorothea enjoyed only in connection with the most obvious manifestations of its absence, the births of her nine children. Miserable during the forty-day purification period following each birth, she resumed attendance at the end of the lying-in period "happy but also sad: happy because she could go to church once more and attend services, sad because she again would be forced to share her husband's bed from which she absented herself whenever she could justifiably do so." Though Dorothea gained a limited amount of autonomy during the last decade of her twenty-six years of marriage when after the birth of their ninth child husband and wife agreed to abstain from sexual intercourse, total liberation and independence came only with Adalbert's death in 1390. Now at last she could follow her commitment to virginity, in her case chaste widowhood, exempted "from the charge of female weakness or corruption, allowing her, as Saint Jerome said, to become like a man" (Petroff *Visionary Literature* 5).

In view of Dorothea's subsequent life history, cynics might argue that she did not get to enjoy her new-found independence for long. In 1391 charges of heresy were brought against her. Because of her "irreverent" behavior during mass-- Johannes himself testified at her first canonization inquiry that in anticipation of the sacrament, she frequently was in ecstasy and, therefore, failed to rise at the elevation of the host--officials at St. Mary's Church suspected her of heresy of the Free Spirit. She was acquitted of these charges, but their implications were obvious: she needed clerical protection such as her Gdansk confessor Nikolaus could not provide. So she at last sought out the "magister at Marienwerder" whom Nikolaus himself had recommended to her more than a year earlier. Her move to Marienwerder bears out Bell's observation that "women who were married, who had paid the marriage debt and had known the flesh could reach God only through the intermediary of a male priesthood, a situation not unlike their dependency at home or in the market place"(84-85). To Dorothea, though, winning a doctor of theology, canon of Marienwerder cathedral, diplomat for the Teutonic Knights, and adviser to the officials of the episcopal see of Pomesania as her confessor and with his help an anchoress' cell, represented the crowning achievement of her independence and authority. Ever since her first journey to Finsterwald (Einsiedeln) in 1384 she had longed to live the hermit's life, removed from worldly concerns. Suddenly this long-deferred dream was within reach.[13]

Caroline Bynum Walker' study *Jesus as Mother* examines the concept of Christ as a maternal nourisher in medieval religious literature and concludes that "women do not use the image of mother-Jesus as one of their primary ways of speaking of union" (162). By elaborating "nuptial mysticism much more fully than did the twelfth-century males with whom it originated" (18), women tend to see Christ as the young, handsome, ardent human lover of the *Song of Songs*. This characterization of feminine medieval mysticism certainly applies to Dorothea's spirituality. Because Dorothea's entire spiritual career, like that of any Christian journeying toward salvation, is a record of ever-increasing abundance, discernment, and enjoyment of spiritual nourishment, references to Christ as provider of food abound. In his lengthy instructions on proper prayer at mealtime, for instance, Christ himself mentions his maternal role, which Dorothea was to include in her recitations: "Help me, dear Lord, to drink and suck from the five wounds you have sustained because of me in such a way that living water will flow from me on judgment day." Actual representations of Christ as mother suckling the infant soul, however, are nonexistent. This is surprising because, like Catherine of Siena, Dorothea, at God's express order, received communion daily and like Catherine would have preferred to nourish her body by feeding solely on Christ's had he himself not prevented her.

The scene most closely approximating an actual depiction of Jesus as

---

[13] The first hermetic community had been established in Finsterwald, Switzerland, around the hermitage of Saint Meinrad. After he was murdered by robbers in 861, his cell became a shrine known as "St. Mary's of the Hermits" or "Einsiedeln" for short. When Dorothea lived there (1385-87), communal houses were still inhabited by hermits. According to Westpfahl, "Die Geistesbildung der heiligen Dorothea von Montau," *Dorothea von Montau: Eine preußische Heilige des 14. Jahrhunderts*, 38-58, Dorothea was particularly attracted to Einsiedeln's four communal houses for anchoresses where she became acquainted with Mechthild von Magdeburg's tract *Das fließende Licht der Gottheit* whose single surviving text was preserved there. She had to wait for fourteen months before her request for enclosure was granted. Johannes testified at her canonization inquiry that in her eagerness to be enclosed, she helped the masons build the wall that would seal her into her cell.

mother is his promise to grant Dorothea the same boon he granted his mother: at her death he would be with her " to receive her soul from her mouth to escort her into eternal life." Scholars comment only in passing on the impact pictorial cycles in parish churches and convents may have exerted on medieval women's spirituality. None of this type of sacramental art Dorothea saw in the churches of Gdansk has survived. The few remaining medieval wall paintings at St. Mary's church date from the fifteenth century, as do the magnificent frescoes of the Franciscan church of the Holy Trinity. The wall paintings at Marienwerder cathedral, on the other hand, date from the episcopate of Johannes Mönch (1377-1409), and experts believe that all were completed by 1400. The subject of one of the paintings in the northwest corner is the dormition of the Virgin depicting Christ, analogous to the topos of the virgin mother holding the infant Christ, ascending to heaven with Mary's pure infant soul in his arms. This rendition can make no claim to originality; Dorothea must have seen similar treatments during her pilgrimages. Still, if it was finished while she awaited enclosure, this painting might have served as inspiration for her vision. For fourteen months she would have had opportunity to contemplate it daily and afterwards could still see it from her cell.[14] Despite the lack of concrete depictions of Christ's nourishment of her body and soul, both Johannes and Christ frequently remind Dorothea and the audience that without God's nurture she could neither have progressed in virtue nor survived the rigors of being groomed for her role as his chosen bride.

---

[14] According to Joh. Heise, these wall paintings based on stories from *The Golden Legend* by Jacobus Voragine, were whitewashed during the Reformation and not rediscovered until 1862. The panels in the southeast corner and along the southeast wall, among them a portrait of Saint Elisabeth of Hungary, Saint Ursula and the eleven thousand virgins, and the three Holy Kings, could not be restored. They now are plastered over again. The heavily damaged panels in the northeast corner are still visible but so faint that their subject matter has not yet been determined. Since their rediscovery and restoration in 1862, the extant paintings have been restored again in the nineteen-thirties (Tadeusz Wisniewski, *Dom und Schloß zu Kwydzyn* 13).

From her cell in the southeast corner of the cathedral, Dorothea could see some of the paintings on the northwest wall because she could pass her head through the grate that connected her cell to the crypt, which in this church occupies the ground floor of the apse rather than the space below it. This arrangement results in a feature unique to Marienwerder cathedral, a two-storied apse, whose second floor housed the choir, thus placing it above the main altar.

By contrast, a wealth of marriage metaphors underscores the gender-specific nature of the spiritual life described in this work. Moreover, by fusing Christ's nature as loving, passionate bridegroom with that of exacting teacher and disciplinarian, *Leben* shapes him into a male authority figure indistinguishable from Dorothea's fleshly husband Adalbert or her spiritual husband Johannes von Marienwerder, whom Christ himself had united to her in wedlock: "I joined you to one another as one unites two people in holy matrimony," he reminds Dorothea on several occasions. They were to cherish, honor, and aid one another, and she was to obey Johannes as she had Adalbert and was "to cleave unto him all the days of her life and not to leave him under any circumstances." *Leben* treats these espousals as dress rehearsals for Dorothea's eternal union with her heavenly bridegroom Jesus Christ.

While men are always authority figures, Dorothea and her soul are always obedient daughters, sisters, spouses. A realistic reflection of late-medieval social rules governing the relationship of men and women, this gender specificity simultaneously reaffirms the relation between Christ the Savior and every soul redeemed through his self sacrifice as spelled out in the gospels and elaborated by centuries of biblical exegeses. To be deserving of the privilege of eternal life, the human soul, whose grammatical gender in German is feminine,[15] like a daughter of good family needs to be taught carefully to prepare her for her life as a wife who will be a credit to her parents and a joy to her husband. Like any woman who marries above her station in life, the soul of the crude, ignorant peasant girl Dorothea needs to be groomed for the exalted position she is to occupy. A painstakingly meticulous bridegroom, Christ refuses to delegate this task to others. "Those to whom I give myself I will educate myself and adorn them with my treasures," he tells his bride. "I will make them pleasing unto me and prepare them as I see fit. No one else can do so in my stead." Dorothea's education

---

[15] This translation will retain the feminine gender of *sele* (Seele-soul) whenever possible to preserve the male-female dynamics produced by this gender-specificity.

extends even to such niceties as polished table manners:

> The Lord came to her to rid her of all bad manners and clumsiness of body and soul, which she exhibited in eating and drinking though she was modest and ate but little. He made her graceful, agile, and vigorous to enable her to behave well and discharge her demanding labors of virtue energetically.

By definition the story of every Christian soul who attains eternal bliss with Christ is a Cinderella story. Consequently, *Leben* relates the marriage of Dorothea's soul to the Godhead after the ugly duckling, cleansed of all dross, has turned into the majestic swan in the simple language and imagery of the rags-to-riches fairy tale. Their "engagement" takes place in St. Mary's church in Gdansk when Dorothea is thirty-nine years old. While she is taking communion, Christ exchanges her old heart for a new, passionate one, which causes her to experience intimations of the *unio mystica* for the very first time: "She felt how the Lord Jesus Christ embraced and kissed her soul and heard the voice of God with which he spoke to her soul from that day to the day of her death." The wedding takes place with great pomp and circumstance, solemnity and merriment:

> Like the daughter of a mighty and powerful king her soul was luxuriously dressed and richly adorned with gold, silver, and precious stones. She and her handmaidens were seated in a comfortable, sumptuously decorated hall. She waited and eagerly watched for her precious, praiseworthy, noble bridegroom and his attendants to enter.

When they do, all dressed in royal purple, leading the bridegroom in their midst, all remove their birettas and bow respectfully before the bride. At the conclusion of the public festivities the bridegroom leads his beloved into the wine cellar of his love to show her "the secrets of his heart that he does not wish to reveal to anyone else." According to Johannes, this espousal took place whenever Dorothea received "the holy, praiseworthy sacrament of the real body of Our Lord Jesus Christ." Like other women mystics who had been married, Dorothea describes such experiences in the sensual language and imagery of a woman familiar with the intimacies of conjugal life.

Johannes von Marienwerder: Dorothea's Confessor and Biographer

Much has been written about the relationship of medieval holy women and male ecclesiastics, especially about the strategies they devised "to avoid...[the] perennial fate of inferiority, insignificance, and silence" imposed on women within the medieval church hierarchy (Newman 2). Even women perfectly capable of recording their spiritual experiences frequently employed male ecclesiastics for this task to allay suspicions of insubordination, for the penalties for being judged guilty of transgressing the misogynist taboo of women as visible, vocal, and informed moral leaders were severe (Petroff *Body and Soul* 176). Hadewijch of Brabant (active ca. 1220-1240) and Mechthild von Magdeburg (ca. 1207-82) were expelled from their Beguine communities. Dorothea herself had to endure the rigor and danger of a heresy trial. St. Birgitta's canonization was subject to review at the Councils of Constance (1414-18) and Basle (1431-39). Marguerite Porete, in the first known auto-da-fé, was burned as a heretic in 1310 after having been forced to witness the public "execution" of her *Mirror of Simple Souls*, a victim of the Dominican inquisitor William Humbert, notorious for his role in the brutal destruction of the Templars that same year (Bryant 204).[16]

Critical assessments of the effects of such strategies vary. According to Petroff, such joint effort inspired "deep love and trust" in both parties and resulted in role reversals granting "more power and authority to the woman than the male ecclesiastic" (*Body and Soul* viii-ix). Furthermore, the woman mystic, compelled by the conviction that her experiences mattered not just to herself, gained protection and official approval through her confessor's collaboration. But

---

[16] Nothing is known of Hadewijch's subsequent fate. Mechthild concluded her life in the prestigious Cistercian convent of Helfta. St. Birgitta's canonization was ultimately upheld, but only because both Councils decided that to "uncanonize" such a popular saint would cause still more injury to the Church. To avoid such problems in the future, though, Jean Gerson, chancellor of the University of Paris and leader of the conciliar party at Constance, stridently warned confessors of female visionaries not to accept any of their revelations as true without first subjecting them to minute scrutiny and not to assign them any importance if they were (Hipler "Johannes Marienwerder, der Beichtvater der seligen Dorothea von Montau" 91). Marguerite Porete's public teaching caused her execution as a heretic even though three eminent theologians had endorsed her *Mirror*.

because they lacked the authority of formal theological education, clerical orders, or male gender, the only justification for women to write was their being an instrument of God (Bowie 41). The logical consequence of making such claims, however, was for women to lose their positions as subjects of their own life histories: to be turned into objects, agents of someone else's message (Petroff *Body and Soul* 177). Petroff considers the frustrations such objectification produced as especially serious in women lay mystics, the most unlikely candidates for sainthood to begin with, because their unusual vocations already placed them at the periphery of society. She interprets the copious weeping of such lay mystics as Angela of Foligno and Margery Kempe as the inarticulate response of women seeking to express themselves in a spiritual milieu denying them a voice (*Visionary Literature* 39).[17] Carol Neel cites Marie de Oigny's efforts to make herself heard as especially pathetic: she carefully chose Jacques de Vitry to serve as her voice only to find herself silenced as he pursued his own agenda of forging her into "the paradigm of a new lay spirituality unique in his own time" (245).

Marie's example demonstrates how medieval women who chose to employ male clerics not only risked "being captured by the rhetoric that inscribes them in a patriarchal mentality" (Petroff *Body and Soul* 177) but also being silenced altogether and/or exploited for purposes other than their own. In no instance is this more obvious than in Johannes von Marienwerder's *Leben*, a record of ultimate scribal authority over what is written about a medieval holy woman's spirituality.[18] Whether Dorothea was illiterate and thus utterly dependent on a

---

[17] Inordinate weeping is a prominent characteristic of Dorothea's spirituality as well. But its causes are complex and less readily assignable to frustration. They transcend the usual pious weeping in pity of Christ's torments and the miseries and sinfulness of humanity because God himself recommends daily weeping as the most effective means of calming the soul and rinsing it clean of minute sins whose accumulation would not merely impede Dorothea's own salvation but that of her supplicants as well.

[18] For a related discussion, consult Amy Hollywood's *The Soul as Virgin Wife*. Arguing against indiscriminate conflation of hagiographical and mystical texts, which she considers separate and distinct medieval literary genres, the author offers a comparative reading of parallel passages from Book IV of the Latin *vita* of Beatrice of Nazareth (1200-68), written shortly after her death

scribe is difficult to determine and irrelevant, for after having been accused of subscribing to the tenets of the Brethren of the Free Spirit, she could not risk renewed ecclesiastical accusations of insubordination or heresy. Consequently, she could not have challenged Johannes' authority had she wanted to because his collaboration in recording her spiritual history provided the encouragement, ecclesiastical endorsement, and protection she needed.[19]

Like other confessors of medieval holy women, Johannes had much to gain from Dorothea's decision to reveal her spiritual history to him. If he could consolidate the interests of Prussia's secular and ecclesiastical authorities in a successful bid for Dorothea's canonization, he could enhance his own reputation as sponsor of Prussia's first native saint and politician of note by being instrumental in solving some of Prussia's most pressing political problems. His theological training, ecclesiastical and secular offices and activities, and polemical skills made him the most likely person to succeed in such an endeavor: his success was such that official efforts in support of her canonization were under way within the year of her death.[20] For the papal commission who would conduct the canonization inquiry he transformed Dorothea's dictations into a series of formal Latin *vitae*. He launches his campaign in the prologue to the first of these, completed in 1396, by pointing out what powerful a weapon the Roman papacy stood to gain in service of orthodox Catholicism through her canonization,

---

by a male cleric, and its source, *On the Seven Manners of Loving*, Beatrice's own vernacular account of her spiritual experiences.

[19] In "Die Geistliche Lehre Dorotheas" Stachnik argues that some of Dorothea's extant letters to her youngest daughter Gertrud are written in her own hand. One of the witnesses at the 1404-05 canonization inquiry also refers to letters Dorothea wrote to her while awaiting enclosure.

[20] In September 1395 the bishops of Prussia's episcopal sees, its four main monastic houses, High Master Konrad von Jungingen (1393-1407), Johannes Reymann, and Johannes von Marienwerder, applied to Pope Boniface IX for Dorothea's canonization. None too subtly, Johannes' so-called "epistula prima" directs the pope's attention to one of her visions which concludes with God's personal seal of approval: "Papa Bonifacius est bonus homo et timet me, et ego diligo ipsum," Pope Boniface is a good man; he respects me and I love him. The applications are collected in the *Codex diplomaticus Prussicus* V and reprinted fully or in part in several studies on Johannes and Dorothea.

urging the pope and the *curia* to

> add this morning star which appeared in far-away Prussia, the farthest hem of the as yet unsewn garment of Christ to the ecclesiastical starry firmament of saints so that through its light the sad darkness of the Schism... may be lifted and the day of grace and of the true Catholic faith dawn in the hearts of those now separated from the Mother Church. (Hipler "Beichtvater" 63 quoting Johannes)

For the ecclesiastical and secular authorities in Prussia much was at stake as well. As canon of the Marienwerder cathedral chapter, Johannes was naturally keen on advancing its fortunes; its reputation and wealth would be greatly enhanced if Dorothea's cell were to become the shrine of a brand-new saint of Holy Church, drawing pilgrims and revenues to this Dominican house in this remote border territory of the Christian universe. As a member of the Order of the Teutonic Knights, he knew firsthand how the Order's fortunes impacted every aspect of public and private life in Prussia. If Dorothea's canonization were to renew the Order's crusading fervor to win the last pagans in Lithuania for the Roman Church, the Knights would not only extend their own sphere of influence in eastern Europe but that of the Dominican Order as well.[21] Moreover, the cult of a native "German" saint would help shore up the political *status quo* invested in the Knights against encroachments of Slavic nationalist interests demonstrated by the rapidly growing political power of Poland and Lithuania, Prussia's immediate neighbors. Diverting public attention from escalating German/Slavic tensions and rivalries, Dorothea's cult might also deflate the impact of yet another threat to the *status quo*, new "heretical" ideas infiltrating Prussia from Bohemia.[22]

---

[21] According to Heribert Rossmann, "Johannes Marienwerder O.T.," most of the canons of Marienwerder cathedral and all the Prussian bishops simultaneously were members and priests of the Order.

[22] These were Wycliffite ideas transplanted to Bohemia, and from there imported to Prussia by such "heretics" as the so-called Doctor Leander, personal physician and political adviser of Konrad von Wallenrodt, High Master of the Teutonic Knights 1391-93, and enthusiastic supporter of John Wyclif's program of church divestment of property and participation in temporal politics. Ironically, to preserve the confessional status quo in Prussia, Johannes von Marienwerder himself favored such "Hussite" practices as daily confession and lay participation in the sacrament of the

Whether Dorothea's canonization could actually have helped accomplish any of these aims is moot. She was not canonized until 1976, the papacy remained mired in the Schism for several more decades, and with the Polish/Lithuanian rout of the Teutonic Knights at the battle of Tannenberg, they and German Catholicism in Prussia entered a long period of decline. Both went down in irreversible defeat in 1525 with Albrecht von Hohenzollern's change of confession and dissolution the Order's Prussian branch. When Catholicism did revive in Prussia during the Counter Reformation, it did so under the auspices of Polish, not German ecclesiastical authority.

Without Dorothea's canonization, all of Johannes' political ambitions were doomed. Conversely, all his private hopes were eventually realized. A graduate and professor of theology of Charles University in Prague, he had seen his promising academic career cut short in 1387 with the triumph of the Bohemian nationalist movement intent on breaking German domination of professorial appointments.[23] Johannes, like many other German professors, left Prague to establish new schools elsewhere. Papal confirmation for founding Prussia's first university at Kulm (Chelmno) had already been secured the previous year, and High Master Zöllner von Rotenstein (1382-90) had entrusted the task to Johannes. Nothing came of this project, however. So Johannes, his teaching career at an end, joined the Teutonic Knights and entered the cathedral chapter of his home town of Marienwerder where he witnessed the nadir of Prussia's fortunes in the wake of the battle of Tannenberg.

In spite of these setbacks, Johannes' relationship to Dorothea secured him

---

Eucharist and church services being conducted in the vernacular. For details on these and other issues see my article "The Political and Social Backgrounds of the Canonization of Dorothea von Montau."

[23] Manfred Gerwing's *"Malogranatum" oder der dreifache Weg zur Vollkommenheit: ein Beitrag zur Spiritualität des Spätmittelalters* (München: Oldenbourg, 1986) offers an excellent overview of the nationalistic struggles between the German and Bohemian factions at the university during the fourteenth and early fifteenth centuries. Rossmann's "Johannes Marienwerder O. T." focuses on Johannes' role and fate in these upheavals.

a place in history. His official eulogy praises him as "gar eyn achtbar lerer der heyligen schrifft...gar eyn selig man seynes lebins, " a most respectable teacher of holy writ... a most blessed man in his life." Subsequent scholarly response to his theological expertise and writings has been laudatory as well, and scholars interested in Dorothea's spirituality will continue to study his works. The inscription on his gravestone in the southeast wall of the Marienwerder cathedral choir reveals what his contemporaries considered his claims to fame, his academic training and his sponsorship of Dorothea:

> Magister Johannes Marienwerder sacre theologie professor
> felicis matris Dorothee confessor
> obiit anno MCCCCXVII die mensis XIX septembris.

When Johannes wrote his vernacular *vita*, he had reason to be optimistic about the outcome of his quest, and his ambitions inform the content and style of this propaganda piece *par excellence*. The Church's insistence on a saintly person's performance of *post mortem* miracles as the *sine qua non* test all candidates for official sainthood had to meet (Weinstein & Bell 141) was as advantageous to Johannes as to every other hagiographer since it necessitated postponing the final composition of a prospective saint's *vita* until his/her death, thus legitimately placing it out of its subject's control. Johannes' manipulation of his material in *Leben* exceeds that of other women's biographers, for not only did Dorothea have no voice in determining the ultimate content and organization of this *vita*: a translation and amalgamation of several of his earlier Latin works composed a decade after her death, it is even farther removed from its subject than the rest.[24]

---

[24] Dorothea dictated her visions, revelations, etc. in German. Instead of composing *Leben* directly from her German notes, however, Johannes worked from German through Latin back to German. While scholars like Toeppen rightfully point out that the language of the vernacular version reflects more of Dorothea's own idiom than do the Latin *vitae*, that idiom appears too seldom and stands in too obvious a contrast to Johannes' latinized diction to permit any other conclusion about the history of *Leben*'s composition. For a discussion of just some of the language and metaphoric ascribable to her, see my article "Dorothea von Montau, the Language of Love, and Jacop Karweysze, 'goltsmyd.'"

Leben could not possibly accommodate all of Dorothea's revelations and experiences recorded elsewhere, so Johannes had to make cuts. What he chose to cut merits attention. Some of his omissions were obviously politically motivated to smooth tensions that had arisen between the Teutonic Knights and ecclesiastical authorities over Dorothea's enclosure.[25] He also omitted all but one of the references to Saint Birgitta of Sweden recorded elsewhere in great detail to ward off perceptions of Dorothea as a slavish imitator of her famous, adored predecessor. Likewise, he cut all spiritual phenomena likely to be misunderstood or misconstrued by lay audiences. Consequently, only one brief passage recalls Meister Eckhart's concept of Christ's birth in the soul of each Christian which eternalizes his unique historical birth by the Virgin Mary:

> At times he enlarged her womb. Then she felt a lovely infant moving back and forth, kicking merrily as if delighted, behaving as though he were given great pleasure and made much to do of.

Other strategies Johannes employs to inspire public zeal in support of Dorothea's canonization further demonstrate his polemic skills. To convince his audiences of the absolute truth of what is being related, he frequently interrupts his narrative with his own comments and the monologues, commands, and commentaries of the members of the trinity and assorted saints. The authority of these divine beings serves him well in legitimizing the unorthodoxy of a woman accused of heresy fourteen years earlier whom the Church now advanced as the divinely-inspired embodiment of divergent, even contradictory strains of spirituality, God's personal emissary to nourish and fortify his troubled Church. To allay doubt about this confusing reversal, God himself refers to her as his latter-day St. Christopher weighed down by the burden of her mission, a burden so weighty that her soul would have collapsed under it had he not granted her "a brief respite now and then to let her catch her breath." Popular enthusiasm for

---

[25] Anneliese Triller's article "Konrad von Wallenrodt, Hochmeister des Deutschen Ordens (1391-1393), im Spiegel der Quellen über Dorothea von Montau," Paul Nieborowski's *Die Selige Dorothea von Preußen,* and my article "The Political and Social Backgrounds of the Canonization of Dorothea von Montau" discuss these rivalries.

Dorothea's canonization proved Johannes right: no devout Christian could ignore the testimony of divine personages.[26]

Ironically, as these voices sing Dorothea's praises, they drown out her own so that the heroine of this popularized drama of salvation ends up playing the part of a minor character. In fact, the "double voice," the dialogue between God and mystic so troubling to Petroff in medieval women's spiritual writings (*Visionary Literature* 23), in *Leben* is reduced even further to divine monologues, silencing Dorothea altogether. Whenever she does speak, she does so solely at God's behest and as his mouthpiece, repeating him *verbatim*. According to Petroff, the affective nature of medieval women's spirituality endows their visions with features similar to those of modern film, namely picture and sound, and makes the retelling of their experiences the "most obvious single narrative in women's writing" (*Visionary Literature* 30). *Leben* generally reduces Dorothea's "films" into abstract briefs. Fortunately, though, most of Johannes works are extant. This provides a rare opportunity to study more than a single *vita* a hagiographer composed about a saintly person and his manipulation of materials to suit his own purposes as well as the needs and expectations of his various audiences.[27]

***

As Richard Kieckhefer observes, "when Johannes von Marienwerder promulgated the cult of Dorothea von Montau, he could be confident that accounts

---

[26] Other rhetorical and stylistic devices Johannes employs to achieve his purposes are the subject of my articles "Male Clerical Authority in the Spiritual (Auto)biographies of Medieval Holy Women" and "Whose Life History is this Anyway? Johannes von Marienwerder's Narrative Strategies in the German *Vita* of Dorothea von Montau."

[27] Printed works include the "Vita Dorotheae Montoviensis Magistri Johannis Marienwerder," the so-called *Vita Lindana* (1396); *Acta Sanctorum* XIII (1883): 499-560; the "Liber de Vita venerabilis dominae Dorotheae," the so-called *Vita Latina*, under the title *Vita Dorotheae Montoviensis Magistri Johannes Marienwerder*, eds. Hans Westpfahl & Anneliese Triller (Köln/Graz: Böhlau: 1964); the "Septililium venerabilis dominae Dorotheae," *Analecta Bollandiana* II-IV (1883-85) and as a separate print edited by Franz Hipler also published by *Analecta Bollandiana* in 1885. The proceedings of Dorothea's canonization inquiries were published by Richard Stachnik under the title *Die Akten des Kanonisationsprozesses Dorotheas von Montau von 1394-1521* (Köln/Graz: Böhlau, 1976). Extant manuscripts are listed in Stachnik's "Zum Schrifttum."

of her mystical experiences would evoke reverence from the masses" (165). But Johannes' political ambitions set unfortunate precedents that have inhibited fair evaluations of her person and spirituality well into the twentieth century. During the Counter Reformation Polish Church authorities restored her shrine at Marienwerder cathedral--her grave, portraits, and other reminders of her had been removed during the Reformation. Yet they made no attempt to seek her canonization, a painfully obvious indication of how firmly she was associated with former German hegemony in eastern Europe even centuries after her death. In 1744 the German Lutheran theologian Theodor Christoph Lilienthal published the *Historia B. Dorotheae Prussiae Patronae* (History of the blessed Dorothea, patroness of Prussia). True to the spirit of Protestantism and the Enlightenment it denounces the cult of saints as criminal, the witnesses testifying in support of her canonization as gullible, the presiding officials as self serving, and Dorothea herself as arrogant and smug. Nineteenth and early twentieth-century German scholarship tends to assess Dorothea's spirituality as Johannes' accomplishment because of her ignorance of speculative mysticism and its scholastic terminology.

From its very inception the elevation of a human being to the status of saint of Holy Church has had political overtones. The tumultuous events of the twentieth century transformed Dorothea's canonization into a political football. On the one hand, saccharine partisan studies of Dorothea now replaced earlier dismissive ones while Günther Grass' satirical "feminist" novel *Der Butt* (The Flounder) mocks both Dorothea and her spirituality. After World War II, Catholic refugees demoralized by the loss of their homelands in Germany's eastern provinces, like the post-war *Landsmannschaften,*[28] sought consolation to come to terms with their losses. They found it in their successful bid for Dorothea's canonization. On January 9, 1976, Pope Paul VI proclaimed her a saint by rule

---

[28] These are refugee organizations, some of them fascist and espousing forcible reacquisition of these provinces ceded to Poland by the Allies. Since the end of World War II they have consistently opposed any peace treaty granting Poland permanent possession of these territories.

of *casus exceptus*.[29]

Admirable in its dedication, post-war scholarship in service of Dorothea's canonization is fraught with the disquieting chauvinism characteristic of many German publications dealing with losses in eastern Europe. But none of it approaches the rabid nationalistic virulence of Paul Nieborowski's 1933 study *Die Selige Dorothea von Preußen*. Enlisting her help in the cause of Nazism, this Catholic priest calls on her protection from "Russian Bolshevism, which, having already poisoned the spirit of much of Germany ... is now arming itself to force its corrosive teachings on us all through the power of the sword" (12). He implores even non-Catholics to embrace this saint "who considered the destruction of eastern anti-Christianism as the *Ostmark*'s sole purpose of existence and to pray with me that once again, as then, Germany may be referred to as the country of 'one God, one nation, one faith'" (13-14).[30] Perhaps the new possibilities for a normalization of relations between Germany and the newly-independent nations of eastern Europe will bring about less partisan, politically charged scholarship on Dorothea as well.

---

[29] Richard Stachnik's translation, "Dekret der Hl. Kongregation für die Heiligsprechungen vom 9. Januar 1976," is printed in *Dorothea von Montau: eine preußische Heilige des 14. Jahrhunderts*, 145-48.

[30] Nieborowski's terminology betrays his political orientation. His is the only study that refers to Dorothea as "von Preußen" (of Prussia); *Ostmark* is a Nazi revival of Charlemagne's designation for what was to become Austria and so used in Nazi parlance as well. His slogan "one God, one nation, one faith" echoes Hitler's battle cry "ein Reich, ein Volk, ein Führer."

The life of the blessed woman Dorothea,
anchoress in the cathedral church of Marienwerder
in the country of Prussia

Here begins the proem of the book
of the life of the blessed woman Dorothea.

Though all the works of Our Lord are great, praiseworthy, and to be esteemed highly, nevertheless, some of his works are to be taken to heart still more fervently, to be considered even more highly, to be noted more explicitly, to be honored, appreciated, and praised still more emphatically: they are those which he has especially selected, endowed more profusely, and made more magnificent in his elect, blessed human beings, in each one of whom the effects of Our Lord were so profound, so notable, and so remarkable that one reads and sings of them thus: "Such a one has not been found who is like this or resembles it."

Such is the accomplishment of Our Lord in the blessed, worthy woman Dorothea especially elected among many works, mercifully endowed, and most wonderfully fashioned; and therefore to be taken to heart more diligently, to be esteemed more highly, and to be praised as more worthy than many other works of Our Lord, above which it is honored and more richly endowed. If one looks at it closely, one cannot find its like in all the world. Who has ever heard or read of human beings deliberately inflicting upon themselves such a variety of very bitter and lengthy sufferings as she inflicted upon herself? And such suffering was not only constantly inflicted upon her by her own hand; frequently she also patiently received many and varied injuries and torments from the world, the evil spirit, her own carnal nature, and especially from Our Lord, who tormented her often and prepared great suffering for her in love through a variety of spiritual and physical wounds as well as extremely hard internal exertion; through great desire, yearning, and pursuit of him, his holy, praiseworthy body, and eternal life, of which much and yet much less is written than actually took place.

However, such delightful secrecy and friendly dalliance as the Lord shared with her; such pure illumination, merciful visitations, unassailable instruction, and effusively great endowment of spiritual possessions as the Lord has bestowed upon her and of which only a part is described in her book; what worldly and insufficiently inspired human being may believe it, all the more so since from time to time it was so much greater than it is recorded, as Truth, which is God himself, often asserted, saying to her: "What you and your confessor describe is scarcely a reflection of the great good I do you and have revealed to you." About her suffering, Truth, Our Lord, spoke thus: "You shall not reveal nor leave behind on Earth your greatest spiritual exercises and self-castigations through which you have won me. You shall keep them to yourself and take them with you into eternal life. There are my dear mother and all my saints who can better judge their worth than all who live on Earth."

From this every gracious listener or reader and anyone not suspicious of a good thing may recognize that the blessed Dorothea's suffering and comfort, love, joy, and spiritual perception were greater than is described here. Therefore, you beastly person or you who discredits the works of God which are incomprehensible to you, be silent and hold your tongue. Do not contradict nor reject God's miraculous works. Let be your slander and your stupid, brazen manner of speech. Learn and recognize as reasonable and discoverable the merciful works God is wont to perform with his elect. Accept and realize that he accomplishes more and that more magnificently than you and I may be able to discern. Be not so suspicious as to think that she or I were so neglectful of our salvation that we, risking eternal harm and perdition, would knowingly speak or write falsehood. To do so we have truly no cause, for, as St. Peter says, were we to hope for Christ merely in this present life, we would be the most pathetic among mankind.

Be not as a judge who condemns a man unjustly before recognizing the truth of the matter. Therefore, first read her life humbly and diligently; consider well the words and works the almighty God has wrought in her. Observe the fruit that has sprung from this. Accept the instruction and testimony of those who knew her well while she dwelled here with us and of those truthful people to whom God showed mercy on her account after her death. And if you cannot get satisfaction from them, prove honestly, if you can, that what is written about her in this book is untrue. Give your reply in writing and let it be known whether it is based on the holy Scriptures, on reason, on sincere love for the true faith, or on envy, ill will, and reliance on your own intellect. Take to heart, you devout, faithful Christians, God's honor, your own improvement, and the reaffirmation of the faith in this blessed mother Dorothea in whom God has wrought merciful works to shame sensuous, carnal people, to comfort and improve Christendom, to awaken or incite to good works those of true faith, and to ignite those whose hearts have grown cold. So that you may not be hindered in achieving your salvation, do not turn to those who scorn and despise her or to her deceitful detractors, for their diatribes are to be considered as nothing more than the barking of a mad dog who devours himself with his senseless barking and disturbs the listeners in their repose. Look up and observe whether the Lord did not speak through his prophet Habakkuk thus: "Behold the detractors and be amazed, for I perform a work in your days, a work you will not believe, even if someone were to relate it to you.

Very well! Be not led astray, but remember the pronouncement of Our Lord in the gospel, which says: "What is impossible for man is very well possible for God." For the Lord rules nature with his mercy and gives a man the strength to do what he would be powerless to do without God's mercy and love, as can be observed in the holy martyrs who willingly and joyfully confronted cruel martyrdom. They were so generously endowed with the mercy of God that to them, according to the highest power of their reason and their love of God, bitter martyrdom and death were more delightful than life. Thus her bitter suffering was hard for this lover of God in terms of her carnal nature, but according to her highest strength of reason, her great love for God, and her desire for eternal life, it was most sweet and pleasant, and she would not have wished to forego it. For in her ears sounded what Our Lord has spoken in the gospel: "He who wants to follow me, let him take up his cross and follow!" And always before her eyes stood the great suffering of Our Lord who had come into his reign through torment. Accordingly, she did not want to come without torment into a new kingdom and into that great eternal reward he promised those who are in agony through his love while they are here. And so, because of his great love, she gave herself willingly to a variety of torments. Thus she was pricked by divine love to suffer, yet through that same love her bitter suffering was sweetened because mercy overcomes nature.

You blessed listeners and readers of this book; consider, weigh, and believe that the Lord of this old world which daily renews itself in vice has renewed in his elected bride Dorothea his merciful, miraculous deeds, for the world as an improvement, for himself as praise and honor, and for those grown cold in his love as kindling so that he may be esteemed and honored greatly in her. To those who do so, God has promised rich rewards.

Here is also to be noted one of the many comforting pronouncements the Lord made to his elected bride Dorothea: "Those who read about my pleasant companionship with you, as your confessors have recorded it, will improve themselves." Now to improve ourselves on account of her life, let us pray like this:

> "Lord Jesus Christ, true light of the world, illumine my soul and drive from it all harmful darkness and ignorance and teach me to know you through a true and just faith, a strong and sound hope, a chaste, burning love. Oh, all-knowing Word! For your praise and honor and for my

own improvement teach me to read this book, to consider your works and goodness described therein in such a way that I will come to know you better, turn to you more steadfastly, cleave unto you more tightly and persistently, be inflamed more hotly by you and intimately united with you in fervent, chaste love that nothing may separate me from you; that I will remain with you forever and will clearly behold you with those angels who are called the Knowledgeable [the Cherubim] and will burn fiercely with those who are called the Burning Angels [the Seraphim] in a delight indescribably joyful and will praise you eternally with all your elect. May Mary, my trustworthy helper in need, that blessed woman who gave birth to you, help me obtain these things through the prayer and merit of the blessed Dorothea, anchoress, your and your adored mother's faithful servant. Amen."

These are the chapters of the first book of the life

of the blessed, venerable woman Dorothea,

anchoress at Marienwerder, as many as there are in number.

34

This is the prologue.

Many things and events force a human being to acknowledge God's grace, wisdom, and might, to serve him in love, and to remain in steadfast service to him: the mirror of creation, suggestions of divine admonitions, punishment of sins, promise of great rewards to the lovers of God, and other things more. Especially the exemplary, holy lives of the saints should draw us toward God's love and his delightful service, for their blessed lives are a living lesson to those who enjoy listening to them or reading them on their own.

That the life of the blessed Dorothea is a fruitful lesson
and delightful to receive.

Chapter I.

Lift up your eyes, incline your ears, all inhabitants of Prussia and all believers in Christ. See and hear how the ancient, the eternal God has renewed his grace in the land of Prussia in his special maiden named Dorothea. Her life, as it is described here, was meant to be for all who encounter it, and indeed through God's grace has become already for many a lesson, a light, and a way to leave the wide road that leads to perdition and a guide to the path that leads mankind to the portal of the heavenly kingdom. Because her entire life has been so richly adorned with the miraculous works and the overflowing grace of her special friend and selected bridegroom, the Lord Jesus Christ, it cannot be described as briefly as the lives of many other saints.

Likewise, it cannot be discussed briefly because of the severe, uncommon spiritual exercises, castigations, sufferings, and unheard-of torments she inflicted on herself from her seventh year until the end of her life; because of the extraordinary, inexpressible effects of God's grace in her and through her, which were so great and so varied that she herself neither could nor dared speak of them without the special bidding and permission of her beloved friend, Our Lord Jesus Christ; especially, however, because of the fierce wounding of her body which lasted up to twenty weeks before her death. Nevertheless, she had revealed numerous details to her confessors before then. Because of all this, every devout person shall enter into her life with sound judgement and desire, as into a winsome meadow, to gather there, with God's help and the strength of individual discernment, the flowers of virtue which she produced with such abundance that they were not only sufficient to secure her own salvation but the salvation of all lovers of virtue.

Her birth.

Chapter II.

The above-mentioned Dorothea was born to honorable, god-fearing parents in a village called Montau in the episcopal see of Pomesania in Prussia. Her father's name was Wilhelm, a man of honorable life. Her mother, named Agatha, was a widow for more than forty-four years after her husband's death. As a result of the charitable works she performed day and night for the poor as best she could in his service, Agatha offered God an honorable life of many years and virtuous deeds. She gave birth to four sons and five daughters who were so prolific that she was grandmother to fifty grandchildren who all lived honorable, prominent, and praiseworthy lives. Among her own children Dorothea was the seventh, a prophecy and portent of her endowment with the seven gifts of the Holy Spirit and the perfection of her entire life for which she was destined from birth, confirmed in baptism, and which she initiated when she was seven years old. [Her baptism] took place on the feast day of St. Dorothea after Candlemas, so the young branch showed early what fruit the tree would bear.

How she was aided since childhood by God's grace.

Chapter III.

Our Lord Jesus Christ, who reveals his secrets to his special friends through the Holy Spirit and who had now also elected Dorothea into this group of God's children, at one time made a revelation concerning her childhood by telling her: "When you were still a child I drew you to me in love; you perceived me and contemplated me; you loved me and cleaved unto me. You kept your heart pure and receptive to me, and whatever I put into it, you preserved therein. If something abhorrent to me sprouted within your heart or entered it from without, it gave way at once and did not cling stubbornly to your heart because you were never preoccupied with acquiring temporal goods. Quite the contrary: you busily kept your heart unencumbered by transitory wealth, for I presented you with more worthwhile possessions to which your desire and love were directed and inclined."

Her steadfast vigils.

Chapter IV.

Because the heat of divine love had so hotly inflamed her in service to Our Lord, Dorothea, from childhood to old age, seldom gave her limbs any rest, unless they were already exhausted through hard work or she was forced to rest in the presence of her mother, her sisters, or the maidservants, for her sisters and the maids would complain to her mother that she seldom slept at night. Whenever the others were asleep, she silently rose, leaned against the wall or the bedstead and prayed or was steeped in contemplation until exhaustion forced her to take a short nap.

This kind of vigil she kept so faithfully even while she was married that when her husband, either with caresses or with threats, tried to force her to sleep, he too did not succeed in making her sleep more than she was accustomed to. Instead, she had to deceive him into believing that she was asleep. Finally, after they had been married for a number of years, she said to him: "Dear brother, I cannot sleep. Therefore you must not order me to." When he recognized her great desire [to wake], he gave her permission to sleep in another bed in the same room, but when she kept on sleeping as little as before, he allowed her to bed down in whatever room she pleased. She had a particularly strong need to gaze at the sky at night. To do so, she sat at the open window without paying the least attention to inclement weather-- snow, hail, rain, wind, or frost. Thus the elected friend of God remained sober and vigilant so that the lion of hell who slinks about trying to espy the slothful to harm them by trapping them in sin would not seize her.

Her prostrations and other spiritual exercises.
Chapter V.

The love of God, which accomplishes great things wherever it is present but which is never present where nothing is accomplished, compelled the blessed Dorothea like a thorn, prodding her day and night to progress toward spiritual perfection, for before she was even seven years old, she already performed certain prostrations under her mother's direction. She fell down on her knees or face and did so joyfully without vexation of spirit or bodily harm. She performed one prostration after another so often that even in the coldest weather her tender limbs were covered with sweat so that this new plant so well watered by the dew of heaven would become fruitful in the days ahead. At night she customarily spread out her arms to form a cross, exerting herself by standing in this pose until she was exhausted. After having done that, she pressed her body against a wall, again assuming the shape of a cross by holding on to the wall, either by pushing her fingers into holes or by draping her arms over nails protruding from it, until she was worn out. Then she immersed herself in other spiritual exercises, such as weeping, praying, lamenting, rejoicing, and singing as time and circumstance permitted and illness did not curtail. One after another she steadfastly performed all these spiritual exercises until sleep overwhelmed her and she had to rest a little.

Also, whenever she had time and opportunity, she castigated her body with a coarse, knotty hair shirt, unmindful of her wounds, which were immediately aggravated through this garment and injured her grievously. For more than the last sixteen years of her life she prostrated herself on planks, stones, or the bare ground. Whenever she was exhausted, she lay down on stones to rest and in place of a pillow put a log beneath her head. Those nights she spent without any sleep at all she passed by taking turns falling on her face and standing up. Then she would incline from one side to the other. Sometimes she stood up, at other times she walked, and at still other times she sat down. She crawled on her hands and knees. Then, by pressing her forehead and her feet to the floor, she would first lift her body into the air and then form a cross by spreading out her arms and then maintain this pose as long as possible. Finally, holding her hands behind her back as though they were tied behind her, she hurled herself on her face. Burning love and a searching desire for Our Lord caused her to mortify her limbs and render her flesh subservient to the spirit, her carnal nature to reason, and her reason to God's grace through these and many other exercises so that everything she had received from God became wholly serviceable to him.

Her fasts.

Chapter VI.

To the person who enjoys the taste of spiritual pleasures, the pleasures of the flesh become distasteful, as God has often demonstrated in his beloved friend Dorothea, who on account of the sweet taste of spiritual blessings considered all temporal goods a foul muck and thus had no yearning or desire for opulent food. Consequently, during her childhood she did not even want to eat milk gruel or other dishes prepared with milk during the mandated fast days as did her playmates, unless she had to do so at her mother's command, and whenever she was forced to comply, such food tormented her far more than any fast. Whenever a fast day approached, she tearfully begged her mother to let her observe it with her. Her mother often became irritated about this and did not want to permit her to fast before she was ten years old. Furthermore, for many years her mother customarily fasted one day each week for the sake of Our dear Lady by taking nothing but bread and water. Inspired by the example of the devout mother, the daughter, though not yet ten years old, desired to keep this fast with her, which she finally gained permission to do through much supplication and weeping.

When she was eleven years old, Dorothea longed to prepare herself with much fasting to receive the body of Our Lord on the seven high feast days of the year, as did her mother. This, however, was not permitted to anyone so young but twice a year, during Advent and before Easter. Those two fasts Dorothea kept very strictly. If from time to time her mother or the maidservants who were older in years and stronger in body wanted to fast for three days of the week, she wanted to fast for four; if they wanted to fast with beer and bread, she wanted to hold a stricter fast of water and bread. From the time she was ten years old until she died she observed her fasts on designated fast days, on Fridays, and during the Advent of Our Lord so rigorously that even during her confinements she did not wish to eat dishes prepared with milk. She considered doing so a sin as though she would break her fast by eating such foods.

When she sat at table with her husband and others ate sumptuous foods, she remained hungry; vegetables and gruel left over from the previous day or the day before that or tiny little fishes refused by her servants were her meal, for she was so horrified by luxurious foods for the body that within the space of half a year she often used no more than one single egg to satisfy her body's needs. She very seldom ate meat, yet many people considered her pampered because of her attractive physical appearance, which in her case, however, grace produced much more forcefully than either agreeable food or nature. The exertions of her pilgrimages and confinements reduced her fasts little or not at all. Especially the two fast periods of Advent and Lent she observed so strictly that she did not even forego them during childbirth but faithfully kept them by flagellating herself with switches and other chastisements. Whenever she could do these things, she made her fasts pleasing to God.

How going to confession and earning indulgences was dear to her heart.

Chapter VII.

From the time she was seven years old, the blessed Dorothea hastened to confession to reveal her sins immediately upon commencement of the fast days. This annoyed her older sisters and the maidservants because compared to Dorothea's childish fervor, people judged the sluggishness of her elders all the more shameful. From the very beginning and continuing throughout her marriage she confessed even minor sins frequently, often twice daily though sometimes less, depending on how her conscience prodded her. In the final years of her life she confessed once a day. Whenever her older sisters wanted to go to church in the village or elsewhere to earn indulgences and her mother forbade her to go with them because of her extreme youth or weakness of body, she was greatly tormented until with weeping and tears she gained her mother's permission to go along.

How even as a child she performed the labors of her elders.

Chapter VIII.

The blessed Dorothea proved in childhood what she would become as an adult. Whenever her sisters or the maidservants ate coarse foods or performed tasks that were rough or difficult, she, though young and small, insisted on doing the same, to partake of that same coarse food, for she did not wish to be scorned by them or called childish, frail, or delicate. And it was most painful to her if at times she was called such things or was forbidden to partake of such food, for, fortified by God, she was convinced she could do the same as everyone else. Whenever she wanted to demonstrate her devout spirit through fasting, going to church in her own village or elsewhere at night during high church festivals, or by performing those previously-mentioned good works before she reached the age of ten, she had to win her mother's permission with weeping and screaming. But the moment she reached that age, she was free to perform these and other good works and put aside childish activities and manners as much as her age allowed.

At what time she took charge of her parents' household.

Chapter IX.

After her older sisters had been given in marriage, Dorothea presided over the goods her parents stored for daily meals and discharged her duties with intelligence and common sense, according to her age. She possessed reason and honesty beyond her years and thus was able to take charge of her parents' household in spite of her tender age. Though extremely young, she was active without being careless, meek and truthful without being dishonest, obedient to her parents and free of contentiousness, cheerful and unflagging in her work. She was diligent and free of dissipation, patient without complaining or grumbling, and out because of her tender compassion merciful to the poor and those in need, for now she entered into an active life to school herself in those works of charity through which the blessed Martha had offered her service to God Our Lord in praiseworthy diligence.

Her pious love of the poor.

Chapter X.

Charity and compassion for the poor and the meek whose conversation and fellowship she so enjoyed grew in Dorothea from the days of her earliest childhood. In sweet compassion her innermost strength was so greatly moved toward the poor that she never turned her face from any of them, no matter how wretched. Rather, she gave alms meekly, as many as possible from her parents' stores, and did so graciously by improving and increasing these gifts as her mother commanded her. She felt such singular love for the poor that she washed their feet and put them to bed herself, and to be with them and speak to them was her special joy and delight. They loved her so much in return that they praised her far and wide. And what prayers and hymns the blessed Dorothea could learn from the poor she learned by heart, reciting and singing them day and night in praise of God along with all her other pious prayers. For holy poverty now began to sprout like a green branch firmly rooted in her heart, as she in future days was to prove abundantly in her works.

How she accepted all things as good.

Chapter XI.

As long as she lived in her mother's house, Dorothea did exactly as her mother told her, without impatience or complaint, and meekly and thankfully accepted what her mother gave her as adornments appropriate for a young maiden: pins, brooches, hats, garments, and other such items of fashion. But she found no pleasure in such ornaments and never scorned any of her playmates who could not afford them. But even though owning such things was a matter of indifference to her, she modestly and politely accepted everything obligingly as it was offered. Even if someone offered her something evil instead of something good, she received it without sadness or sorrow, as she certainly demonstrated during her marriage.

How the joys of the world were painful to her.

Chapter XII.

In human consolations, in worldly joys and dancing she found little if any satisfaction because her desire for the heavenly treasures that attracted her made her abstinent, and human festivities were bitter to her, as can be shown by four-fold proof. The first is this: even when she was still very young and was taken to banquets, she sat there, neither eating nor drinking, but so tormented in her heart that she frequently wept for sorrow. Thus the joy of the world was turned into grief for her. The other proof is this: Whenever she was forced to dance even for just a little while, she fled from the joys of the world into a corner as soon as the opportunity presented itself and there bewailed the vanity of the world and being prevented from contemplating spiritual joys by such contemptible activities. The third: After she was married and bound to obey the orders of her husband and found out about upcoming festivities and worried about being invited, she jabbed her feet with needles until they festered to have visible proof of her inability to attend and thus a reasonable excuse to present to her husband as well as the revellers who believed her injuries were due to frostbite or some other cause. The fourth: Whenever she had to attend such festivities while she was married, though she seldom did, she always appeared with numerous wounds all over her kneecaps and calves.

While still very young and newly married, she at times had to do as other young women, her companions, did and dress up with shoes and stockings and other such things to conceal her austere life more effectively. But when she had to dance in them, the vigorous movement made her wounds bleed so severely that her shoes were filled with blood. Thus dancing caused her extreme pain. Later the pain of these wounds increased so severely that she could no longer wear tight shoes. Therefore she wore straw clogs lined with coarse felt hidden underneath her long gowns. But during the winter these shoes injured her not a little when they stuck to the scabs of her wounds. Tearing off these scabs as she moved, they reopened the wounds and started the flow of blood anew. Aggravated by frostbite, these wounds produced even more new pain, similar to the agony they caused her in the heat of summer. Thus her delight with dancing was counterbalanced by cold, heat, wounds and pain.

The beginning of her sufferings.

Chapter XIII.

When the blessed Dorothea was seven years old, carelessness caused her to be scalded all over her body with boiling water to such a degree that her mother, greatly tormented by compassion, had to nurse the child in a cradle. But God Our Lord, the benevolent comforter of all the afflicted, visited her with the mercies of his comforting presence and strengthened the blessed child Dorothea during that time and from then on through the last hour of her life, so that from that time forward she never experienced a waning but a steady waxing of her virtuous life. For often she felt in her desire for God a tremendous pull that seemed to draw her upwards body and soul. It also kept her constant desire unadulterated by perishable delights for through the eyes of reason she never lost sight of God's benevolence and kingdom. As a sign of this, she enjoyed contemplating the starry sky at night as her future home where she hoped to dwell forever with God and his saints.

How God explained the pain of her wounds.

Chapter XIV.

It happened on account of the great mercy of Our Lord Jesus Christ, the bridegroom of his elected bride Dorothea, that several weeks after the day of the holy virgin Agatha [February 5] in the year of Our Lord 1394 Dorothea was blessed with burning love, heartfelt prayer, and abundantly flowing tears. During this time the Lord especially wished to reveal the bitterness of her sufferings by saying to her: "Go back and contemplate the life filled with difficulties and the pain of great wounds that you have lived since childhood. Do this so you may praise me especially for these favors that allow you to leave a useful memento to the world. "You are well aware that your life was mine, not yours. You also feel that without me you could not have endured such severe, painful wounds. And you recognize through experience the truth that with your own strength you could neither have lived like this nor have told anyone the least bit about it. But now you have my permission to announce boldly how from the time you first gained cognizance of me I have worked miraculously in you. Consider how I kept your wounds open, brimful of bitter pain, whose scabs sometimes itched as though they were working alive with gnawing worms. At other times they delivered such sharp jabs as if they were shot crammed full by sharp arrows. Sometimes they burned as if ignited by fire. At times they swelled until they broke open; at still other times they bled freshly and profusely with excruciating pain as though they were indeed fresh and new. During such torments your eyes were so full of bitterness that even when you were asleep they seemed filled with smoke and soot. Because ever since childhood you endured so many and such serious wounds, you would have become lame, crooked, and ravaged by the foulness of your wounds had I not miraculously sustained you. Yet because of my love for you, you never spared yourself, for you trusted me steadfastly. For this reason I wanted to sustain you diligently." These and many other such revelations the blessed Dorothea received from Our Lord.

How she castigated and wounded herself.

Chapter XV.

What a conqueror she became over her body through God's love anyone may hear and marvel about, for she flagellated her body often with rods, whips, thistles, thorny branches, and with hard, knotty, barbed scourges. Also, as she reached the age of seven, she often burned herself with boiling water and from time to time with red hot iron and burning candles. At times she injured and wounded various parts of her body with boiling hot oil, mainly her shoulders, arms, hips, sides, loins, knees, calves and feet. With such devices she inflicted one wound beside the other from her shoulders down to the hems of her sleeves and from the hips upward as far as her clothes covered her body. And she treated her breasts in the same way until all these individual wounds looked like one single big wound and her body resembled a plowed field. She initiated her self castigations with such instruments in her youth and continued them even after she was married, practicing them both day and night.

She often mortified her flesh with knotted scourges studded with iron nails until she suffered great injury and the blood flowed freely. These nails at times tore her lean, chaste flesh so mercilessly that it was wounded in strips like fissures and pieces of her flesh stuck to them. Furthermore, she wounded her knees by kneeling on hard boards or sharp splinters. Such torment was most painful to her for neither the wounds on her knees nor the burns healed quickly. At one time, when she was still a child, she burned her ankle so severely with boiling water that she sustained a dreadful wound and became extremely ill. When she was ten years old, she once burned both feet so severely with boiling water that she had to sit in a dunghill and cover the burn with dung to draw out the pain. She had to remain sitting in that dunghill for a long time, more than three quarters of the day. Self-castigations with such and still other devices she began in the seventh year of her life and practiced them afterwards all the days of her life. The aforementioned self-mortifications are difficult to listen to but were even more difficult for her to endure and may seem scarcely or not at all believable to those who enjoy the life of the body. Nevertheless, in her desire to attain eternal blessedness, the praiseworthy Dorothea was so enraptured by God and so firm in her hope that it was sweet to her to endure all this through the superior strength of her soul.

How she aggravated her wounds with hard instruments.

Chapter XVI.

Remember, reader of this chapter, the words of Our Lord in the gospel, who says: "That which is impossible for man is very well possible for God." For God often accomplishes with man and through man that which otherwise would be impossible for man to do or endure. Therefore, accept God's omnipotence and take note of the strong disposition of Dorothea, the maid of God, who was not satisfied with the wounds she inflicted upon herself but whom love and her need to suffer the pains of the crucified God forced to renew these wounds to add suffering to suffering. She was accustomed to pricking her wounds with nettles, hard, coarse broom twigs and jagged nutshells, stinging herbs, and other hard instruments, which is gruesome to hear but even more gruesome to endure. She did this so her wounds would be kept open and fresh, and that, therefore, God would increase her suffering and its rewards.

This same renewal of her wounds she accomplished by other, equally painful methods, with the result that those parts of her body covered by her clothes were frequently torn, wounded, and smeared with blood. She brought this about with a coarse, knotty hair shirt, which she wore next to her skin, or a coarse woollen shift. When the rough fibers of the shift were pressed into the fresh wounds and stuck to them, the pain she suffered was far greater than that caused by the hair shirt. Occasionally she also made it a habit to submerge her open wounds in meat or fish brine. During the winter she also submerged her hands and feet, even her entire body up to the navel or the chin, in freezing cold water until the water froze so hard that she could pull her limbs from the ice only with utmost difficulty. Furthermore, also during the winter, she occasionally seated herself beneath a waterspout until she was partially or totally splashed with the cold water and her clothes froze to the ground. These castigations she began when she was eleven years old and continued them for twenty-six years. If God, who orders and directs all good things with strength and wisdom, had not attended her with special grace, she would have been completely destroyed by the cold.

But as miraculous as God's effect on her was in these instances, it is not to be considered any less miraculous that she did not lose her sanity through her above-mentioned vigils during which her spiritual exercises, works, and self-castigations kept her from sleeping for a whole week or two at a time. In fact, these vigils caused such sufferings that her head rang as though a great flock of birds were whistling and raging within. Oh, how miraculous is this woman's strength! When has it been heard in our time that such a manful heart was in a woman's body? Who through such manly exertions did not seek the fame and praise of the world, the favor of worldly princes, the gifts of lords, temporary rewards, while she, through temporary pain, sought to drive away eternal pain and through insignificant suffering obtain eternal joy? Oh, what a wise purchase did she engage in when she bartered corporeal goods in exchange for spiritual goods, earthly goods for heavenly goods to possess eternal instead of temporal treasures!

Be silent, you smug, beastly, carnal, sensuous, weak, lost, wretched creature and do not contradict or condemn the miraculous deeds of God which he can perform but your mind cannot grasp, and which he has performed in his beloved maiden Dorothea--to your disgrace, to Christendom's solace, to the faithful as an incentive, to the hearts of all people as a marvel of his unfathomable providence. He performed such works in a weak woman to prove to a world grown old in sin, rejuvenated in wickedness, grown cold in love of God that even the lovers of the world may see the fire of divine love burn to warm their cold hearts and gain God's favor.

The wounds God himself impressed upon her.

Chapter XVII.

God, the creator of all things, Lord of Lords, whose property was Dorothea's soul, also wanted to prove in her what right he had to her. Because she, wounded with the sword of God's love and his bitter martyrdom, subjugated her tender body so fiercely to her spirit through such self-castigations, the dear Lord Jesus Christ, her bridegroom, also wished to impress his own marks on her as symbols of their inseparable love and therefore also wounded her on her shoulders, arms, chest and back; on her shoulder blades, sides, calves, and knees. As she fell asleep, he impressed one, two, four, six, or eight wounds at once and so rapidly that she herself was unable to state the number of the wounds with which Christ had endowed her body. Whenever the wounds she received from Our Lord occurred in the fleshy parts of her body, they were deeper than those in other places. It also happened at times, though seldom, that she received wounds from God in such a way that suddenly at some part of her body a swelling appeared which started to burn, rage, and swell until the tightly-stretched skin ruptured and an open wound appeared.

In such a manner both the wounds she received from Our Lord and those she inflicted upon herself were renewed often. When she was nine years old it happened that through Our Lord a horrible, big wound appeared on her spine and tormented her so severely that she had to walk bent over and could not straighten up for a long time. Many people were convinced she would remain crooked for the rest of her life. And that wound remained open until her seventeenth year and often bled so fiercely that the blood hardened on her garments, which was a severe pain for her small body. For many years she dressed it with bandages morning and night so the blood would not drip on her bedclothes, dress, or elsewhere and thus reveal the presence of this wound. Thus she suffered constant, grievous pain from God's wounds on the one hand and wounds inflicted by her own hand on the other. But the wounds from Our Lord caused her the greatest pain, and she was burdened with the flow of blood and physical agony both day and night.

Nevertheless, she remained joyful and playful and with the blitheness of her spirit overcame the ailments of her body and revealed her sufferings to no one nor complained about severe pain until God himself wished them to be known. To hide her sufferings better, she herself washed her blood-soaked clothes at night. Had it not been for God's special providence, she could not have hidden these torments, especially from her mother, sisters, and servants whose company she had to share all day long. But when God decreed that scabs, scars or other manifestations of injury become noticeable on various parts of her body, she explained them as signs of nature cleansing itself in her in this way, as it does in others through boils, pockmarks, and the like.

In such a manner, with such severe wounds, pains, and self-castigations she impressed upon her soul the constant memory of the holy wounds and scars of Christ the Lord, in which she read as in a book the love and the suffering of Christ Our Lord and the obligation of giving thanks to God the Father for such a boon, who proved his love for all mankind in that he did not want to spare his own son but allowed him to be wounded to death for the sake of mankind. She also did not wish to be unmindful of a saying of Saint Paul who spoke thus: "If we suffer with him, we shall rule with him." If Christ had to suffer and could come into his kingdom only by so doing, how could any ordinary human being expect to enjoy someone else's kingdom without suffering? For is it not only not easy but truly impossible to live in this world according to the pleasures of the body and gain divine joy in heaven, that is, to go from joy to joy? This impossibility this wise woman recognized and followed the narrow path which the Lord Jesus Christ and all his dearly beloved friends walked who passed through the narrow portal of this life's misery and in so doing earned the privilege to rule in the spacious palace of heaven in the perfection of all joys.

How she was comforted in such sufferings.

Chapter XVIII.

Her wounds customarily produced in her five-fold torments from five-fold causes. At times she was plagued by burning sensations; afterwards they burst because of severe cold. Sometimes they raged as if pierced by darts; afterwards they swelled up, tore open, and bled profusely. From such ferocious pains the tender maid before and during her marriage derived such comfort from God that he made the small glands in her neck swell, which she then could blame for the pain caused by the wounds she chose to endure secretly but whose torment was nevertheless so severe that she had to take to her bed for some time. Sometimes she also suffered from illnesses affecting her eyes, from chills, or something of that sort. Though quite painful to others, to her love these would have been too insignificant to be considered suffering for God's sake. Still, they comforted her greatly because they allowed her to conceal those great wounds that overwhelmed and confined her to her bed. At times such an illness appeared twice or three times a year, generally when the pain of her wounds was so excruciating that she became bedridden. In her bed she often slumbered for twenty-four hours at a time as if in a faint, though actually in intense sweetness, as her soul was so highly blessed and pierced with spiritual pleasures that it seemed on the verge of melting since in such situations she enjoyed God's inexpressible comforts in so many different ways.

Whenever she had spent two of three days in such comforts and joys of the spirit, the wounds again served their purpose in the aforementioned manner, with stabs, swellings, and raging and tormented her so cruelly that she could neither lie down nor rest for three, four, or more days. Yet in the midst of this God's presence provided a special comfort which so saturated her soul that her body's suffering was notably reduced. For several days afterwards, as the tempest of pain calmed, her wounds healed, though never all of them, for several always remained open as a steady source of spiritual discipline. With those she rose cured from disease, fresh and restored, unchanged in color, for whether she lay ill or rose from her sickbed, she was always rosy-cheeked and beautiful of face. You who are so full of worldly wisdom, examine and mark in this that grace can do more than nature! Believe it and grant God full honor, if you want to have use of him for the betterment of your lives!

How devoutly she prepared herself for divine services and holy days.

Chapter XIX.

God alone, who understands all hearts, knew with what energy and devotion Dorothea prepared herself for the holy feast days all of Christendom celebrates together: how she initiated them through the integrity of her conscience and steadfastness of faith, how she observed them with sincere love and appropriate ceremony, what steady hope and complete confidence concerning her future rewards she received from them -- not only as an adult, but already in the days of her childhood. For when she was still just a child, she already began to avoid vain things and develop a fondness for attending church and church services. Both day and night, according to the time of year when the Church's holy days occurred and were celebrated, she participated with devoted passion, the mark of a devout daughter of the Lord who enjoyed entering her Father's house where she wished to learn her Father's will and fulfill it.

As the Church's holy days approached, such as Christmas and Easter, whose celebration began at midnight, and she was prohibited from going to church at night because of her childish frailty, her desire to participate was so intense that she bemoaned her absence violently and could not be comforted. No one could calm her, and she was unable to sleep for longing. She took the body of Our Lord for the first time when she was eleven years old on the Saturday before Easter and kept vigils until the Easter mass was to begin, waiting attentively by the door for her mother to rise for church services so she would be ready to accompany her. However, no matter how much she begged, she was prohibited from doing so because of her childish constitution. Because of this restriction she wept such bitter tears that she remained sleepless the entire night, and her father could find no words of comfort to stay her weeping although he remained at home with her until she received special comfort from God in the form of spiritual joys in her soul.

It was a miracle that on Easter day her wounds burst open and bled so profusely as though they were being formed anew, and because of this, she had to hide at home in one of the storerooms so the ample flow of blood would not betray the presence of her wounds. Especially noteworthy was that from the time she was seven years old-- when she was drenched by boiling water-- for the rest of her life she had such great devotion and desire to attend the church services on high feast days and holy days that she yearned to do so with such entreaties and diligence that many people thought she had become insane, especially if her desire to go to church was refused.

From that time on and all the rest of her days, whenever the feasts of Christ and of Our Lady, the feast days of the martyrs and many other saints approached, she either suffered from many new wounds or the old wounds renewed themselves with special torments--stabs, raging pain, swellings, and other such, as has been described before. With these she approached the coming holidays. And in the same manner as in other people of devout heart joy is increased in anticipation of the high festivals of the Church, in Dorothea, the elected friend of God, suffering increased through renewal of her wounds and their pain as the high feast days drew near. And the closer they approached, the fiercer the pains grew. They were like heralds dispatched ahead of time who with piercing darts announced the impending joys of the spiritual feasts to come. Whatever her sensual nature suffered in bodily discomforts, though, God, the comforter of all those in distress, did not forget his faithful maiden since she, especially after having reached maturity, on such occasions enjoyed a special advantage over many other devout people in spiritual foretastes of heavenly bliss, for before and during the holy feast days of Christendom the joy of the saints and of eternal life were revealed to her in a special way.

Her mighty struggle against the evil spirit.

Chapter XX.

With poisonous speeches and suggestions the ancient foe of human blessedness began to attack and wage war against the young maiden Dorothea who so longed for heavenly possessions. He shot sharp arrows of temptation into her heart to turn her mind away from worthwhile activity and prevent her contemplation of heavenly bliss. This he initiated through malicious suggestions like this: "Turn away from God, for it is useless to perform good deeds. You will not reach God anyway." When she was at her prayers, he spoke thus: "Why do you want to pray and exert yourself, interrupt your sleep and suffer cold, when none of it is of any use to you?" Whenever she gazed longingly towards heaven, he said: "Why do you look to heaven? You will never enter it anyway." Whenever she cried and sighed, he whispered to her: "Why do you cry and make yourself miserable? It is better for you to be merry with human beings than to devour your youth with wasted labors."

With such ideas he tried her youthful years so that he might deceive her and turn her from her service to God. When she wanted to attend church, give alms, endure distasteful things patiently, or perform other good works, he practiced his thousand wiles on her, in hopes of turning her from her good intentions and tormented her exceedingly in this fashion. But with the help of God's mercy, she did not give in to his evil suggestions but cleaved to God with still greater diligence. And as in her ardent desire for God she became ever more diligent in performing good works, the enemy assaulted the maid of God with ever greater temptation. The insinuations the fiend whispered to her were so powerful and painful that out of her own free will she would have chosen to tolerate large wounds on her body rather than to suffer such vicious suggestions from him.

There was still another reason why the temptation of the deceiver was so hard and painful to her, for she did not yet understand the power of the tempter in such a struggle and how difficult it is to withstand him. But God the Lord brought her aid during the temptation and strengthened her weak infancy against the ancient foe with such grace that she was victorious over him. When she was sitting alone in pious contemplation, in heartfelt prayer or sang a hymn of praise to God and in doing so started burning with love and desire, the evil spirit could not tolerate it but became more daring in his wicked temptation and venomous suggestions. Her piety was so painful to him and his temptation so unbearable to her that, had the world been hers, she would have gladly given it to free herself of this burden.

The reason why she suffered such severe temptation, she assumed, was that she had not dedicated herself sufficiently and extensively enough to good works. Therefore, the more she was tempted, the more her spirit was driven to perform good works. Her love for God increased; her desire became hotter. She satisfied the needs of the body even less than before; the wounds and pains of the flesh she regarded as still more insignificant and castigated herself even more severely to be freed from the temptations of the evil spirit and more firmly anchored in the divine foundation of virtue. It is a miracle that she was not beguiled by the wiles of the wicked fiend to wound and castigate herself so as to mortify and injure herself beyond proper measure and appropriate discipline. And therefore he often attacked her all the more fiercely when she was immersed in the passion of the spirit to poison and deflate as much as possible the bliss of her spirit with his bilious insinuations. Her struggle with the wicked spirit started when she was nine years old and took place daily both before and during her marriage.

Even though the temptation of the enemy weighed heavily on Dorothea, she was nevertheless of good spirits and in the company of others exhibited a cheerful disposition. Also, though she assumed her flesh to be the source of such mighty temptations, they did not stem from her flesh but the malice of the wicked enemy, for she confessed that she had never felt any temptation of the flesh, and that is quite believable since she began to torment her body with wounds and other hard castigations even before nature corrupted by original sin could manifest itself in her. Thus her flesh did not incline toward sensuality because of the extreme pain to which she subjected it. Furthermore, reason started to tame and master sensuality in her at such an early age that the donkey, that is the body, could not get its way but had to be obedient to the spirit. For this conquest she also had extraordinary help from heaven because of which her flesh is not to be blamed for the temptation from the seventh to the thirty-ninth year when her heart was torn from her body and renewed (how that happened is known only to God). Rather, during those years she hurt her body grievously so that she might overcome the fiend's temptations which she suffered especially keenly during her conjugal life.

Whenever because of her great devotion she visited churches and traveled from one to another to earn grace and indulgences, the envious spirit spoke to her thus: "Why are you going about and search out various places like a fool? Why don't you remain quietly in one church and tend to your prayer with devotion and without hindrance?" If, however, special devotion seized her and drew her up to God so that she, remaining in one church, silently hid herself in one corner, the jealous spirit asked: "Why are you not seeking out this or that church where many indulgences are to be had?" to cool her heart inflamed by divine love and shatter her spirit's blessed calm with restlessness.

In these various deceits the Holy Spirit assisted her with his help and instruction and by calming and destroying the fiend's malicious guile, as God revealed to her ten weeks before her death: "When you turned to me in sincere love, the evil spirit started to hate you. It was because you were so hard-pressed to resist him that you initiated your strict regimen. For against your bodily enemies you would have been victorious more easily because against such foes you would have had the aid of friends. Those enemies you would have recognized more easily, their deception, power, strategy, presence, and absence."

Here is to be discerned an open affirmation of the blessed Dorothea's saintliness whose enemy the evil spirit became because she resisted his wicked intention, did not obey his venomous suggestions, but contradicted him entirely. Obviously no temporal lord assaults the fortress he himself has fortified and holds in uncontested ownership with attack and battle; however, the one he still hopes to win he attacks with assault, war, and siege to conquer it. In exactly the same way all whom the devil possesses in complete ownership and who do his bidding are immune to his temptations. But God's servants and handmaidens who contradict and avoid the pleasures of the body and the delights of the sinful world, the tools in the work of the evil spirit, he tempts and rages against so that he may overwhelm and possess the fortress of their souls which the Prince of Peace, Christ the Lord, holds through his ever-present grace. The stronger the fortress, the stronger the assault. Excellently fortified was the fortress of Dorothea's soul with its deep moat of humility, its solid walls of strength of character; with its surrounding wall of caution, the high towers of angelic protection; with the many assault engines and defense mechanisms of various virtues. Therefore, the devil's temptation of her was all the greater and her victory all the more painful to him. To all people who hear the story of the holy life she lived in those days in praise of God Our Lord her example shall be all the more inspiring.

Her praiseworthy marriage.
Chapter XXI.

Not only virgins and those who live chastely enter into the kingdom of heaven but also married people who with true faith and good works earn God's grace. Therefore it is well to consider that not through blind circumstance but through God's ordinance the beloved bride of God Dorothea was betrothed to a human bridegroom so that the holy state of matrimony as it is supported and validated by the Church be further sanctified and confirmed through the holy life of those of God's children who remain in the state of matrimony, as it happened in former times with Saint Elisabeth [of Hungary, October 16], Saint Hedwig (St. Jadwiga) [November 19], and many other blessed people, both men and women who were married. Furthermore, married life was helpful to the blessed Dorothea insofar as she became all the more humble through the heavy load of conjugal burdens, and God was praised even more highly in the fruit her married life brought forth as she, for his praise and honor, became more skilled in all matters ordained proper in God's service.

The chaste, modest virgin glistened like a beautiful lily in all her worthiness and until her seventeenth year faithfully guarded the chastity of her body and heart as a precious hidden treasure by protecting her spirit from all evil desire. Because of this she never suffered attack on her reputation, either seriously or in jest, for having kept bad company. For she was sober, moderate, humble, outgoing, gracious, pleasant, and peaceable; disputes she brought to positive conclusions, and therefore she had many suitors. Her oldest brother affianced her to an honorable, clever artisan, rich enough according to his state. She agreed to the engagement as a maid obedient to her superior, in fear of God, not out of desire for future delights of the body. After that, according to the traditions of the Church, she was married and led into her bridegroom's house, into the city called Gdansk in the episcopal see of Leslow. After the marriage rites had been completed according to the custom of the land, Dorothea, true to the angel Raphael's admonition, remained untouched by the bridegroom not just for three nights but even longer, and she on her part always remained untainted by the desires of the flesh. Thus there was established between them a chaste and honorable marriage adorned with the threefold treasure of conjugal life-- fidelity, a wealth of children, and a holy union of uninterrupted cohabitation.

How she remained faithful to her husband.

Chapter XXII.

Her husband Adalbert, out of his heart's devotion travelled to the holy places in Rome and Aix to win God's grace. In his absence the blessed Dorothea was even more eager to accomplish praiseworthy works because at such times she could better enjoy the pleasures of her heavenly bridegroom who for her sake had been wounded to death and for whose love she then more daringly renewed her wounds and performed other castigations that she had to conceal carefully when her husband was at home. But whether he was at home or not, she conducted herself so blamelessly that she offered to God her dedicated service and to her husband pleasant companionship and fidelity.

The birth and upbringing of their children.

Chapter XXIII.

The comfort and joy of married people is the birth and good upbringing of children. So that the blessed Dorothea with her husband would not be denied this bliss, God blessed her with the fruitfulness of nine children that she bore her husband. Moreover, this blessed woman afterwards labored diligently to give birth to these same children spiritually whom she previously had born into the world physically so that they would be her fleshly as well as her spiritual children. She was not one of those foolish, faithless mothers who raise their children from infancy into the service of the devil and teach them how to dance and flirt before they are able to recite the *pater noster*. Curses, crude manners, and vice are their delight; thus they send their children into everlasting damnation through two kinds of sin, those of the parents who raise them poorly and their own that they acquired when they were young and retain even in their old age.

It is fit for faithful parents to provide their children with sustenance and discipline. Such this faithful mother Dorothea did for her children by instilling in them the sweet name of Jesus Christ with her milk. For whatever she did with her children, the name of Jesus was always in her heart and mouth. She also rose early with great anxiety and like the holy Job offered devout prayers for each child individually, shedding many tears for them. From infancy she taught them to fear God and avoid sin, as the excellent Tobias taught his son. She did not punish her children carelessly over their misdeeds as Heli did his son but castigated them sensibly and strictly, according to the nature of their misbehavior. With words and deeds, good habits, and examples she enticed and guided her children toward a desire for the kingdom of heaven. Her diligence, concern, labor and exertion to bear her children to God were greater than they had been in giving them physical birth.

Equally dedicated was her effort on behalf of other people whom she, according to God's exhortation, was to bear to him in spirit through fervent prayers and excellent guidance to a new, virtuous life. Weeping and praying, she diligently interceded with God for her spiritual children while punishing and admonishing them and doing what she could to draw them to God. To increase her reward, God granted her the grace that those unmindful of her instruction by word were many times won by her shining example of virtue which she so excellently presented to all her spiritual children.

Their life together.

Chapter XXIV.

The sanctity of marriage, which means the impossibility of separation, was evident in their union, for no human being but God himself severed the bond of matrimony between them through death. The maid of God lived united with her husband in holy matrimony for twenty-six and a half years and kept her marriage vows in such chastity that she never demanded her conjugal rights from her husband. But in fear of God and in keeping with the law to render unto Caesar what is Caesar's and to God what is God's due she paid her marital dues whenever her husband demanded. Physically she became the mother of children, but she remained a virgin in spirit to do justice to her carnal bridegroom and at the same time not to withhold from her heavenly bridegroom the service that was his by right. Finally, though, when she conceived and gave birth to a daughter, they both realized that it would be pleasing to God if they abstained from conjugal activities to serve God in complete chastity and with an unencumbered spirit. They agreed to it and remained with one another for ten years without conjugal activities until death separated them; and the daughter became a nun in a convent.[31]

---

[31] Upon moving to Marienwerder permanently, Dorothea entrusted the twelve-year-old Gertrud to a Benedictine convent in Kulm.

The holy exercises she performed during her marriage.

Chapter XXV.

From youth until old age the servant of God Dorothea busied herself to serve God with all her might, for the love of God called her so insistently that she paid no heed to the comfort of her body. Whether she was pregnant or not, near giving birth, or nursing an infant, she worked, she fetched and carried, she climbed stairs and bent over, and whatever was appropriate for her to do she did in good spirits and with complete trust in God. Nor did she curtail the chastisement of the body in terms of fasts, genuflections, self-flagellations, and other torments, even when she was in childbed. Lying in childbed, she seldom had peace and comfort in her house, first because of the hard work of supervising servants, then because of the infant's yelling and screaming, and also because of her own physical pains and various burdens and labors.

Furthermore, she was ailing in both body and soul from intense longing because she had to forgo church attendance for forty days; this long absence caused her great irritation. When the lying-in period was over, she most devoutly went to church with the infant, happy but also sad: happy because she could go to church again and attend services, sad because the care of the infant would severely curtail her church attendance and because she again would be forced to share her husband's bed from which she absented herself whenever she could justifiably do so. To do so she frequently sat by the cradle and rocked her child all night long. During the winter when it was cold, she wore nothing but a single shift covered by an old, threadbare coat but paid no attention whatever to the labor and the freezing cold but suffered them on purpose to stay away from her husband's bed. She also did not consider that all winter long, both before her marriage and afterwards, she had never been warm.

Early in the morning after tending to household affairs and the needs of her children, she commended the children to God's care and left for church. Generally she was the first person there, arriving before the church doors were even unlocked. If anyone preceded her she was mortified and punished her sluggishness, for she insisted on being first in waking, praying, and serving the Lord and never to be tardy. She did this not out of greed for fame but because of love she felt for God. Often it happened that she spent long periods of time kneeling in weeping supplication in front of the church before it was unlocked.

When the church finally was opened, she entered the house of the heavenly Father with appropriate respect and hid in a corner and there multiplied her exercises, her genuflections, and her prayers with such heated spirit and physical exertion that even in the wintertime when she was dressed only in a thin shift and a coat sweat poured from her and bathed her entire body on account of the great heat. Generally she settled down eventually to quiet prayer, contemplation, and meditation, totally enraptured by God, her spirit so inflamed in profound meditation that it seemed as if she were sitting in a hot bath. For this reason she often had to cool herself, both winter and summer, by fanning her face with her coat, by sitting on cold stones, or by leaning against them.

No matter how determined she was to remain at church until all masses had been celebrated, at times she was prevented from doing so by the wails of her infants, which she recognized even while she was in church by a sign such as this: when she felt the milk trickling from her breasts, be it while she was in church or elsewhere, she hurried without delay to her child. It was most annoying and painful to her, especially at night, to go home from church through the refuse without a light. And when she was prevented from her early morning church attendance by her husband or other matters, it was as severe an injury to her as if a sharp sword were cutting her apart. Such suffering she endured until she received a special comfort from God.

Yet Dorothea did not cease her suffering on account of such comfort, for as it reduced her burden, love of God increased her practice of painful self-castigations because of the foretaste of future consolations she perceived in them. Therefore she beat, stabbed, tormented, and wounded her body with various tools and in a variety of ways until nothing or very little of it remained whole. Beneath her clothes it was drenched with blood, so every turn and movement was painful and bitter; yet for all that she did not stop the labors she had obligated herself to perform. Whenever she did not perform such castigations on her body, she was saying her most heartfelt prayers and went from one church to another to gain indulgences, listen to sermons, and be present at the celebration of the mass. She also visited the poor on whom she practiced the works of charity both physical and spiritual, for herself and others, whenever she wept copiously about the sins of human imperfection, the problems of the poor, and the misery inherent in this transitory life.

Then she felt, as it was later revealed to her by God, that God the Lord drove and commanded her like a laboring beast is driven to torment herself in this manner and in so doing without tarrying should move ahead to traverse the road towards eternal bliss from one painful exercise to the next, from one labor to another, so that she would enjoy little respite. And whenever she desired to rest for a moment and refresh her tired limbs or ease her wounds, the Lord seemed to manifest himself to her by driving her with blows, admonishing her to return to work, castigations, and vigils. Therefore she slept seldom and little. All of this was painful and bitter to her for many years, yet no matter how exhausted her body became, sleep was even more painful to her than waking.

How she received comfort from God.

Chapter XXVI.

After a great storm everything becomes very calm, and after a heavy rain comes a beautiful sunshine; likewise God gives his beloved great joy after great sadness and after great labor great reward and rest. This God also did for his faithful servant Dorothea. When she had castigated herself so severely and had worked hard for many a year, the Lord sometimes granted her rest for one hour, two, three or even a little more in sweet slumber during which she felt that her spirit was engaged in delightful pleasures and that God entertained a sweet dalliance with her soul. That was a matter of intense joy to her even though she did not yet realize what this dalliance of Our Lord meant. Her heart jumped notably for joy, and she prayed fervently in her sleep. Whatever she could not accomplish in prayer while she was awake because of many deterrents, her spirit wanted to accomplish while she was asleep, and that was brought about through her long-standing custom of praying diligently and her longing love of God.

As she became aware of the presence of this kind of sleep, she developed a great longing for it; and that was not surprising, for in such sleep she experienced the start and growth of a great love for the stark joy of divine consolation, holy desire, and God's strong pull of her spirit through his hot, burning love. To such sweet foretaste of future bliss she was admitted in this present life for more than sixteen years, and as soon as she realized through this spiritual taste how sweet the Lord is, the entire world became more distasteful and bitter to her than ever before.

How through ecstasies of spiritual sweetness
she was estranged from her physical senses and became
incapable of discharging her everyday responsibilities.
Chapter XXVII.

As Dorothea was drawn by God's mercy to such enjoyment of contemplation, she burned so fiercely in divine love that for her it was much more a joy than an effort or an annoyance to interrupt her sleep, to forego partaking of food for the sustenance of her body, or to omit whatever else is necessary for the body's comfort. She now recognized that divine sweetness immeasurably exceeds all fleshly gratification and that one compared to the other in respect to their strength resembles the entire ocean opposed to a single drop of water. God so increased her holy desire that as a result she began to hate the world and its glory even more. Concerns about temporal affairs; wearing luxurious clothes, and to own a great variety of them for adornment and worldly comfort; to attend banquets or other kinds of human entertainments was disgusting to her and so cruel to her spirit that physical revulsion seized her over the cheap tawdriness of such occasions.

From time to time she was also so filled with God's sweetness that she behaved as though she were drunk and was occasionally overwhelmed by such satisfaction of the spirit that she lay as in a stupor, removed from the control of her external senses so that people thought she had fainted or had fallen asleep. When she was thus in ecstacy and her husband, to whom things brought about in this manner were unknown, called her and she failed to answer him, he blamed her stubbornness, not the workings of God's mercy. This is why when she once was thus in ecstacy, he again and again doused her with water, which she, however, did not feel at all until much later when she found herself wet without knowing that water had been poured all over her. It also happened on other occasions that when she was thus strongly drawn to God while being pulled back and forth by a crowd, kicked by rushing feet, rudely jostled or subjected to other kinds of blows, she nevertheless remained lovely in appearance and cheerful of face.

Occasionally when she was supposed to go into a certain room and do something at her husband's behest, the sweet grace of God overcame her and she sank down, remaining seated at a place in the attic, unmindful of her husband's request. Likewise it happened that when her husband asked her to buy meat or fish, she would buy eggs or other goods. For the same reason she also from time to time lost her way; when she was supposed to go to market, she went to church or somewhere else. Similarly, she at times was so completely drawn into herself by the effects of God's grace that she did not recognize even things that at other times were most familiar to her, as happened once when she held goose eggs in her hands but did not realize they were goose eggs even though she looked at them intently, on account of which the other women who were there made fun of her.

Occasionally she also was drawn into such high contemplation by God or blessed in some other manner that she could not retain enough control over herself to walk or move from one place to another. In spite of this she was in good spirits and happy, and sometimes, because of exceeding joy and spiritual delight both at home and in church, could not refrain from uttering a few words expressing her heart's delight in the presence of rude people who on account of their animalistic nature knew nothing of such kinds of divine grace, and ignorant of spiritual delights, assumed that she had become mentally deranged.

How once her husband injured her because of food.

Chapter XXVIII.

Adalbert, her husband, was a choleric man, by natural inclination and because of his arthritis. As long as his wife, the blessed Dorothea, fulfilled his wishes, he was favorably disposed toward her serving God diligently before dinnertime as she wished and was able. To prevent her being hindered from doing so by the care of children, he himself stayed at home during that time and diligently supervised them in her stead. Eventually, because of her ecstasies and the counsel of her spiritual advisors she little by little, though reasonably, began to remove herself from the conjugal embraces of the marriage bed, the intimate companionship customary among marriage partners. Because of this and other good works she constantly performed in love of God, her husband at one time became furious and threatened her: "If you don't cease your wandering about and see to the care of your household with greater effort than you have done so far, I shall tame you with shackles and chains." Then his rage overwhelmed him. For three days he kept the honorable housewife Dorothea fettered and in chains, a prisoner in his house. But she interposed the spiritual shield of patience and thus deflected the grim volleys, strokes of anger, and curses and endured them without complaint or counter argument so that her husband, mistaking her holy patience and silence for defiance and arrogance, severely beat her on the head with a chair. All of this she endured for both their sakes with great patience and suffered it gladly for in that very temptation God did not abandon her without comfort but internally pacified her mind beyond temporal sweetness.

The four kinds of spiritual ailments love caused her.

Chapter XXIX.

The *Book of Kings* tells us how Ammon, the son of King David, fell ill because of the love he felt for the beautiful Tamar, his half sister. If, then, impure love is so powerful to sicken the person it overwhelms, how much more powerful is the holy love the almighty God grants his lovers, which also overcomes them in such a way that they too must yearn for him, and that ever so much more since his beauty, his nobility, his sweet embrace and passion surpass the desires and joys of all living creatures. Little wonder, then, that when the blessed Dorothea was seized so forcefully by the divine love of her own crucifix she could find no satisfaction in anything external; she too started yearning for him out of passionate love.

Starting in the thirty-second year of her life she occasionally suffered four kinds of sickness because of her longing love for God. The first type of illness grew out of her fearful torment of great love, which compelled her to contemplate how she could make herself equal to her only lover who here during his time on Earth had been despised and rejected as though he were a criminal and how to equal him in his abject humility. Therefore she wished to be released from all earthly, perishable things which she now considered putrid carrion, for the flower of worldly glory had now withered and died in her heart.

The second illness, more severe than the first, she endured because of her great longing for the perfect life as the Lord has taught it in the gospel: it consists of voluntary poverty, misery, and the destruction and contempt of one's own being. And while she was united with her husband, she worried greatly about how to pursue the elements of perfection in the future. However, she satisfied her great longing as opportunity permitted, and from time to time seated herself among the beggars in front of the church portal in a threadbare coat, her head and face covered with a cheap piece of cloth in order not to be recognized by acquaintances, and there accepted alms. And when a piece of bread was given to her, her spirit was so overjoyed by the effect of God's love through which she had received it that neither honey nor any other delectable food would have tasted as good and sweet to her. Sometimes her confessor encountered her sitting there like that among the poor and recognized her. She then invited him most graciously to share this gift of her "Dear Friend." And for everything she received by begging in this manner, she reimbursed the poor doubly or threefold.

The third spiritual illness attacked her through her great longing to receive the body of the Lord. But since the body of Christ in the sacrament was not given to her as often as she desired, she was robbed of her strength and languished on account of her great desire for the body of Our Lord. But as soon as she received it, she recovered her strength, which was obvious in the body's ability to stand and move as well as the beauty of her facial hue, which had faded during her yearning for the divine sustenance.

The fourth ailment, her longing for eternal life, was the most severe of all to oppress her. When she was in the throes of this illness, she was oppressed so severely that she often had to take to her bed. The other three weakened her to such a degree that she sometimes could barely stand or move about; the fourth, however, incapacitated her so she could neither stand nor walk. So with exercises appropriate to her desire, she pursued eternal life until nothing else was on her mind but to be released from the prison of the body and take up residence with Christ her Lord.

The lovely miracle that happened to her

on the feast day of Our Lady's Immaculate Conception.

Chapter XXX.

This miracle happened to the blessed Dorothea in the thirty-third year of her life, on the feast day of St. Mary's Immaculate Conception [December 8]. Very early in the morning she went to the parish church in Gdansk, which was established in honor of Our Lady St. Mary, and remained there for about four hours in continuous, rapturous prayer. After that she wanted to go to the church of the preaching friars and there perform devotions over the noon hour, as was her custom. But when she stepped from the churchyard into the adjoining lane, she right away felt a hindrance, as though a wall were stretched in front of her to prohibit her progress.

Immediately she perceived this as a divine mark of warning and without delay hurried home and went to a storeroom which she had not entered for half a year and there encountered a fire so extensive that even with much help from other people she extinguished it only with great difficulty. Her house, household goods, and four of her children would have perished in the fire had she not received this warning from God and his mother Mary who had impeded her in the lane with her presence because the blessed Dorothea was particularly devoted to her. That it indeed had been the Virgin Mary who had protected Dorothea from this harm, Mary herself revealed to her more than fourteen years later, admonishing her to keep demonstrating great affection toward her and to commemorate the day of her immaculate conception each year with great reverence.

Their pilgrimages to Aix.

Chapter XXXI.

Saint Paul says: "A blessed woman blesses her husband as well." This is what the blessed Dorothea did, who through her good example inspired her husband to good works, which is apparent in this: When all their children but one daughter had died,[32] they sold their house and all household goods, and to serve God with unencumbered spirits, they divested themselves of all the vanities of the world. And at Whitsuntide of the thirty-eighth year of the blessed Dorothea's life, they went on a journey to Aix and committed all their possessions to acquaintances, except for their daughter whom she entrusted to the care of

---

[32] Paul Nieborowski and a few other scholars argue that in addition to Gertrud at least one more daughter (Agatha) survived to adulthood and maintains that this daughter and her children were living in Gdansk at the time of Dorothea's death in 1394. Recent scholarship credits this idea to faulty translation of Latin records.

spiritual rather than worldly friends.

After they had completed their pilgrimage to Aix, they traveled on to Einsiedeln, also called Finsterwald, to the chapel of Our Dear Lady. In that chapel the special servant of the holy Virgin Mary conceived such special devotion to God and his mother that it was not enough for her to have been in it only once. She returned three times by the same road to receive more blessings and enjoy still more contemplation. The first time they had traveled three German miles on foot. Still they returned to the chapel. The second time they had traveled a whole day's journey from there and had already taken up quarters for the night when a woman arrived on horseback who wanted to travel to that same chapel. Because of her great love to St. Mary, Dorothea followed the woman on foot on the muddy roads and there renewed her contemplation before returning to her husband. The third time, when they had completed their pilgrimage to Aix and were traveling towards Cologne, both of them were inspired to return to Aix, which they did. There, in Our dear Lady's church in Aix, they fulfilled their good intentions in God's honor with great love. As a result, in the course of this particular journey the blessed Dorothea came to Our Lady's chapel in Einsiedeln for a third time so as to knit the tight knot thrice that tied her to the service of Mary, the most worthy empress and mother of mercy.

How God preserved them both from two serious injuries.

Chapter XXXII.

One day it happened that husband, wife, and their horse boarded a small ship to cross a big, deep lake. Be it that during the journey the horse stamped its feet or leaned too far to one side to cause the boat to take on water; they all together would have drowned, but there is no doubt that the blessed Dorothea with her prayers earned their rescue from Our Lord God who made the water and waves obey his command. After that, around the days of Saints Simon and Jude [October 28], they suffered tremendous delays on their way home as well as dangers because of water and highwaymen. One time in particular they came into the hostelry of a turner who outwardly greeted them with friendly demeanor; secretly, however, he prepared his malicious weapons against his peaceful guests and would have murdered them for their property had God in his infinite mercy not sent a carter who arrived just in time and in his devotion to justice protected the guests whose innocent blood the guilty host meant to spill. This episode Our Lord renewed in Dorothea's memory nine years later and bade her to be thankful to his mother Mary who at such times had been the protectress of her and her family.

Their return from Aix to Gdansk.

Chapter XXXIII.

On the feast day of Saint Martin [November 11] in the thirty-eighth year of the blessed Dorothea's life, they returned to Gdansk after having seen the holy places and having committed themselves more deeply to serving God. Dorothea, the servant of God, was then drawn higher with love and longing for God, received God's comforting visitations more frequently, and recognized God's comfort more clearly. Not surprisingly, delicious food became disgusting to her and whenever she smelled it, it caused her severe pain. Meager food and clothing, on the other hand, she loved and desired more than ever as a way to castigate and starve her body rather than pamper and spoil it. She also wished to suffer more intensely and be shunned instead of enjoying physical comforts and honors. What sufferings the Lord imposed on her to suffer at the hands of her husband or others she endured joyfully.

All night long she did not rest in bed, but with a variety of exercises appropriate to the inner as well as the outer being she devoured the night. Frequently when there was heavy frost, when it stormed, rained, or snowed, she sat by the open window, leaning out to observe the sky. Since childhood she felt a keen desire and love for observing heaven and did so indoors and out, day and night, wherever she happened to sit, stand, or walk. Her castigations, self-disciplines, her hard and heavy exercises grew and increased just as she increased in years and devotion. In equal measure, though, the foe of blessedness increased his temptations of her, especially during the two years or so before and the four years after the exchange of her heart. She resisted him with God's help and drove him away with many hot tears.

Book II

Here begin the chapters of the second book of the life of the blessed Dorothea, anchoress at Marienwerder.

How her heart was drawn from her body and another put in its place.

Chapter I.

The Lord has worked and completed a merciful deed in the blessed Dorothea, as he promised to grant through his prophet Ezekiel, through whom he spoke thus: "I will give you a new heart and put a new spirit into you and will bring about that you walk in the spirit of my commandments and uphold and protect them." This renewal was accomplished in the blessed woman Dorothea like this: It happened in the thirty-ninth year of her life and the tenth year before her death within eight days of the holy day of Candlemas [February 2]. She experienced severe longing and desire for the glorious holy body of Our Lord Jesus Christ, which to receive she had prepared herself with great diligence.

But during that same praiseworthy preparation the spirit of suspicion and hesitation assaulted her heavily, which already for two years before that holy day had assaulted, troubled, and dismayed her most woefully. Now she came into the church of Our Lady in Gdansk very early in the morning, as was her habit, and knelt before the high altar and with great devotion and tenderness in divine, hot, burning love recited fifty *Ave Marias* in praise and honor of the praiseworthy Virgin Mary, revealing her distress, suffering, and sadness. Now take note! As she did this and with sincere love offered her prayer, a great press ensued, for a large crowd of people were jostling each other to get as close as possible to the high altar to witness the holy body of Our Lord about to be raised. This commotion forced her to continue her prayer in praise of the honored Virgin Mary standing up.

As she continued her requests during the silent mass, Our Lord Jesus, her mighty lover, came, pulled out her old heart, and pushed into its place a new, hot one. The blessed Dorothea felt very well that her old heart was being extracted and that in place of that heart an extremely hot piece of flesh was shoved into her. In receiving this piece of flesh or new heart she experienced such rapture and joy that she could never truly relate it to anyone. This removal and renewal of her heart was performed by Our Lord Jesus Christ, to whom all things are possible, and later he often revealed this to her. That he wrought this especially through his mercy has been proven through other great mercies subsequently bestowed upon her. For all grace, virtue, and delightful gifts she received through this renewal were greatly enhanced and adorned with fierce, hot burning love and brought to a high degree of perfection.

With this renewal of heart the Lord bestowed on her a love which encompasses other kinds of love and good things, which the Lord enumerated especially during her last year of life: "The first good I gave you when I pulled out your heart was the overflowing love. This is an immeasurable love, also called a satiated love; a sweet, happy love, well ordered, good tasting, fragrant, fruitful, impossible to lose, never overcome, and undying. At the time I snatched your heart from you, you understood nothing more about the satisfaction of spiritual desires and joys but that you were in eternal life. Nevertheless, you immediately changed into a totally different person because through that love I pulled you into eternal life for the first time. Through this rapture you recognized at once how good it would be to be with me." She was at once illuminated in her rapture and well instructed so that she understood better and more thoroughly the life of the saints as they had lived on earth than a great learned man could have taught her in an entire year.

The blessed Jesus taught her that from then on she had to guard her heart diligently so it would remain honest, clean, whole, and unimpaired; to open her inner senses while closing her outer ones to everything but the absolute necessities of life; and to live in accordance to his will. If she let be all temporal things, she would become wealthy and possess all things with him and should be transformed into a different being. In the instant the new heart was given to her, she was enraptured and her soul so deeply united with God that she was oblivious to all external things. She felt how the Lord Jesus Christ embraced and kissed her soul and from that moment until her death heard the voice of God as he spoke to her soul, generally internally though occasionally externally, to reveal secret, hidden things to her. She could not have endured not hearing this voice on any given day for the distress it would have caused her to assume that inertia had distracted her.

Here one needs to take note that the renewal of Dorothea's heart not only took place spiritually but physically as well. God's own revelations previous to this event and what she herself said about it confirm this. Her confessors also have understood it that way, as is evident from their frequent conversations with her about this event. It is very well possible for God to renew and change the heart in this fashion, just as he changed Adam's rib into a woman, Lot's wife into a pillar of salt, water into blood, and in Moses' day a rod into a snake. He also transformed water into wine, bread in to his body, and wine into his blood. Many other signs and miracles he has performed with his saints. With them and through them many a dead man was raised from the dead and many a blind man illuminated who until then had never enjoyed sight or perhaps had no eyes at all.

Moreover, one can read in the *Life of Saints Cosmas and Damian* who in Rome detached a diseased leg from the body of a sleeping man and attached in its place another that they had cut off a moor who just been buried at the churchyard of St. Peter of the Chains. This was proven true, for when the dead man was dug up, he was missing one leg while the other man had acquired two different legs, a white one and a black one, which he kept all the days of his life. Therefore, through this story we take to heart the word of Saint Augustine who says this about God's miracles: "His might and his will are the cause of miracles; let us concede to God that he may do things that we with human reason are incapable of comprehending."

The many other merciful gifts that followed the renewal of her heart.

Chapter II.

After the exchange of hearts Dorothea at all times enjoyed unclouded insight, burning love for Our Dear Lord, and zestful enjoyment. She was enraptured frequently and intensely and was illuminated by a divine light through which she discerned mighty, secret things in heaven and on Earth, which she saw and understood sometimes in her imagination, sometimes, and that was generally the case, without the power of imagination but through her understanding or reason. These insights occurred at one time more clearly than another. After the extraction of her heart and through the Lord's teachings, she despised many things which before had been very dear to her, considering them now putrefying refuse. Her life, now so strongly awakened by the Lord, was adorned by a hot, burning love and illuminated by a penetrating light which began to glow before God, whom it pleased greatly, as he indicated to her: "Formerly you hid yourself from yourself by putting others in front of you to whom you paid more attention than you did to yourself. Now you shall place yourself squarely before you and behold yourself and how you are made. Remember how you have spent your time in the past, what good things you failed to perform then and what evil you did commit so that you may pry loose what is punishable with the file of repentance, live righteously, and please me."

As she had been instructed by the Lord, she placed herself in front of herself, and as she examined herself honestly, she espied a number of traits unpleasant to God, and the more diligently she looked at herself, the more plainly she recognized what was wicked, harmful, and useless in her. Therefore she started to confess details of her entire life in the way the Lord taught her: not everything anew, for on many occasions she had already confessed all the sins she could remember with great contrition and gentle tears. Now, renewed in spirit, she did it in a new way. For the merciful Lord was present to aid her with his grace and taught her how to recognize her sins, their magnitude and number, and how to confess them in clear, appropriate words. He also taught her to confess things that oppressed her or duties she was loath to perform, such as not wanting to clean a bowl, for instance. Our Lord also taught her to recognize and confess a number of sins she had committed earlier.

This kind of confession she practiced until she received assurance from the Holy Spirit that all her sins had been forgiven. When she had won this promise, there arose in her a strong, steadfast hope that her soul upon being separated from the body would go to heaven without delay. Before she received this assurance and measure of hope from the Holy Ghost, she never ceased her confessions but kept them strictly for perhaps five years, until God the Lord, her comforter, started sending the Holy Spirit as a special comfort to his elected bride whenever she was highly distressed even about very small sins. On the Sunday before Shrove Tuesday, two years after the exchange of hearts, she was illuminated so intensely that she became transparent, able to see herself through and through as if she were gazing through a crystal with healthy eyes. For the very first time she beheld her entire person for then she could see all her sins, no matter how small, and discovered a number she had never noticed before. From that year of her life, her forty-first, until her death she was generally illuminated so strongly and clearly that she could see through her body with her spiritual eyes. Likewise, from the time her heart was pulled from her body until the end of her life she experienced greater longing and desire than before to see and receive the body of Our Lord and desired most passionately to go to heaven to Christ Jesus, her lover, who daily wounded her soul and heart, now with the arrows of love, now with love's steel spears.[33] And in the injuries caused by these projectiles she now felt pain, now sweetness, now love and longing. At times, in the throes of agony, she experienced all these sensations simultaneously in soul and in body.

In such wounding through love her spirit grew stronger in longing and remained in rapture longer than before, and the Lord demonstrated the richness of

---

[33] A few portraits show Dorothea holding a bundle of spears. The majority, however, portray her pierced by arrows and spears. See the Appendix for the oldest picture of Dorothea made from a woodcut for Jacop Karweysze's 1492 print. His initial "K" appears in the front center floor tile.

his grace more abundantly, openly, and freely, granting jubilation to her heart and powerful illumination to her mind. She was often so filled with the rich, inexpressible sweetness of divine desire that whenever she experienced it, she did not know how she could bear to remain in it, for her spiritual desire made her tremble so vehemently that she could in no way stand, sit, lie, or walk, but was extremely restless. Because of this agitation she now attempted to stand, then to sit, now to lie, and to walk. She would wring her hands because of her extreme desire, love, and joy, just as a person in a state of great suffering and sadness will do.

How the Virgin Mary cast a most delightful thing into her arms.

Chapter III.

During the first or the second night after the previously mentioned feast of Candlemas, the purification of Our Lady, after having received the blessed body of Our Lord, Dorothea turned to Mary the holy virgin in devout prayer. She burned hotly and implored her with great humility to bring her beloved son and not deny her. Then, when she had prayed much in burning longing, she addressed her like this: "Oh, most beloved virgin, honorable mother of God, blessed above all women, answer me, show and give me your most beloved son, for you will suffer no harm from doing so. When you presented him in the temple, you permitted Simeon the Righteous to take him into his arms, and before that, when you laid him to sleep in the manger, you showed him to the shepherds and the three kings. I beg you, grant my prayer through the grace God granted you and the grace you granted the shepherds and the kings." Behold, after much imploring and many endearments inspired by Dorothea's having being set afire with God's love for the holy virgin, she mercifully was granted her prayer by the merciful mother of God, and as a sign that her prayer had been granted, Mary placed into her arms a most delightful thing that Dorothea received with great reverence and delight. She was set ablaze with the fire of divine love and filled with inexpressible joy in which she remained for many days and which made her exclaim lovingly: "O, dear rose, laugh; laugh, dear tender rose." Ecstatic with love, she could not stop saying these words for days on end; instead, she repeated them many times, and these repetitions brought her spirit ever-increasing sweetness and joy.

How the Lord taught her to turn to the contemplative life.

Chapter IV.

After this, in the course of another night it happened that Dorothea paid neither attention to God's voice, though it sounded mightily in her ears both inwardly and outwardly, nor even noticed it in particular. Rather, as she was wont to do, she prayed, genuflected and disciplined her body with exercises and painful castigations. Then the voice of God spoke to her: "You must not exert yourself so severely with running about and not cry out so much when you are in prayer. Instead, listen to my voice in quiet and in silence and taste the wholesome sweet fruit of the contemplative life!" With these words of her beloved her soul was at once softened and elevated above itself in rapture and remained thus transported in contemplation for five hours.

After these five hours, she came to herself again, filled with inexpressible joy, and on account of the uncommonly intense sweetness she had drawn from this contemplation, she frequently spoke these words: "Oh, Lord, with your dew bless me, Lord; creator of all creatures, bless me. You who have redeemed all mankind on the cross, bless me! May the Holy Spirit bless me with all the gifts of virtue and sweetness to achieve perfect blessedness." This prayer she recited for many days with a devout, joyful heart and did not readily wish to say anything else, not even at the time when she strove to complete her customary number of prayers. The sweet bridegroom Jesus Christ revealed to her many prayers sweeter than honey, many spiritual love songs, and many sound teachings that agree so perfectly with the holy scriptures that no expert of holy writ could punish her. They are so sweet that no devout person may find fault with them. With God's help much more will be said in far greater detail of these and many other things at the appropriate place.

How the name of Jesus was exceedingly sweet to her.

Chapter V.

The blessed name of Jesus was very sweet to Dorothea. It happened often that during mass, at other times of day, or on other occasions when she heard the name of Jesus, she was set ablaze by the fire of divine love, much like a flaming torch. At those times she was often softened and highly enraptured. On the Wednesday of Easter week of the previously-mentioned year a devout priest concluded the mass by singing, "Through Our Lord Jesus Christ," as is the custom. At that moment it appeared to her that the sweet name of Jesus which she bore in her heart and the name of Our Lord the priest was singing met one another and fused, injuring her heart as severely as if a sharp dart had been shot into it. She immediately became enraptured and from then on bore the honored name "Jesus," so forcefully impressed on her on that occasion, with great, hot love in her heart. This same event occurred once more that very same day during a mass celebrated by another priest and many times after that whenever she heard the honored name of Jesus reverently exclaimed in church.

After having plucked out her old heart, the almighty God was so often so gracious to her that in his merciful presence she felt as good as if she had been in eternal life. That is, she felt so well that she could not express and explain it in words other than: "It seemed to me as if I had been in life eternal." And when she was thus so mercifully endowed, the singing in church, due to the strength of God's grace, seemed so sweet to her that she thought she were hearing it in eternal life. Such singing, she claimed, she heard often, both that of the saints and that of the angels. All the while she enjoyed this overflowing grace and spoke the honored name Jesus in church, it pierced and wounded her heart through and through the moment she heard it. It overwhelmed her heart so thoroughly to convince her that had she not joined those chanting the name of Jesus, her heart would have been torn asunder and perished.

How she was often effusively comforted and her nature
weighed down by God's comfort.

Chapter VI.

As often as Dorothea felt the Lord visiting her with his healing mercies
with which he drew her to him and raised her spirit to unite with him in joyous,
pleasurable delight, she was submerged in overflowing spiritual graces and her
soul burned sweetly and was hotly inflamed. And then, in the midst of divine
pleasure and consumed by flames of burning love through grace, she now and
then was granted to see Jesus her bridegroom, either through contemplation or in
rapture. She felt his embrace of her soul was gentle, his kiss exceedingly sweet,
his whisperings merry, and his union with her soul profound. In the vibrancy of
her inner senses--now awakened, opened, and ignited by God--she sensed how
Jesus revealed himself to her soul with deep love, wooing her soul in many ways,
at one time more affectionately than another, of which much could be said.

How the Father and the Son and the Holy Spirit worked mightily in her,
caused great activity in her, and awakened many emotions in her through the
sacrament of the blessed body of Our Lord, the attendance of the Holy Spirit, and
many degrees of love-- much more is written of that later. Generally, every night
after the removal of her old heart the Lord spoke to her sweetly and kindly in a
voice she heard inwardly with the ears of her soul with such great desire and joy
that the long nights seemed very short, so when day dawned she was most
distressed, for she feared to be hindered in her delightful dalliance with God.
Therefore, she often covered her face and occasionally hid in a corner at home or
in church. Through the effusiveness of divine passion, her soul was not only
softened and made fluid, but frequently overwhelmed so she could control neither
her body nor her soul. On occasion she was mistress of her soul but not of her
body, which at such times was so severely weakened by the emanation of
sweetness from the soul that she could not have moved even for a great reward;
and if the whole world had been hers and destined to perish in the sea unless she
moved, she could not have done so unless the Lord had made it possible by

distancing himself and his overwhelming desire from her.

Once, when she was troubled about her nature being so greatly weighed down while her soul was being comforted so abundantly, the Lord spoke to her about this: "Can you not fathom that I am a burden to your nature when I give myself to you so abundantly in a kind of joy so far beyond the imagination of any creature that you can only say that you can neither know nor comprehend the manner through which I am with you? And even though I don't pour the totality of sweetness and desire that are in your soul and heart into all your other limbs, your nature is nevertheless burdened for I am a heavy weight on it. This you have often felt well enough and have become aware of in yourself as well as in others when you or they lay spent, seemingly unable to live another day. Yet, even though your sensuous nature was weighed down that you on account of the burden of my desire, could not pray, walk, sit, or stand, you would not have wanted to forgo my effect on you, which so burdened you, for all the riches of the world.

"This very same weighing down of sensuousness whenever the spirit is so effusively comforted you may also observe in Saint Christopher who picked me up as an insignificant small child. But when he entered the water, I became so heavy that he thought he would drown, and because I had become so heavy to him, he was delighted to set me down. So it is with your carnal nature which is so burdened by me that it fears to perish unless it were presently relieved of its burden and therefore is gladdened when I absent myself long enough to let your body rest a little and catch its breath."

How divine pleasure produced a variety of differences and effects.

Chapter VII.

Spiritual comforts tend to be immeasurably greater than physical ones. For this reason people who taste spiritual sweetness scorn physical pleasures because the spiritual ones are so joyous to them that they cannot even adequately describe them when they are presented to them to be tasted, as David well realized when he said: "I was mindful of God and have been made joyful, and my intellect has been dissolved." Likewise, the blessed Dorothea after experiencing great spiritual comfort and bliss often said: "I cannot really say how I felt or how well I felt." And Our Lord also spoke about this to her: "You know not how I am with you and affect you. Tell it, if you can." And she described it as best she could. Sometimes she said: "Through extreme passion body and soul melted, and the soul, because of hot, burning love and desire, flowed much like molten ore and in spirit became one with Our Dear Lord." At other times she said: "The passionate comfort was so intense that I forgot all external things and everything that had been revealed to me as well."

From time to time she was filled with divine sweetness. It kept increasing until she thought her heart would be torn apart immediately. At other times it felt as though her heart was being crammed full and stuffed. On one occasion she said: "So effusive was the spiritual sweetness in my soul that it spilled over into all my limbs, which as a result seemed fat, even bloated, as though they had been glutted." Sometimes she also observed, "because of overwhelming passion I could neither speak nor pray; I was beside myself." Another time she said: "Because of overflowing passion, I had to leave the table or wherever I happened to be and remove myself from those around me. This happened to me especially during the first year after the removal of my heart while I was visiting the Carthusian house near Gdansk. When I had seen their dwelling and was attending mass in their church, I was set aflame with overwhelming love and filled so profusely with great sweetness that I could scarcely walk from the church to my room in their hostelry where I remained until evening, unable to speak, move, eat, or drink. The women who were with me believed I was physically ill and so needlessly put herbs into my mouth. One of them said: 'Do not fail to make your confession.'"

How she was severely punished by God.

Chapter VIII.

Her sins of commission and omission, even when they were insignificant, did not go unpunished by God who punishes and castigates those he loves. Often he illuminated her thoroughly, surrounding her with a clear light to make her sins manifest to her: her conversations had not been pure and holy; her prayers had not been entirely devout; her obedience had not been constant, sweet and affectionate; her speech had not been sufficiently careful so that now and then her words were or appeared to be insincere, unjust, wanton, arrogant, insinuating, or slanderous. Thus he corrected her and said: "As you know very well, you have been a Christian in name only for you did not lead a Christian life by following me in the proper way. As you also know very well, I possessed true humility and wisdom and did not conduct myself irresponsibly nor lived an irresponsible or wanton life but suffered poverty, disdain, unhappiness, sadness, misery, and much torment. But you did not protect yourself entirely from external distractions by following me and surrendering your life entirely to me. You also did not abandon everything I have forbidden you, nor did you always do what I ordered you to do."

In this manner he upbraided her for the evil she had committed, the good she had left undone, the virtue she did not possess, and the virtuous desires and the fruit of virtue she lacked: "As you know very well, the things of this world are transitory and perishable; as you know very well, here all is baseness whereas everything in heaven is eternal and imperishable. As you know very well, here are want and sadness but there blessedness and comfort. As you know very well, here sadness and bitterness hold sway while joy and sweetness dwell there. As you know very well, here all is strife and temptation, danger, and uncertainty while there all things are at peace and safety and certainty reign supreme. As you know very well, here are shame and dishonor, there praise and honor. You know very well, this is no permanent place while heaven lasts forever. Why, then, do you tarry here without exerting and extending all your might toward the land of which you know that it contains the fullness of good in everything?"

Whenever the Lord instructed her on these and various other matters, she sat dejected and wept and sobbed in utter abandon. She sighed deeply and cried unto the Lord for forgiveness of her sins, begging him humbly to grant her his mercy once more, to help her not to anger him again but to allow her to stay with him always and conduct herself according to his holy will and do its bidding above everything else. In such prayer, crying, and weeping she often labored intensely and for a long time until she became quite drained and had no more tears left, for the great bitterness of her suffering pressed frequently so many tears from her that she had none left to shed.

At last the most merciful Jesus took pity on her, for he beheld the pain of his bride. He drew her, thus penitent, into a great sweetness and surrounded her with a clear light. He illuminated her internally and externally, saying: "Now look about and take heed that you have not yet come very far from the world. You are free to retrace your steps and turn to the right or to the left, as you like. Notice, three roads are ahead of you: choose one, whichever one you want. One goes to the right and leads to purgatory; the other goes to the left and leads to hell; the third leads straight ahead to heaven. If you elect it and journey on it steadfastly from one virtue to another, I will help you faithfully, but you must diligently and persistently stand by me and never swerve."

When the Lord instructed her thus or accused her of the sins she had committed, she was so self absorbed and so removed from external things that she knew nothing of the things of this world or what happened through other people's actions. But she did understand clearly that according to God's will she was to travel the third road, and therefore she implored the Lord to help her, for she had a burning desire and an eager will to follow him in the proper way and to accomplish his holy will.

How they were robbed.

Chapter IX.

When the blessed Dorothea was in the thirty-ninth year of her life and the twenty-second of her marriage, her husband took to heart that it was not safe to remain among those with whom he formerly used to squander his time and wealth uselessly. He realized that if he remained with them, he would find it difficult to remove himself from their bad habits and his own. So he settled his affairs and his property, and on the feast of St. Lawrence [August 10] he moved with his wife Dorothea and his youngest daughter, the only one who remained him, to Aix-la-Chapelle because he meant to stay-- as indeed he did-- in yet another town called Finsterwald to serve God more peacefully.

Dorothea was the driving force in this decision. She had implored her husband to move to the aforementioned town with her, for she entertained hopes of winning him over to God's service much more easily there. Now it so happened that they spent nine weeks and much money on their way because war and unsettled conditions were so great in the lands through which they traveled that few people still remained living in their houses. So Dorothea and Adalbert often had to seek protection from robbers among the sheep and cows grazing in the church yards. Not for a single day during these aforementioned nine weeks of their journey could they be certain that after getting up in the morning they would actually arrive at their night's lodging with their possessions intact. Often they were advised to turn back if they wished to keep themselves and their belongings safe. In the towns soldiers and outriders threatened them frequently: "Tomorrow we will take your daughter from you," remaining silent about what else they meant to do.

The blessed Dorothea was in fear day and night about this; in worry, labor, and exertion, terror, great dread and numerous pains about how, with God's help, she, her old sick husband, her young, small daughter, and their entire possessions might get through war-torn lands. Sleep fled from her eyes, and on the journey to Aix she did not enjoy a single good day in respect to her physical well-being. Spiritually, however, she was greatly comforted by God, and never more so than on the day they were robbed by robbers who took their clothes, money, the wagon with the team of horses, and wounded her husband severely. Dorothea and her daughter they left with nothing but a shirt and a flimsy skirt.

However, she herself explained how this day was nevertheless comforting to her: "When the robbers appeared, I was sitting on the wagon, greatly blessed by God. I was lifted up high in pure contemplation, liberated from the ignorance of worldly creatures, to gaze into the mirror of the Holy Trinity. During this vision I was so abundantly filled with divine sweetness and joy that I forgot all external problems and paid no heed whatever to temporal affairs." As she was thus inexplicably comforted and strengthened by the Lord through such a high degree of divine love, the robbers attacked. As they were being robbed, she, for God's sake, hoped to forgo all bodily and worldly comfort for the rest of her life and joyfully beg for her bread door to door in poverty of spirit. At the time that would have been more comfortable to her than to possess many worldly goods. When the robbers were gone, she brought her wounded husband and her little daughter to the town in Brandenburg[34] which lay closest to the forest where they had been ambushed. She deliberated how she would send her husband and the child back home again with the little money her husband had been able to conceal from the robbers. She herself meant to remain in foreign lands, living in misery as a poor beggar to see just how sweet the Lord would be whose sweetness she had now tasted so often.

How they recovered their property.

Chapter X.

But her husband did not want to return home. He insisted on traveling on and on trying to recover his property, for he had heard it said in town that the robbers who had robbed them were being held prisoners in yet another town also located in Brandenburg. But since he himself could not go there because of his illness and injuries, he forced the maid of God, Dorothea his wife, to claim the property that had been taken from them. He ordered the servant who had driven their wagon to go with her. Yet Dorothea, the clean, chaste, and modest maid of God, in her desire to be poor, would much rather have foregone all earthly wealth

---

[34] Brandenburg is a province of northern Germany whose principal city is Berlin.

than claim their stolen property. She also would have preferred to have traveled on far enough so as not to know where the robbers had gone with their belongings. However, for God's sake she had to be obedient to her husband, so she went and found the robbers imprisoned. Out of heartfelt compassion for them she insisted that no suffering be inflicted on them but that they be released, which nobody wanted to do unless they were made to give back everything they had taken. While she, in the company of their servant, went to the place where the robbers were kept prisoners, several forward women surrounded and embarrassed her by saying: "You abandoned your old husband so you may indulge your lust with the young servant." Several felt sorry for her, though, and defended her. But they, too, were made a spectacle of by many people there who gawked at them both, Dorothea and her servant, suspecting them and pointing their fingers at them. One reason for this ridicule was that Dorothea appeared young, beautiful, and well-proportioned even though she was not as young as she appeared. Her attractiveness was due to the hot, burning love and the divine comfort of God, with whose help she endured all things cheerfully.

The robbers, upon promising to return the property, had been freed. Dorothea, barefoot, followed them with her servant through woods and across fields without fear. The thieves, however, conspired to murder them both and had spoken of it in an inn along the way, as the hostess, an honorable woman who would have liked to see Dorothea stay with her and let the servant follow them by himself, told her. But Dorothea's trust in God was such that she did not fear to go with them, and the highest protector on whom she relied for her safety did keep her so no harm came to her. And when wagon, horses, clothes, and all that the robbers had taken from them was hers once more, she, after much suffering which she endured patiently, as has been just described, returned to her husband with the servant.

Her patience during their journey.

Chapter XI.

To allow her husband to recover from his injuries, they remained laid up for a considerable length of time in a certain town. While they were there, he was often angry with the blessed Dorothea. Especially on two occasions he fell into such a grim rage that he beat her mercilessly: first because once she did not want to go to the market to buy twine since the market was crowded with robbers and outriders, and again because she could not quiet the child, her little daughter, whom she had with her at all times, even though she tried her best to calm her. He beat her on the head so fiercely that all the people who saw it were dismayed, and the hostess had such compassion with Dorothea that she wept bitter tears. But Dorothea accepted and endured it cheerfully even though she had been beaten on the head so severely that she suffered from it for many years afterwards.

When her husband was healed and healthy again, they continued their journey. Then one of their horses fell ill. Thereupon her husband dismissed the servant and ordered Dorothea to drive the wagon. This office she discharged humbly and conscientiously. She walked along in a short skirt and led the wagon; she cleaned and greased it; she watered the horses, fed them, and hitched them to the cart. She led her little daughter and her old husband through the provinces, market places, and towns where people often gathered in droves about her as if to witness a miracle. And when they noticed her husband, that he was old and grey and had a long beard, they laughed, and many of them spoke derisively, some with amazement: "Dear sister, where do you want to take your Joseph? Are you taking him to the fountain of youth?"

Such sarcastic words and many other useless comments and deeds, being waylaid by robbers, and other vicissitudes of travel Dorothea bore patiently, even joyfully. Along the way she was often enraptured, which made her oblivious to the world around her, so that she frequently lost things. Ultimately, being drawn so completely from external matters to God, she was neither aware of nor concerned about anything physical or external. And this happened because of what the Lord revealed to her more than seven years later when he said: "The Father and the Son and the Holy Spirit dwelling together in people blessed with internal grace frees them from the cares of temporal possessions, and because the entire trinity dwelled in you and had taken possession of your heart, you were not allowed to worry or be concerned about temporal matters."

Their life in a foreign country.

Chapter XII.

When they arrived in a village called Finsterwald on the Rhine and became acquainted with a group of spiritual people, many of whom Dorothea met within the next year and a half, the Lord worked great mercy in her and allowed her to taste and recognize his inexpressibly great joy and grace. She was steadfast in devout prayer, moral vision, and divine contemplation. Her food and rest were minimal, her labors, weeping, sweating, and burning love monumental. Hunger, thirst, heat, cold, her husband, and the evil spirit tempted and tormented her; she bore this at all times patiently. For the year and a half they were there, the people were often panic struck because war and unrest ruled there. When the enemy was advancing, or it was said that he was approaching, they rang the bells in warning, and the people came running together, now into the church, now out of the church, and there was much crying, screaming, unrest, and lamentation. But even at those times Dorothea, unperturbed, remained seated in the church from morning until noon and from noon until after vespers with Our Lord who comforted her, just as she did any other time.

Her steadfastness and virtue were admired greatly by a number of people who loved and honored her because of these qualities and wished she would stay with them forever. But in this hostile environment and for lack of even basic necessities her husband frequently became quite despondent and impatient, and in his great wrath behaved in so hostile a fashion toward the blessed Dorothea as if to suggest that he wished her dead. Occasionally he wanted to divide their meager possessions with her and move away. She, on the other hand, was gracious and placid and had great confidence in God, whom she accordingly begged faithfully to protect and keep her and especially her husband.

Because of these civil disturbances, bread and every other kind of food became very expensive. So her husband often went elsewhere to a different market place or town to eat and drink to his heart's content while the blessed Dorothea and her child had nothing more to eat all day than one piece of bread scarcely as large as a fist and scarcely enough for one of them. But God helped her, so even though they both ate of it, it satisfied their hunger and both had enough all day.

It happened once that one market day Dorothea was ordered by her husband to buy bread for an entire week; she failed to do so and forgot about it because of the great bliss in which she found herself at the time she was supposed to be buying the bread. Next day, when she was to prepare food for her husband, she had nothing but a tiny piece of bread. So she made half of it into a puree and served it to her husband with the other half. She fed the child with what was left over and gladly did without any nourishment. Her husband, however, was still hungry and started grumbling. Because of his profound despair he was even more discouraged than usual. Dorothea, on the other hand, with great trust in God, awaited his comfort in good spirits.

Now behold what happened! A grocer's wife in a town not very far from there who had seen Dorothea and her husband scarcely twice, at God's prodding, sent them three large loaves of bread and a big cask of wine that very day. When they saw that, they both thanked God, but the maid of God was especially glad. Her husband then realized that this merciful deed was not a reward for his merit but his wife's and therefore gave her unlimited leave to serve God. He even offered to mind the house, for from then on he did not wish to hinder her in her prayers nor be angry if she remained in prayer for a long time.

In that place she suffered many other injustices at the hands of her husband and much sadness and hardship through the temptations of the evil spirit who all the time they lived there tempted her incessantly from her virtuous labors and would have liked to plunge her into despair and mistrust of God. But the most gracious Lord fortified her against that by providing her with his merciful gifts in this spiritual contest. One of these gifts the Lord commanded her to describe fully.

When they had been in Finsterwald for a year and a half, the inflation got out of hand, and it became so difficult for them to secure their livelihood that her husband considered returning home to Prussia. Dorothea, out of love and passion, would have loved to remain there as a poor beggar for God's sake. Finally they agreed and through mutual good will were of one mind that Dorothea would remain there while he, her husband, and their daughter would travel back home to relatives and friends. And to secure written permission to do so from the priest, they then went to the aforementioned priest at the church in Finsterwald to ask for a letter. While they were waiting for him to arrive, Dorothea was at her prayers, and it was most pleasing to her that she should remain there in misery, far from her worldly friends. Then God granted her such overflowing spiritual desire that she could not contain herself; she had to laugh out loud for joy and happiness and with a loud voice kept rehearsing the words she planned to say begging for bread door to door: "Bread, for the sake of Our Lord."

At that moment she thought that she had never before felt such inexpressible joy and desire for divine grace. But while her husband waited for the priest and she was so richly showered with God's gifts, he changed his mind and regretted having granted her this freedom. Therefore, when the priest arrived, he complained about his spouse, claiming that she wished to be rid of him and stay there, and begged the priest to order and instruct her to travel home with him.

Their move from Einsiedeln.

Chapter XIII.

The priest knew that according to holy writ it is not appropriate for one married partner to leave the other against his will, and therefore he insisted on her returning home with Adalbert. Dorothea obeyed and traveled homeward with him, experiencing exertion, fatigue, and suffering day and night. During the day she braved hardship and struggle through water and snow; treacherous, filthy roads; and the dangers attending travel through forests and over land. At night she had to wash and dry her and her husband's clothes whenever and however she might. All that time her husband slept soundly because of fatigue while she had to stay awake so they would not lose their belongings or be harmed in body or through loss of property even though she, too, needed rest and sleep.

During the day her husband generally rode on horseback with the child, leaving Dorothea to travel on foot to follow them. She often fell far behind, wretched and alone, for she did not always walk at a steady pace, now sauntering leisurely now hurriedly running after them , and in her haste to catch up, the maid of God often fell into deep ditches, snow drifts, or puddles. And no one would have been there to help her escape had Our merciful God not aided her. He was her protector who shielded her from robbers, murderers, and other misfortunes and supported her with his comfort whenever she was dejected or in pain.

Occasionally, because of warfare or other dangers on the road, her husband sold their horse because he did not want to risk losing it and then walked with her whenever he could not secure a fare by ship or wagon. Then Dorothea had to carry his clothes, which he, on account of his age and illness, could not carry himself. The elected bride of God was so overburdened and her strength so depleted from doing this that she felt ill for many years afterwards. But the Lord, who in all her suffering did not leave her uncomforted, nine years later reminded her of the good things he had done for her on that journey: "Consider how well I guarded and protected you when you walked through fields and forests, water, dirt, and snow and had no external comfort and had been abandoned by everyone. Still, you were not despondent because of that nor oppressed by all that chaos. Nor were you unreceptive to the gifts of my grace in spite of all the hard work and exhaustion you endured on the way but remained gracious and receptive to them."

How they were protected to keep them from drowning.

Chapter XIV.

On their home journey it so happened that they traveled from a town called Harburg toward Hamburg on ice which here and there was covered with water. A sleigh came after them, pulled by three horses and driven by two handymen with whom they arranged to travel for several miles. As they sped across the ice, water spewed through the holes, which indicated the weakness of the ice. But the sleigh driver was careless. Roughhousing with his companion while traveling on the ice, he yelled at the horses, driving them with the whip, and occasionally even drove them on by throwing a heavy stick at them.

Suddenly the midmost of the three horses--they were hitched to the sleigh one behind the other--broke through the ice and fell into the water. Adalbert noticed this and was terrified, yelling to his wife: "Hurry, get off the sleigh right now." When Dorothea heard this without, however, knowing anything about the horse's crash through the ice, God inspired her to hurriedly grab their staffs and satchels with her left hand and her daughter with her right. She jumped off the back of the sleigh, landing on her face and knees, still ignorant about the accident. Her husband also dropped off the sleigh and onto his knees. As Dorothea, still lying on her knees looked up, horses and sleigh had already sunk beneath the ice. All she could see was a little piece of the sleigh's tail end.

Then the horses raised their muzzles out of the hole. Her old, sick husband started to crawl toward them to see if he could help them, but because of the extreme cold and his own weakness, he could not even pull himself up on the ice without another person's assistance. Dorothea came, grabbed him by the feet, and laboriously pulled him away from the hole. He was drenched and would have drowned had she not helped him. She raised him to his feet, took him by one hand and their daughter by the other, and with great difficulty and through great danger brought them across the ice to the bank. In this manner the sick man was protected and his life preserved by his faithful spouse.

When they reached the dike, their little daughter of five, who through the entire episode on the ice had not said anything at all, started speaking: "Oh, mother," she said. "You must not assume that it was you who helped me off the sleigh so I would not drown; the dear Virgin Mary helped me. She hurriedly pulled me off the sleigh and put me on the ice and so kept me from drowning." The girl spoke so intelligently that both father and mother listened to her and marveled over the wise speech of the child, who went on to say: "We may very well say now that we are reborn." Dorothea, the mother, wanted to test her steadfastness and said: "Why do you say that the dear Virgin Mary has pulled you off the sleigh when I took you off with my own hand?" The child replied: "But I saw the beloved Mary, how she approached and took me off the sleigh." Approximately eight years later Our Lord deemed this sign through which he had protected them from drowning a great miracle.

After this much effort, discomfort, and exhaustion but a lot of divine comfort as well, they arrived in Lübeck where the Lord, after Dorothea had received his holy worthy body with great devotion on Sunday, worked a great good on her. For many days in a row she sat in a small church from daylight to dark. And there the Lord granted her such overflowing sweetness that she was often enraptured and without interruption listened to the voice of God whispering to her graciously and sweetly, dallying with her affectionately. And sometimes when she in her transport did not answer the Lord as he was speaking to her, her heart became enlarged as though it would burst. In this manner she was admonished to respond and dally with the Lord as best she might. This also happened to her in Rome for fully eight weeks during which she had to answer God's voice, speak to him, and dally with him every place she went, regardless of her situation or troubles. Oh, what a great merciful grace is in this, the highest, most worshipful majesty who does not disdain to converse with the ashes, the earth, the dust.

How in Gdansk she was often in ecstasy and therefore suffered greatly at the hands of her husband.

Chapter XV.

From then on the Lord was even more merciful with her day and night, on board ship as they traveled across the sea toward Gdansk and in Gdansk, too, and she was miraculously filled with love, worship, and divine affection. And to be alone with the Lord, her bridegroom, removed from other people, and to drench the bed of her conscience with tears, she sought out corners and hiding places wherever she could. She did not spare her body but disciplined it with much kneeling and many genuflections, castigations, and wounds.

When acquaintances were building a small house near St. Catherine's Church for her and her husband there in Gdansk, she was often sent there by her husband to do something. Often she stayed there for three hours but nevertheless returned without having done what she had been ordered to do for she was so greatly preoccupied with the Lord that she was unmindful and forgetful of external things. Therefore, she seldom accomplished what she was supposed to. Sometimes when she entered the aforementioned little house or some other dwelling, she seated herself behind the door or in a corner and immediately was enraptured. When her husband found her sitting there, he often beat her; sometimes he pushed her, and at times he complained to many people about her, accusing her of being idle and incompetent for he wanted her to be busy and efficient in taking care of daily affairs, which she would have liked to be, according to his demands, had she been able.

Sometimes she prepared fish uncleaned, unscaled, or in some other unappetizing manner, oblivious to their being unpalatable that way. Once when she was drawn high into contemplation and remained in that state for a long time, she failed to prepare a mess of fresh fish, which, unlike other foods, need to be prepared immediately. As she was busy trying to get them ready quickly, her husband came, and, very impatient, beat her so severely on the mouth that her upper lip was cut badly by the teeth. Her mouth swelled shut hideously, which disfigured her greatly. But even though she had been badly mistreated and beaten severely, she endured it patiently and smiled at him pleasantly and affectionately. She was fond of him, so she prayed devoutly to God on his behalf and prepared his fish speedily. Everyone present who saw this marveled at that woman's patience, how she remained gracious and in good spirits and untroubled in mind.

Another time when she was in church, her husband ordered her to buy straw. But immediately afterwards she was drawn into great sweetness and burned in the ecstasy of hot, burning love, elevated above herself, and in that state was given to drink until she was spiritually inebriated. In this wise time got away from her; so she failed buying the straw but came home happy and in high spirits. This infuriated her husband, and in the fury of his rage he hit her so hard on the chest that blood shot out of her mouth and she kept spitting blood with her saliva for many days afterwards. Still, she did not grumble and complained to no one about this but joyfully bore it as yet another trial the Lord had imposed on her.

Because of this and other domestic disturbances two priests, their confessors, came and punished her husband severely for his wrath and lack of charity and the cruel injustice and discomfort he had inflicted on his bedfellow, as it had been reported to them by other people. When the husband had to abandon his ill will, he succumbed to a serious illness which rendered him bedridden for a long time. While he was confined to his sickbed, no one's aid and service satisfied him except that of his wife Dorothea who, in the course of this illness and the many other confinements that troubled him because of his arthritis, served him pleasantly and graciously day and night as best she could. She patiently endured staying up all night by his bedside, his impatience and his yelling when she did not do quickly enough what he wanted or how he wanted it, no matter whether it was day or night. After he recovered, he usually accused her of having given alms too freely and of having squandered his property, and for this reason he finally took the keys from her and left nothing at all to her authority. He himself went to market to purchase what they needed.

It was most agreeable to the blessed Dorothea not to be encumbered with temporal affairs any longer. When she, at the behest of God's commands and revelations, had told all this to her confessor so he could commit it to writing, the Lord immediately wounded her with many arrows of love and ignited her with hot, burning love and said: "You must love me greatly, for I have so often pulled you away from your husband; while he was still alive and thought he possessed you, I drew you and possessed you. It is appropriate for you to speak highly of me for I have helped you, often without your knowing it, and have come to your assistance throughout your life, which was full of pain and torment. Now weep heartily and thank me profusely. My suffering and torment were greater than yours. But you performed a service of love for me, too, when out of your own free will you left the house you just as well could have kept. But you loved poverty and misery and for my sake and in accordance with my will were happy to be deprived of all transitory things all the days of your life." When Dorothea heard this from the Lord, she shed sweet tears and thanked Our dear Lord, as she had been commanded.

How in the churches dedicated to the Virgin Mary
she was mercifully showered with gifts.

Chapter XVI.

Of God's merciful visitations which Dorothea experienced in the churches dedicated to the glory of the holy Virgin Mary something has been written already and still more is to be written in praise and honor of the gracious queen Mary. In the forty-first year of her life, Dorothea visited the church of Our Lady in Köslin [Koszalin, Pomerania] where she and her sisters were allowed to spend the night, which she desired so intensely that even in exchange for great riches she would not have spent the night anywhere else. During that same night the Lord visited her so mercifully that the night seemed short to her and she wished it had been much longer. Until high mass was concluded, she sat immovably in front of one of the altars in the fullness of divine sweetness and longing, of which she became spiritually inebriated and oblivious to her surroundings so that she did not realize the lateness of the hour.

After high mass the sisters, her travelling companions, came, shook her, and said: "It is time for us to go." She rose and went with them but was so inebriated that she stumbled and could not find the way so familiar to her before. In truth, she had been made drunk spiritually, well wined in her bridegroom's, Our Lord Jesus Christ's wine cellar, where she often before and afterwards became so intoxicated that she lost her way and went to a different place than where she wanted to go. Her sisters were startled by her drunkenness, confusion, and stumbling and wondered, "what might be the cause of this?" But one among them was more intuitive than the rest. She praised God profusely for his grace. Dorothea herself remained on the cart all day, submerged in dalliance with the Lord, and until late that night did not partake of the tiniest morsel of bodily sustenance.

That same year at the feast of the Holy Cross, [September 14] Dorothea returned to that very same church, and because of the great number of pilgrims who had come there to attend the fair the next day, she could not find lodging anywhere. Forced by circumstance, she and her sisters were directed to take shelter in a corner of the church were the donkey that served as the church's draught animal was stabled. He moved over to make room for them. She prayed, meditated, and performed her devotions diligently. She felt a special joy in reciting a few *Ave Marias*, through which she hoped to implore the most worthy queen Mary to intercede for her and secure God's love, sweetness, and joy for her supplicant. When she had prayed for a long time but nothing she craved was granted, she thought, "it would have been better for me had I stayed at home instead of being here without love and comforting grace." Nevertheless, she did not abandon her efforts nor grew lax in her prayers but trustingly assaulted the ears of God and his dear mother with her laments.

Now, take note! While her sisters were sleeping next to her and the people in the church were jostling each other, making much noise, she was enraptured in divine love by the Lord, who granted her exceeding great mercy and inexpressible great desire and joy in which she remained rejoicing and praying throughout the night, so removed from external events and focused within her own being that she did not even notice the noise and hurly-burly of the crowd. Moreover, she was brightly illuminated by the divine light. The Lord taught her many things and told her that there was no one in church to whom he had given as much grace, love, and passion as he had granted her.

During mass she felt divine grace increasing tremendously within her, and intense spiritual delight so exhilarated her that she did not know where to go, what to do, how to behave, or how to conceal that extraordinary happiness God granted her from those around her. So to conceal herself, she hid in a corner where she remained until all the masses had been celebrated and felt great longing to remain in this state of sober drunkenness for a great while longer. However, the sisters who had accompanied her there looked for her until they found her thus hidden in that corner. They dragged her along with them although she would have liked to stay there to await the end of the divine visitation there. Later she regretted having followed them instead of remaining there, immobile, to experience all of God's merciful comfort.

Another time, on the eve of the Assumption of the Virgin [August 15], she and her husband made a pilgrimage to the above-mentioned church. It so happened that just as they arrived at the inn where they planned to spend the night, she was removed from external things and filled internally with intense love and sweetness through the grace of Our Lord and therefore refused to alight the wagon when her husband called and ordered her to do so for she thought it more appropriate to listen to what God said to her than to extricate herself from God's dalliance at the behest of her earthly husband and be encumbered with external matters. As she hesitated, her husband became grimly infuriated and threw a tantrum over her disobedience. She became frightened by this and begged God to advise her whether or not it would be permissible for her to remain with him and to defy her husband's command. Thereupon Our sweet Jesus answered her, saying: "Extricate yourself at once from my delightful dalliance and be obedient to your husband's wishes." When she heard this, she climbed down from the wagon, despondent because she had to forego her delightful dalliance with Our God. And this she had to do often, both before and afterwards, to obey her husband, serve him faithfully, and receive hard knocks while serving his needs, for well-observed obedience is more pleasing to God than sacrifices.

From this it can be seen that this blessed, devout Dorothea was so greatly and notably blessed in many churches of Our Lady, as in many others, that it would be cumbersome to describe it all. Therefore I will leave it at this.

Her long illness, which originated in the sufferings of Our Lord Jesus Christ
Chapter XVII.

In the forty-third year of her life, from Candlemas [February 2] to the feast of the Assumption of the Virgin [August 15], there was not one day when Dorothea was not bedridden, incapacitated by disease or love. Especially during the fortnight beginning with the feast day of St. Dorothy [February 6] she was so deeply and completely drawn into the suffering of Our Lord Jesus Christ that because of the intensity of her pain she could not even turn or sit up in bed. Nor could she eat or refresh her body in any way. Steeped in such great, bitter sadness and anxiety, it seemed to her that if the intensity of her bitter pain were to last one more day, she would have to die, unable to endure it any longer. But after the fierce torments of the day, the most gracious Lord comforted her so lovingly and profusely through the night that the delight of this comfort not only obliterated the bitterness of her suffering but at times transported her to such heights of pleasure that she forgot all external things. Whenever she was thus comforted during the night, she thought she might very well have been able to refresh herself if someone had been there to give her something she would have deemed suitable to eat.

When those two weeks had passed, the Lord plunged her in such great, inexpressible joy that her body could not tolerate it. For this reason she was extremely ill for yet another six months, seldom able to stir from her bed except on the days the Lord allowed her to receive his holy body. During that time she developed the intense craving for Our Lord's body that she felt from then on more than ever before. This longing was the gift of the Lord, who drew her soul up high and kindled in her a flaming desire for him, bestowing on her the wings of contemplation on which she soared high above all creatures to contemplate her maker. Thus highly elevated in contemplation, she heard the sweet song of angels for the very first time and beheld many secrets, which were also made known and explained to her by God. While she thus lay ill, the Lord flushed her with the fire of love, which made her countenance rosy and attractive. But she was also racked by heavy internal labors. They caused her veins to protrude, pulled taut like the strings of a musical instrument, and made her pulse race. This inner labor flowed from the heartfelt,deep compassion she felt for the suffering of Our Lord and from the heat of flaming love which made her glow like a fiery ember.

Fierce love and pains made Dorothea so anxious that she thought her heart would tear apart. She labored as heavily in all her limbs as do people smitten by a raging illness before they get to enjoy the cooling relief of perspiration. In such a manner she struggled with all her might and limbs before she started to sweat. But whenever she did perspire, her sufferings in body and soul were reduced. That year and thereafter she tended to sweat often from the fire of divine love. It also happened frequently that body and soul were flooded by the influx of divine sweetness and melted by fierce desire. But as soon as sweat and sweetness ceased, she experienced the same internal labor and pain as before. At times they were so bitter, so severe, and so protracted that she was convinced her strength could not endure should they last even one more day.

During this time, as these pains and comforts from God took turns, changing back and forth and being repeated so often to cause her bitter suffering followed by delectable comfort, followed by still more suffering alternating with solace, Dorothea started craving the sustenance and fruits of heaven. More than anything she desired the grapes of heaven. Whenever she expressed these wishes and refused to partake of any other kind of food, those who were with her and heard her say this insisted she would die and was, in fact, already engaged in death's struggle. This they also assumed: that her veins and all her limbs jerked so violently because she fought death so fiercely. Often, though, as her physical being was weighed down by the bitter pains of her internal labors, her soul was drawn up high in joyous ecstasy to God who delighted her beyond words by flooding her with his sweetness until it inundated her body and all her limbs. Sweet nectar with the merry taste of grape must started flowing freely in her mouth. Whenever this juice filled her mouth, she took great care to prevent it from spilling. She was especially careful to keep it from spilling when she felt the flow of this sweet liquor after having received the holy body of Our Lord. She often tasted this sweet juice as she received or had received the holy body of Our Lord or when he comforted her profusely after having visited her with bitter pains or plied her with drink until she was spiritually inebriated. Many other things in addition to those described above took place as well, as, for example, her inability to stand, one of the effects of love, sweetness, and inebriation, which can be contemplated and understood in the light of what has been described already and what will be written later.

The heavy internal labor, which is useful though exceedingly rare.

Chapter XVIII.

Internal labor originates in God through hot, burning love and is felt first in the soul, which then, through this love, becomes greedy for the sacrament of the true body of Our Lord and for being with the Lord irrevocably in eternal bliss. The soul then also grows restless and, full of anxiety, starts laboring with all her might. The soul's forces, in turn, become increasingly tense in pursuit of the blessings the Lord causes the soul to desire so fiercely. Through this internal labor the Lord forcefully drew Dorothea to himself. While she was thus being drawn, she passionately longed for the Lord. In this state of hot desire, Dorothea became ignited and burned first in her soul, then in her heart and mind. Then she suffered exertion, heat, unrest, and weakness in all her limbs. At times her veins pounded, as will be described in the next chapter. Her heart jumped as though it were raging. Whenever this internal labor did not manifest itself externally through sweat, tears, screams, prayer, genuflections or castigations, it was all that much harder and difficult to endure because her inner forces had to work unaided. Whenever these external forces cooperated, her internal labors were reduced.

But even though Dorothea's internal labors were so excruciatingly bitter and severe and she would have labored far less had she spent the entire day praying, weeping, genuflecting, sweating, and performing other physical exercises rather than exerting herself for a single hour at her internal labor, she did not want to be deprived of it on account of the love with which God granted it and the great, useful joy she received and felt through it, as the Lord pointed out to her when he spoke to her thus: "Your internal labor is more useful to you and more pleasing to me than your external work, for it overcomes carnal nature and makes the spirit agile. It overcomes the world and the evil spirit. It robs people of the joys of the flesh and the world and makes everything worldly bitter. In this manner it kills the flesh and quickens the spirit. The strength of those who perform inner labors of this kind is consumed more thoroughly than if they had physically exerted themselves all day long. Thus, whoever performs this inner labor for one year overcomes human carnality more effectively than by performing external labors for many years. Internal labor is the slayer of vice, pride, greed, lechery, anger, envy, hatred, sloth, disobedience, impatience, and unbridled vanity bred of worldly fame. It drives away such evils as worldly ignorance, servile fear, and worldly renown. It also engenders and causes good. It cleanses the spirit and enlivens it. It nurtures virtue. It fosters deep humility, brings about chaste, child-like obedience, and regenerates the individual.

"Internal labor tramples and overcomes lassitude, disorderly or beastly conduct, faulty reasoning, and all other improper thoughts that turn man's will from God. It provides good, holy thoughts and creates a hot desire for God, sound hope, and unshakable trust. It causes and creates the hot, burning love and all the other kinds of love rooted therein. Internal labor makes all kinds of love recognizable by differentiating one from the other. It also inspires languishing love and overwhelming love, which transports people into rapture. Even more, it creates internal activity. It moves people toward God and makes them God-like so that God becomes well-disposed toward mankind and the individual at ease with God. Thus it unites and ties human beings to God so powerfully, developing such a great trust in God that they fear neither to behold and receive God in the sacrament nor to die. Rather, because of the great desire and trust they have developed for God, they would desire to die rather than to live if the decision were theirs." Furthermore, the Lord said: "This inner labor, however, is rare indeed, and those who perform many heavy external labors only seldom progress toward the internal work."

How she accepted alms as a beggar among beggars.

Chapter XIX.

Our Lord, who ruled and instructed her, taught Dorothea to suffer exertion, love, and disdain gladly for his sake and ordered her to go to the main portal of the church of Our Lady in Gdansk, seat herself among the beggars in front of the church, and beg for alms. She was at once amenable to this command, and on All Saints' Day [November 1], clad in ragged clothing, she obediently begged for alms among the poor from the passers-by even though she had no need of them. Every time someone gave her alms, she received them graciously and effusively thanked not only the person who had given her the gift but also the Lord Jesus who came to her in the form of the gift, who, as it seemed to her, mercifully came to her each time she received a gift of charity. She was joyful and well-pleased about this, but greatly annoyed when the beggars complained that they, who were in need of this charity, were suffering from the cold and received nothing.

There she also received such great, gentle comfort from God that she forgot all physical need. She assumed this comfort which God's mercy so abundantly provided for her had been bestowed on the others as well, for she could not have accepted any temporal goods, no matter how great, in place of the mercy God showered on her there. She felt so good that she sat there for five hours until all the beggars had risen and gone away without her being aware of it, for the divine favor in which she found herself drew her into heavenly contemplation. Because she loved the alms she collected in this manner so intensely, she could not bear to relinquish them to others. She kept them for her own use and in their place gave much more to the poor. During one such episode she received twenty-three gifts of charity.

Our Lord's commandment to be satisfied with life's bare necessities.

Chapter XX.

From that time on the blessed Dorothea desired more than ever before to be poor and to divest herself of all worldly property. As her desire to be poor increased and grew, she was not only horrified to behold her wealth and the adornments of her clothing but nauseated at the mere thought of wearing her stylish veils or coats, and her heart ached. Whenever she went to church in a pleated coat, she became so agitated and anxious that she had to retrace her steps and take it off. Whenever she had to concern herself with worldly affairs, it was a pain rather than a pleasure to her. Yet the Lord did not deign to release her from these chores, as he told her afterwards for many years, until the time should come which he in his omniscience had assigned and designated and she had developed such a great longing to be rid of all temporal things and forgo them that she would become terrified of them. Until then she was to live in such a way that she would accept nothing more than the absolute necessities of life among the temporal goods God had provided for her. Human conversation and precious things she was to do without.

From then on she called "creature comfort" or "worldly comfort" anything above and beyond the necessities absolutely essential to sustaining life as regards food, drink, clothing, sleep, rest, human conversation, aid or advice, warmth, bathing, and other things. This was precisely the kind of comfort from which she was to remove herself and forgo it for God's sake. For the more a human being would remove himself from the comforts that provide the most pleasure, the more divine comfort he would enjoy. And the more a person would receive such [worldly] comforts, the fewer divine comforts he would have. And because the Lord wanted to comfort her gently and more frequently after her husband's death than before, he desired her to be poor and free of all transitory goods beyond mere necessities.

For this reason he did not even permit her to stand on a bear rug her confessor had spread in her pew at night without her knowledge to make it easier for her to endure the severe cold of that winter since she customarily came to church early in the morning and did not go home until after vespers. As she came to the pew and, as was her custom, wanted to enter it, the Lord said to her: "Do not step on or stand on this skin but fold it up and sit on it." He told her the name of the man who had spread the bear skin there and instructed her how she was to pray for him. When she had done so and was seated, the Lord said: "When he comes and asks you, 'why do you not step on this rug which was laid down for you so that you would be less bothered by the cold,' answer him and say: 'My dear Lord does not allow me to step on it or make use of it because it is not essential to my bare, naked need. And even if I use of temporal goods only what my basic need requires, I still have to take great care to return it to the honorable Lord who has provided it for me with dutiful service and appropriate thanks.'" In this manner she was illumined by God to recognize what her needs were as regards food, drink, and other daily necessities. And among minor items a cushion was pointed out to her that her needs did not require. Before and after this time the Lord often stripped her of anything unnecessary.

How the Lord commanded her to be generous;
how, if she had no alms to give, she was to distribute spiritual wealth.
Chapter XXI.

At another time when she was set afire with divine love which does not seek its own enrichment and yet left Dorothea abundantly rich in spiritual wealth even though she had no temporal wealth beyond what her most basic needs required and was thus unable to give alms to others, the Lord said to her: "You must show yourself loving and gracious to all those who are desirous of some of the wealth I provide for you and deny it to no one but dispense it amply. And should you find yourself unable to give to the needy real goods or perform real services for them, give them spiritual goods for there are many who are poor in spirit, who do not possess sufficient grace either in this world or in purgatory and therefore are in need of great mercy. Acquire those mercies from me through diligent prayer and faithful supplication. For such people are much poorer spiritually than anyone is in body."

As the Lord told her this, there appeared to her many people who were thus poor in spirit and lacked that joyous grace, as she could very well discern spiritually, and they begged her privately to pray to God on their behalf. This she did faithfully according to the Lord's command. Once when she left her pew in church to go home, she saw a blind man whom she had noticed before and whom she would have liked to give a penny, had she had any money, to comfort him. As she felt this intense compassion for him without having anything with which to comfort him, the Lord said to her: "Pray to me on his behalf and say:'Jesus Christ, my most beloved Lord, give yourself to this blind man!'" Kneeling down, she did so immediately. Then the Lord said: "This you must always do: Whenever you see a poor person in need without having any temporal goods to give, pray to me for that person!" In a similar manner he often instructed her to pray now for the living, now for the dead and commanded her to share with them the spiritual wealth he had bestowed upon her, for he had empowered her to pray for them all.

The story of how she was punished severely for having committed a venial sin by greedily feasting her eyes on a mess of fishes.

Chapter XXII.

On the eve of All Saints' Day [October 31], as she was in her cell, she was extraordinarily illuminated by the divine light to behold the joy of the saints and indeed witnessed their delight. For the duration of the vision and through the merciful visitation of Our Lord, she was so filled with divine sweetness, desire, and rejoicing that all her limbs were in motion because of the extraordinary intensity of her joy. She could not even keep her feet still. At her customary mealtime after vespers she would have liked to remain without bodily nourishment to experience all the more fully the grace granted her, had the Lord permitted it. However, he did not wish to allow it but said: "If you were merely blessed with my gifts without encumbrance from your internal labors, you would be so full of joy that you would be incapable of rising from the place where you are seated to eat your meal. Now, however, you have to nourish yourself on account of your great internal work. For if you don't do so, you will have to worry about injuring your mind through lack of nourishment and losing your sanity altogether. Now rise and feed your body. Eat and drink! In this manner I often commanded the holy Birgitta to eat and drink and strengthen her body so that she might live on Earth all the more strongly in my service."

When Dorothea heard this, she got up and ate from a piece of cold fish she had in her cell. But while she was eating that, the boy who served her brought her a hot meal of such size and delectable preparation as to terrify her. Nevertheless, she did not immediately turn away her face but feasted her eyes on it even though she had little desire for it. Because of this, a protest arose in her spirit, which did not want this seductive meal of small fishes deliciously spiced with saffron. Mightily annoyed, her spirit was displeased with her flesh and sensuality, that she had gazed upon the delicious meal too long and had been delighted with it.

Thus a struggle ensued between spirit and flesh, between reason and sensuality. Moreover, a severe displeasure arose in her mind with the man who had sent her enough of these delicious fishes to last her for three meals. So the Lord bade her say to him: "Dear brother, what have I done to you, how have I offended you that you are so angry with me? You have done me more harm than anyone since I came to live in this cell, for with these fishes you attempted to drive my beloved lord from my table. And this I will not suffer you to do, for Our Lord himself says: 'Those who look for my comfort and await it will receive it. Those, who are concerned with satisfying their bodily needs have to forego my heavenly solace.'"

With that the battle between spirit and flesh was resolved, and she was taken up into great delight. At the fourth hour past midnight,though, she became terrified because of the fishes she had looked at and tasted the previous evening, worried that she might have to endure still other punishments for having done so. At the fifth hour the Lord set her ablaze with his love. She wept and sweated profusely until she was wet all over, as though water had been poured all over her and she were sitting in a hot bath. She sat immobile, not daring to stir in fear of the Lord's severe punishments and threats. She did not even dare to put on her veil, belt her gown, or drape her cloak about her, for she was so frightened and weary of God's punishment that she could scarcely make use of her senses. At God's behest the meal that had been brought to her that evening, a sauce and a dish of small fishes, was called up so realistically that she could not avert the eyes of her soul from them but had to contemplate them in great agony, much against her will. The Lord said to her: "Since you desire to look at this, behold and contemplate it so you will be satisfied."

She sat in great pain of the wounds she incurred in her soul in consequence of her misdeed and wept piteously with deep sighs and sobs from the bottom of a heart full of bitterness. This bitterness did not diminish but was increased through God's punishment of forcing her to contemplate that dish from which she could not turn away for more than two hours. More than anything she would have liked to turn away from it, for she felt a great, burning desire to contemplate the Lord, but she was prevented from doing so, for, unfortunately, an impediment had been raised between the Lord and her because of her sin. For this reason she was wounded by bitter pains, filled with bitterness, sickened and oppressed so heavily that she could not raise herself. In abject humility she pressed herself to the ground even more tightly, body and soul, weeping bitterly, crying to the Lord, begging him to deign to send her soul's physician, her confessor, so she might show him the wounds of her soul and he could administer the medicine of an appropriate penance.

When she had thus wept, cried, and tormented herself for two hours until she had no strength left and her confessor had still not appeared, the Lord said: "When he does come, say to him: 'Beloved son, why do you tarry so long? You assume that I am well and healthy; but the wounds of my soul hurt me so bitterly that I, because of this fierce pain, cannot even veil myself, belt my gown, and drape my cloak about me.'" As the Lord spoke, she shed even more tears and was consumed by pain as never before since moving into her cell. Soon after this her soul's physician arrived. When she had revealed her wounds to him through an honest confession and he had anointed her with a healing absolution and penance, her soul's wounds healed at once, and the Lord filled her soul with great bliss.

Nevertheless, because of the great, bitter pain she had endured through these wounds that had impressed themselves so deeply in her soul, her sobbing and sighing continued long after the pain had ceased. Further, she feared to drive the Lord away or deprive herself of some grace if she veiled herself, tied her belt, or covered herself with her cloak and therefore dared not do so until she had asked her confessor's permission. Normally she did so without his leave, but now she did not dare do it without his express permission. When she had clothed herself after having received it, a great peace came over her, and the separation her sin had erected between God and her was also removed. Immediately she was overjoyed and illuminated, and her inner senses were opened so she could observe the bliss of the saints in eternal life, and she heard them clearly as they sang their sweet song with which they praised Our Lord. It resounded so sweetly and forcefully in her ears that she scarcely heard the singing in church.

The Lord came to her comfortingly and mercifully in the sacrament of his body and said: "Now you may praise me more than ever before. And you may well eat what is given to you through my will with one stipulation: that you don't ever put more on your plate than you can eat. The rest leave in the pan. If it is in a bowl already, place it far from you and do not look at it for long or mark its quality or delectable appearance with pleasure. Rather, when you have eaten a tiny morsel, take another if you have need of it, as if you were eating with half-closed eyes. If I had so desired, I could very well have prevented the appearance of the food from harming you. But I wanted to visit this temptation on you and to punish you severely for giving in to it so that those who would hear about it and recognized that they had sinned more grievously than you should take it to heart and mend their ways by considering: 'If God Our Lord has punished his elected bride so harshly for having looked at these little fishes prepared and served so carefully and appetizingly with a desire so obviously originating in her sensuality rather than her reason, how much harder will he punish us who have eaten so much more deliberately and full of self-indulgence and in the lust of eating have forgotten God?'"

How her inner senses were quickened and opened.

Chapter XXIII.

The soul has five internal senses through which she is united with God in love, vitalized, increased, and rejuvenated, just as the body has five external senses through whose use it ages, falls ill, and passes away. The soul's senses, however, are much more alive, and the purer and free of sins the soul is, the more keenly receptive they become. Now mark this in God's bride Dorothea: how exceedingly alive and alert her inner senses were, who even through a minor sin felt spiritual discomfort and immediate injury, which pained her more severely and which she bemoaned more piteously than any visible, severe injury on her body. In truth, this was a real indication of the spiritual life that started shining in God's presence when her heart was renewed. And she became all the more clearly and unerringly aware of bitter pains being as great or greater from the wounds and damages to her soul as those inflicted on the body, suffering them in her soul just as her sensual nature suffered because of bodily wounds and damages.

From this time on, not only the inner sense called touch was alive and sensitive in her, but all her other inner senses were vibrant, open, and active, too, though at one time more so than at another, depending on the effects of ever-present grace, which was abundantly bestowed on her until the end of her life. Her inner sense of taste was awakened to become discriminating and sound. Through it she tasted eternal things, recognizing that God was sweeter than honey and that heavenly delights were inexpressibly more delectable than all delights the world has to offer. In the sacrament of the body of Our Lord she received and savored a variety of fruit, marvelous desire, and sweetness through which her soul was nurtured most tenderly and lastingly. For her spiritual wounds healed; her lassitude, hunger, illness, and anxieties were dispersed, and she received many other blessings which will be recounted later.

Furthermore, in the course of her internal visions Dorothea was generally illuminated so clearly that her own conscience and soul became transparent to her. Furthermore, she could see into the hearts of many other people whose sins, thoughts, wishes, inclinations, and temptations she discerned clearly. When she revealed these to some of them, they admitted that it was as she said. Here it is not to be assumed that seeing and punishing the sins of others was a joy to her: it was painful to her and she would have liked to have been relieved of this task, had it been God's will. But when she beheld and contemplated heavenly things and the countenance of her creator, which is a spotless mirror, it was an unspeakably great joy to her.

She also possessed a keen sense of hearing through which she perceived the lovely sweet dalliance of the Lord and his whisperings to her soul. The Lord spoke to her soul in three ways: At times through a spiritual vision of a real parable or picture, which explained a number of hidden heavenly secrets. At other times he spoke to her in a human way when he appeared to her in his human shape on the cross, in his resurrection, or in another of his human forms. At such times he spoke words to her in such a way that she heard and understood them more clearly and completely than when one person hears another speak and understands and retains what has been said. The third way, the way the Lord employed most often when he spoke to her, occurred internally in her soul when the Lord revealed the truth to her without the aid of parables, real or spiritual creatures, or other aids or inclusion of creatures. Then the Lord proclaimed the truth solely with his voice, which he taught her so comfortingly on such occasions. In these lessons no words traveled through the air and none were received in the ear. Her soul's sense of smell was likewise sound and keen. Through it she joyfully perceived the sweet smell of her bridegroom and frequently, with great pain, the stench of sinners, for the sins of sinners stank most foully in her nostrils and pained her most excruciatingly. More, many notable things happened from which a keen observer can discern clearly how lively, sensitive, and delicate her inner senses were. And this the hot, burning love had accomplished in her. It subdues and calms the raging fleshly desires that commonly besmirch the inner senses and darken them rudely and furiously. Opposing those desires is the flaming light which arises from the treasure of divine love. It cleanses the inner senses of their spots, appeases them, drives out their drunkenness through its illumination, and refines and opens them.

How on her way to Rome she was miraculously showered with gifts
and mercifully preserved.

Chapter XXIV.

The most merciful comforter, Our Lord Jesus Christ, a gracious and pleasant companion on all her travels, through his mercy adorned Dorothea, his elected bride, with innumerable good deeds. Among those was one, which she enjoyed throughout her entire journey to Rome and from Rome back to her home again: she burned hotly in love even though the fire of love at one time was not as hotly ignited as at another. And that happened sometimes in the midst of sincere, bitter regrets, sometimes in the course of devoted, intense prayer; at times it occurred in the course of a rigorous self-examination, at other times in the course of her contemplation of heaven or while she was enraptured. Many times she burned through the transmission of the Holy Spirit, whom God Our Lord often sent her in the course of her journey now in the form of burning love, then as a passionately desirous love; now as wounded love; now as hot, burning love, then as inebriating love or languishing love; sometimes with overflowing love and still other degrees and effects of love than those mentioned above. Nevertheless, it must be realized that ultimately there is not more than one single love, even though it bears many names and produces a variety of effects, which Dorothea recognized clearly through her labors and intuition, which made her experiences comprehensible to her.

Dorothea, through a variety of love's effects, was also so strong, quick, and energetic in body and soul that seldom anyone walked ahead of her, even though she had often been ill and had suffered much before the start of the journey. She also said one thing about which people may wonder, that on the entire journey to Rome and back and during her stay there she was never aware of having slept at all, except for one single night, the second night after her arrival in Rome. That night she slept after having received the body of Our Lord Jesus Christ, and her strength was markedly increased on account of it. Otherwise, whenever those who traveled the pilgrim road with her had fallen asleep, she arose and seated herself at the foot of the bed or in a corner not far from her travel companions with whom she had retired as if to go to sleep and then passed the night without sleep in prayer, self-examination, joy, exultation, or sadness of spirit; in weeping, lamentation, dalliance, contemplation, or in rapture of spirit. Only in rapture did she experience something akin to sleep, which the scriptures refer to as spiritual sleep.

On the way to Rome she wore shoes most of the time; in the city, however, as she visited the churches for two or three hours before daybreak, she walked barefoot on the sharp pointed stones and paths, and this she did in such great hot love that she felt none of the pains that assailed her. Here is to be taken to heart what the Lord said to her more than four years after her pilgrimage to

Rome: "It is to be esteemed more highly and as more miraculous that I preserved your honor on the way and you did not fall into sin than that I kept you alive in your mother's womb so that you were not stillborn."

Her illness in Rome, which lasted longer than eight weeks.

Chapter XXV.

Starting on the day of St. Luke the Evangelist [October 18], Dorothea daily visited the seven main churches of Rome with great devotion and emotional fervor. After eight weeks, the Lord, through the Holy Spirit, brought about a renewal of her spirit. She began to ail in body and to decline in physical strength without suffering any physical discomfort or pain. Eventually she became incapable of visiting the holy places and churches where she had nurtured her love. By that time the holy desires she had acquired had grown there to such a degree of perfection that she ailed more from love than from bodily pains, both while being bedridden as well as later when she arose and was restored to health. This illness lasted for more than seven weeks.

During this time she could neither walk nor stand and seldom turn from one side to the other. She lay there as though she could not move at all and was left for dead by her relatives and acquaintances. She was taken to a hospice for the sick. There she was drawn into a deep contemplation by Our Lord who filled her with his passion and performed much good in her, much of which she discerned right there. But later the Lord revealed to her much more of all the good he had done for her there, of which he allowed her to say only very little. The food she ate during those weeks was so little that had it all been collected, it would scarcely have added up to a pound, and her drink would scarcely have been more than is what is contained in a cup. Now, if someone had taken clear note of the lack of food and drink in her, he would well have realized that her illness was not human, as indeed it was of a supernatural kind.

In the course of this illness she was often enraptured, frequently for such a long time that she was not herself even long enough all day to be able to ask

for a drink of water. Even so, her face remained rosy. Now, while she lay with
the sick in the hospital for eight weeks and the attendants despaired of her life,
behold, the physician who heals all our diseases! All the while he renewed her
internally with his love. He also kept her internally, having drawn her from all
external things. He filled her with great delights even as she lay ill and often
embraced her soul gently, finally granting her the strength to rise again. After she
managed to sit up, she asked for something to eat. And this was accounted a
miracle in the eyes of those present who knew she had lain there for so long
eating scarcely anything yet still remaining rosy-cheeked, retaining a complexion
more wholesome than ever before.

She remained seated on her bed for three days, free of bodily pain but
unable to walk. After those three days, the Sunday came on which the veronica
of Our Lord was to be displayed, but which she would not be able to attend on
account of her body's weakness, even though she desperately desired to do so.
She hired two strong men who were to take her to St. Peter's church. But when
they tried to convey her there as best their strength allowed, they could not lead
her without help, nor even raise her to her feet. So they left her lying on her
knees in the middle of the road and went on their way. How she had become so
heavy was kept a secret from her at the time. Later she was taken to a stable near
that road where she remained for twelve days. There she learned to crawl and
pull herself up on the great stones and beams lying about. She practiced until
twelve days later, though with great difficulty and other people's help, she could
walk on a cane to St. Peter's cathedral to see the face of Our Lord.

All who saw her were amazed that she could not walk even though she
was not disfigured and did not look ill at all. Dorothea herself assumed that she
would never again be able to walk, and therefore she thought to herself: "I will
stay in Rome and beg for alms on the stairs of St. Peter's cathedral from the
passers-by." She was not troubled by her inability to walk or about the fact that
she had no food to eat, nor yet about having to beg if she were to leave Rome
before receiving money from home. All the seemingly disgusting things that

happened to her, her illness and other such reversals, she bore with the same unperturbed calm.

When she had been in the above-mentioned church of St. Peter for several days and with the aid of a cane had learned to walk again, she sought to do and accomplish what would win her the grace to be gained there during that year of jubilee. But she found herself incapable of reciting the *Pater Noster* or the *Apostles' Creed*, even though she had learned both correctly as a child and had rehearsed them in the proper Christian spirit ever since, having recited them daily for many hours until she had been smitten by this particular illness. Her forgetting these basic articles of faith, however, was a consequence of the great change that had come over her while being confined to her bed; the protracted ecstasy she experienced during this confinement and for weeks afterwards; the profound union of her soul with the Godhead; and the constant, merciful visitation of God, who graciously sustained her throughout the aforementioned time and who bestowed upon her more abundantly than ever before the delight of his unlimited grace. Eventually, she easily relearned both *Pater Noster* and *Creed* and firmly committed both to memory.

During the last year of Dorothea's life, when the Lord revealed that she was to write down all that happened in Rome, he said: "Now I will tell you why I let you suffer the gruesome stench among the diseased while renewing you internally with my love. I rendered you incapable of walking and innocent as a child untarnished by any stain. Earlier that same year, while you were still at home among your friends, I had made you very ill with my love and then well again. Had you become as infirm then as you were in Rome, you would have received comfort and aid from your family and therefore would not have paid as much attention to your sickness as you did when you were left in wretchedness, uncomforted by your loved ones, without a single person to see to your needs faithfully.

"More, I robbed you of your strength with my love. I removed all those near you and all your acquaintances and forced you to use up all the supplies you had brought with you to satisfy your needs, for it was my will that the foundation of your true, constant patience be tempted, tested, and made manifest, and to see whether you would be unmindful of the good I graciously provided for you there and before that time. And had you turned from me even a little or had shown the slightest sign of impatience with me, I would have esteemed you not at all. However, you stood firm, without impatience, and desired nothing but me, that you might win and keep me, never to lose me, and for this reason I comforted you without ceasing, leaving you to yourself not even for a moment. I have revealed this to you to be written down so that those who hear it may improve themselves and will not be seized with impatience, no matter what suffering they may be forced to endure, and that they will not forget me even in their suffering, for I am a sweet comforter to those who suffer in patience."

Why the blessed Dorothea came to the church in Pomesania,
that is to Marienwerder.
Chapter XXVI.

Later the praiseworthy woman Dorothea became acquainted with many secrets of Our Lord and tasted and felt the great, inexpressible sweetness and joy of Our Lord, the excess of his goodness, deeds, and wealth by which she often felt buried, even devoured, to such a degree that she did not know how she was conducting herself externally. Furthermore, at times she was incapable of concealing her overabundance of joy, desire, and rejoicing. Instead, it showed itself openly in front of people in church, sometimes in her laughter, gestures, voice, and words; she could not contain herself. On account of this, some who heard and saw this and were not improved through the grace which God had bestowed on her, were moved to resent this and turn it into something despicable. They brought these matters to the authorities who summoned and interrogated her. She acquitted herself humbly before them but without revealing the great good God had done to her, for then and long before then she had felt in dire need of a wise man to whom she could entrust and reveal the secrets of her heart. Now she was told about such a man to whom, however, she did not want to bare herself and entrust herself totally without the advice of her confessor.

Master Nikolaus, a preacher in Gdansk, had been her confessor for many years. He advised her to travel to Marienwerder where she would find a canon at the cathedral, a master of holy writ, who, he was convinced, could guide her in her questions and matters of conscience. As master Nikolaus was advising her thus, she became most pleased with that suggestion, and the master he had spoken of appeared to her at once in the shape and figure in which she first saw him more than two years later.[35] The reason why she did not seek him out immediately, even though she was determined to do so, was that shortly thereafter in the year of Our Lord 1390 a year of jubilee was to be celebrated. So, following the advice of her above-mentioned confessor, she journeyed to Rome first, arriving there on the feast day of St. Luke the Evangelist [October 18, 1389], before Christmas of the year preceding the jubilee, and she remained there until the following Easter. During that time her husband died during Lent. When she returned from Rome the Sunday before Whitsuntide, she still desired to seek out the master in Marienwerder, and the Lord drove her hard to do so. But even though she had the firm intention of following the command of Our Lord, she was prevented for yet another year before going to the before-mentioned man at Marienwerder.

How she came to Marienwerder to the man who had been recommended to her.
Chapter XXVII.

St. Paul taught his disciple Timothy how a true widow should live, saying: "She who is a true widow without consolation should put her hopes in God and be in holy prayer day and night, for the widow who lives in lechery is dead." To this teaching the blessed Dorothea adhered diligently. Now that she was a widow,

---

[35] Johannes von Marienwerder is here referring to himself in the third person. For more details on narrative strategies such as this in *Leben*, consult my article *"Whose Autobiography is this Anyway?"*

she steadfastly practiced righteousness and looked about for a place where she might serve the Lord without hindrance from her friends and worldly affairs. And to fulfill her resolve to seek the instruction and advice of the man who had been recommended to her, she journeyed to Marienwerder on the Monday following the feast of the Holy Trinity in the year of Our Lord 1391.

When she arrived in Marienwerder, she immediately went to the cathedral church of St. John[36] the Evangelist and took a seat behind the portal, a humble place where the Lord visited inexpressibly great mercy upon her and ordered her to speak of it in this manner: "When I came to Marienwerder for the first time, such abundant sweetness came over me that I deemed the Lord himself had transported me there since all the days of my life I was never so courageous as to have dared to travel by myself even a quarter of a mile on an unfamiliar road. But when I first came to Marienwerder, I was not afraid to travel all by myself on a road totally unfamiliar to me. From Mewe (Gniew) I traveled on a path to Marienwerder so energetically and joyfully and in such a short time that I don't know whether one should call it walking or flying. When I arrived at the church and sat down behind the door, my beloved Lord visited me with his opulent mercy and sent me his Holy Spirit, invisibly, with his hot, burning love through powerful illumination. He consoled me so excessively with his spiritual passion, joys, and various blessings that I thought, 'Oh God, Lord King of all creation, if you comfort me this mercifully in your great love and tender mercy in this church as you are starting to do now, I will never leave but serve you eternally within.' It seems to me that I have never been in any church where so much joy and sweetness were bestowed on me.

"After this, on the eve of Corpus Christi, I felt such severe, hot desire and hunger to receive the body of Our Lord that I could scarcely endure it. So I went

---

[36] Marienwerder Cathedral is dedicated to St. John the Evangelist. Above its main entrance on the south side of the building a Venetian mosaic commissioned by the Pomesanian bishop Johannes Mönch commemorates one of the scenes of his martyrdom described in the *Golden Legend*, his being boiled alive in a cauldron.

to that man on whose account I had come and begged him to hear my confession and give me the body of my dear Lord on the feast of Corpus Christi. As he heard my confession for the first time, I immediately conceived a greater love for him than to any other person. At once I loved him as sincerely as a brother and trusted him so explicitly that then and there I would have revealed all the secrets of my heart to him had the Lord taught me how to phrase them properly at that very moment. I remained there for a week in his pleasant company and revealed to him in perfect confidence what was in my heart, as much as my dear Lord allowed me. During that same week the Lord daily granted me great mercies. He granted me hot burning love, he illumined my understanding clearly, and through this illumination he revealed to me which of the many things he had worked in me I was to communicate. He poured great joy into my soul and bestowed many other benefits with which he comforted me inexplicably and extensively all that week but most powerfully during mass on the feast of Corpus Christi.

"On the Sunday following Corpus Christi, I became so inebriated spiritually by heavenly sweetness that I was unable to find the short way from my hostelry to the cathedral, and, coming from the church, was equally incapable of finding my inn. I was too embarrassed to ask anyone to show me the way because I feared people would notice my drunken state and hold it against me. So I followed the others going there until I arrived at the church without drawing attention to myself. After having received so many blessings there, I returned from Marienwerder to Gdansk, downcast all the way because Our Lord reminded me of many secrets I was to have put before the above-mentioned man while I was with him but which I had forgotten to mention. Day and night for fifteen weeks I was driven by the Lord to return to him. I enjoyed no rest or peace of mind until after XV weeks I did come back to him. During that time the Lord drew me so forcefully to receive his holy body, which I could not partake of frequently enough to satisfy my hot desire and fierce hunger for it, until both hunger and desire were so great that I was sometimes ill and bedridden. My strength left me, and I longed so much to receive the body of Our Lord that I gladly would have given the entire city of Gdansk, had it been mine to give, in exchange for it, if, by doing so, I could have earned the sacrament according to my desire, as my most beloved Lord has often confirmed."

How she returned to Marienwerder and pledged her obedience.

Chapter XXVIII.

Because of her great longing, which was best known to the Lord, Dorothea returned to Marienwerder on a heavy cart loaded with crates and other heavy, bulky items the carter was taking to the fair that always takes place there on the Sunday after St. Michael's feast [September 29]. The cart overturned as she was riding on it, and in that accident she was hurt so seriously externally on her limbs as well as internally that she would not have recovered from her injuries and easily could have died had the Lord not granted her his special protection and nursed her himself, as he later told her. There in Marienwerder she opened her heart to the master of whom she had thought so often and who from then on was her confessor, always revealing as much to him as the Lord inspired and ordered her to say.

She also asked him for a cell. But when he did not hold out much hope for her being given one there, Dorothea often thought of abandoning the place to search for another within her homeland or in a foreign country where she could be enclosed, if the Lord had permitted her to do so. For by that time she had long desired to be enclosed in a cell, unencumbered by the world and external affairs. But she was not accommodated at once because the cathedral chapter of Marienwerder had to examine her life: whether she was honest and enjoyed a good reputation. For this reason her request was also not forwarded immediately to the lord bishop and his cathedral chapter but only after more than a year and six months had passed. During those eighteen months her revelations and all the other great works the Lord had performed in her were examined by the aforementioned master of holy writ, her confessor, to whom I will refer from now on with the letter B, and by another man, who at that time was the prior, a doctor of canon law, whom, for brevity's sake, I will designate from now on by the letter P,[37] just as I will refer to the blessed Dorothea by the letter D. [This examination] was to determine whether God was the source of [all her experiences].

During this time the Lord drove her and ordered her to swear to him that she would remain with B for the rest of her life, never to abandon him. As the Lord ordered her thus, he showed her the path to eternal life as though he were saying: "You must not fear that this is a hindrance toward eternal life; quite the contrary: it will be an advance." The Lord also ordered her [to remain there], to put her mind at rest, which was often troubled and vacillated whether to stay there or go elsewhere. From the time she had taken this blessed oath during the octave of Sts. Peter and Paul [June 29] in the year of Our Lord 1392 the Lord drove her to be obedient to B as well, saying: "You shall humbly kneel at his feet and beg him in God's name to accept you and take you fully into his governance. You shall subordinate your will entirely to his. Whatever he asks you to do, do, and whatever he prohibits you from doing, do not do."

When she understood God's will clearly, Dorothea went to the church on the fourth day after having taken the oath recorded above, and after praying devoutly and deeply with tears streaming from her eyes, she committed herself to the authority of B, just as the Lord had commanded, who afterwards appeared to her most lovingly in spirit and said: "You both shall often take to heart how I have brought you together. I have united you just as two people are bound to one another in marriage, and for this reason each of you shall take on the burdens of the other and one help the other so that you both may come to eternal life; you shall know that no other person has been nor ever will be commended as highly to B as you have been." This was brought about by the obedience which she, at

---

[37] Johannes here refers to himself as B [*Beichtvater* (confessor)]; since his fellow canon Johannes Reymann, Dorothea's second confessor, was the prior of Marienwerder cathedral, he designates him by the letter P.

the behest of Our Lord, showed her confessor.

The three letters that she read and the master who instructed her.

Chapter XXIX.

In the school of self-discipline and self-castigation under the master who has his lectern in heaven and his school on this earth, Dorothea studied and learned how to win a clean conscience. When she had achieved this, she was illuminated and very knowledgeable. She was instructed by the Lord to read three letters. The first one was black, the second red, the third of pure gold. In the black one she read the number and severity of her sins and how far she had been led away from God because of her trespasses. There she discerned the nature of her sins, their degree, their frequency, and where, when, with what intent, determination, and purpose she had committed them. On the second letter, the red one, she read the abundance of wounds on Christ's body, their profound bitterness, and all his sufferings. In the third, that is the golden one, she read the joy of the saints in eternal life: the distinctive honors, joys, and adornments they enjoy in God's presence.

Concerning these three letters, the Lord said to Dorothea: "When I tore out your old heart, I pressed three letters into you: the black one recorded your sins. This letter you were to read until you came to the subject of penance and complete forgiveness of sins. You did read the chapter in which I tell you that all your sins are forgiven. But it would have behooved you to read the entire letter so diligently as to eradicate once and for all the bitterness of your heart through the inflammation of love to make the other two letters all that much more completely a part of you and all that much sweeter. Had you done so, you would have marshalled your intuitions far more productively and directed your path toward eternal life in the direct way one shoots at a target." By saying this to her the Lord indicated that she was done reading the black letter, and the other two appeared most brightly before her. God said: "Never again shall you read the black letter. But read the other two as long as you live. All people who seek to be blessed eternally shall read their black letter until they come close enough to me to hear the sweet voice say 'your sins are forgiven.' There are few who finish reading the black letter while they still live on this Earth but many finish it in the torment following this life."

Afterwards the Lord said: "Had you always been truly obedient to your master (whose school you attended and whose teaching you received), you would have learned even more from him than you did. Now gather up the writings I have taught you and study them diligently. I have taught you to overcome the world, the evil spirit, and your own carnal nature and will. I have opened your internal senses and taught you to discern, see, hear, smell, taste, and feel the eternal treasures I have prepared for you. Now consider what a solemn, strict, wise, honest, gracious, and erudite schoolmaster you have had whose school you attended for such a long time, and how many pleasant benefits you have received. All writings you have studied under him, that is me, you may honorably and without shame bring before your two masters B and P, whom I sent to you so they may weigh them and check them against holy writ and examine whether they are correct. For I don't want you to leave error (falsehood) behind. And all who will read the writings you have received from me will proclaim that you had an excellent, exacting, and purposeful master."

How she was dead to the world for more than thirty years.
Chapter XXX.

Without mortification of the flesh human beings are not receptive to God or suitable for the contemplative life, which requires following one's creator up the mountain into the presence of God's glory. For the wise man says: "The body, which is perishable, weighs down the soul and drags it earthward." And St. Paul says: "If you live according to the flesh, you shall die; if, however, you kill the sins of the flesh through the spirit, you will live." For this reason Dorothea from the time she was a child mortified her flesh and its beastly demands. She resisted its wicked inclinations and disciplined herself toward the good. She patiently endured the bad that happened to her for the sake of the good in order to live for God, dead to the sins of the world, the evil spirit, her own will, and carnality.

This the Lord himself acknowledged when he said to her: "I am teaching your soul to die and to cleave unto me. To accomplish this, I am sending you my Holy Spirit often. He kills the flesh and quickens the spirit, so he will kill you and teach you to kill yourself more and more. No one can kill himself as successfully and then keep on dying as he to whom I send my Holy Spirit. I also often inspire great love in you so you may die entirely as regards perishable things, for nothing can kill you quite as well in respect to temporal things and awaken the desire for eternal goods in you as my great love. From it springs proper self-mortification through which one lives spiritually, becomes receptive to God, and committed to the contemplative life. I have taught you to die and to live-- to die to the world and its temptations, to die in your own carnality and its desires and aims to live spiritually for me alone.

"You never could follow me entirely until you had totally killed off your carnal nature. You have mortified yourself in spiritual exercises, self-castigations, and disciplines for about thirty years now. This you have done not only according to reason but beyond reason as well. You never did spare yourself in these self-castigations and self-inflicted injuries, for I too drove you to them unsparingly." The Lord God pointed this out as if to say: "I added my own wounds to yours." He continued: "You might as well know this: in truth there are not many who equal you in zeal for spiritual exercises and self-castigations. But you shall not reveal and leave knowledge on Earth of the greatest exercises, castigations, and disciplines through which you have won me. Rather, you shall take them with you into life everlasting. For there are my beloved saints who can weigh these things better than those who dwell on Earth and generally assume that it is easy to earn eternal life, not taking to heart that even my dear chosen mother did not achieve that distinction for nothing but came to it through exertion and hard labor."

How the spiritual eyes must dim in death before a human being
dies totally into the spiritual life.

Chapter XXXI.

Part of the death of a human being's carnal nature is that the spiritual eyes dim in anticipation of death, just as the fading of a creature's bodily eyes precedes the death of the body. This dimming of the eyes, as the Lord instructed Dorothea, happens "when people, because of great divine love, desire, and longing love eternal, spiritual things so intensely that temporal, physical things become grievous. From time to time it happens that such persons, because of great longing, hot love, and desire, weep hotly or that something else works so strongly in them to make them feel a potent grace flow through their eyes into every limb. They are made aware that this work of mercy kills off their love for perishable things, rendering them contemptible or annoying through this special divine love. When that happens, the eye of greed for temporal things dims and these people come to resemble the blind, as though membranes were pulled over their eyes to make temporal things invisible. Simultaneously, in respect to spiritual matters, it is as though a membrane has been pulled from the eyes of reason. Such a blinding of the eyes has to happen frequently, now against one thing, now against another, for a man's eyes, when he is thus to die, will not be dimmed against all worthless things all at once. Rather, they dim gradually: first one, then the other.

"Those whose spiritual eyes dim in this manner are often in spiritual torment, but their real eyes will not be dimmed in death." This the Lord revealed to the blessed Dorothea, further telling her that her spiritual eyes would be dimmed toward certain necessary temporal things as they had already been dimmed against unnecessary ones. When it happens that the eyes of a person living a holy life are dimmed, such a person may very well assume to have reached the proper goal of life at last. But few people ever reach this point in their lives. Furthermore, the Lord said to her: "For two reasons will I dim your eyes. First, because you have a tremendous desire to die to all perishable things that oppose me and your own well-disciplined will. The other is that you have a burning desire to be good to others and to live a holy life. For the sake of my love you often did not warm yourself and have not eaten nor taken drink, nor have you gossiped with others, though, according to your sensual nature, to which, however, you refused to submit, you would have liked to do all these things. In this manner you did blind your eyes and left behind temporal goods for my sake. At that point I started to kill you and your eyes started to dim."

How the spiritual eye is restored to health.

Chapter XXXII.

Jesus Christ taught her how to teach her spiritual children, and commanded her to speak to them thus: "My dear children, mark now whether you have experienced the same degree of bitterness and regret over your sins as you experienced lust and enjoyment through them. Consider whether you have carefully weighed the magnitude and number of your sins as well as their various kinds and whether through illumination of divine light you have been able to recognize how deep the wounds caused by your sins really are. Note how the pain and cruelty of sin finally drove you to confess and uncover fully how you committed your sins internally in your hearts and externally in your works so that your confessor, the physician of the soul, could apply his craft of healing to your souls' wounds. Only when you have done this so often that you can feel yourselves being cleansed will you for the first time feel complete certainty that the blindness in your souls has been pierced by the thorn of contrition. This is the first lesson.

"The second lesson is this: Mark whether you flee from sin because of your sincere love of God and true fear and horror of evil or because of mere cowardice. Then weep bitterly over your sins and note whether you are truly following the Lord and cleave to him with all your might. Doing this, you will earn a greater light than ever before, which will illumine you to witness and bemoan in sincere empathy the martyrdom of Our Lord-- his death and all he has suffered. When you have done all this, you will have progressed on the path toward God, and the blinders will have been removed from the eyes of your soul. Such progress depends on the desire and effort to do good, to increase in virtue to cleave to God; on doing his will and on making yourself over in his holy image to resemble him rather than on increasing your external works.

"The third lesson is that while you are progressing and are moving from one virtue to the next, you win for yourselves a still stronger light with whose help you may behold God's infinite great mercy granted to you so clearly, abundantly, and fairly that you will not be able to refrain from weeping. Tears will start from your eyes and pour forth in boundless gratitude to thank God for the great good he has done you. When that happens, your spiritual squinting will have ceased and you will have progressed farther and climbed higher in the increase of perfection.

"In the fourth lesson, mark that in your increase and ascent toward perfection you will be illuminated even more clearly than before and will burn hotter still in God's love so that, on account of true love and the taste of divine sweetness, you will start to weep copiously, lament vigorously, and long incessantly to behold the glory of God, for those who come this far climb the mountain of the Lord and begin to discern and contemplate the glory of the Lord. Upon beholding God's glory, the infection of the inner eye disappears without delay and all blinders, thick or thin, are removed from their eyes immediately. To such seekers the correct paths to eternal life they must travel will then be revealed, and as they do, they will be returning from a foreign country, retracing their steps into their father's land. Actually, though, they are returning on a road different from the one they took before, for they who went away wantonly return chaste; those who departed full of greed return full of the gentleness of charity and contempt for temporal wealth. In the same manner it happens with the other paths that lead people astray and those that return them to life. In this fashion the Lord taught me to walk the narrow roads and paths to eternal life. He taught me to turn back on the sinful paths since I had traveled them not in a lucid state of mind but in pride, spiritual emptiness, or sinfulness. These same paths I was now to travel straight toward him without being sidetracked, without deceit, in deep humility, spirituality, sanctity, and obliteration of my own self."

How her labors were heavy, intense, joyful, and fruitful.

Chapter XXXIII.

From the time she was a child, Dorothea's life was full of work and activity. Her labors were intense, hard, heavy, full of effort, varied, and the result of great love. For this reason they were profitable, producing great spiritual wealth for her and others, as the Lord proved to her on many occasions. He said: "What can you say of my work and my effects? I will surpass your description through that which I inspire in you. If all your internal and external powers and senses could read and write, they still could not describe all the works and effects I have brought about in you from your earliest youth. I will tell you even more: Neither could they comprehend or describe the variety and beneficial nature of the works and effects I bring about in you now, for those shall remain hidden from your worldly contemporaries just as the works and effects I cause in my elect in eternal life are concealed from them. Now say to your B and P: 'My beloved sons, my prayers, vigils, fasts, and genuflections are my least significant labors. The labors I perform and endure when I cannot weep are much more taxing, for then all my energies are stretched and extended until they resemble a string stretched to its utmost limit.'"

Moreover, the Lord said: "You must never assume that you have done enough. On the contrary: always exert yourself to do even better work, to live more saintly still, and never let any time pass during the day without performing good works. Then, when night comes, you will still think you have done little and still have much to do. And indeed, when evening falls and there is still some strength left in you, start your labors anew, for you will still find plenty to do. You shall not regret this, for you must at all times be active and busy with works." As the Lord said this, she noticed many new and unfamiliar effects of the Lord through which her strengths became extended like the strings of a musical instrument. Then the Lord said to her: "Until now you have been filled with works and activities at all times and never spared yourself because of any physical defects. Therefore, I, too, will not spare you from now on but will constantly perform my works in you. In you I will awaken such great desire for me and such powerful effects and noteworthy external labors that all people on Earth shall be made aware of it.

"Those who shall aid others acquire spiritual wealth and help me maintain this world cannot be idle or work sluggishly or drowsily. They must be ready at all times and shall not spare themselves. Now implore me that I help you and set you afire with hot, burning love! The person ignited with this love cannot tolerate being idle but is fruitful and accomplishes great deeds. It is easy to say 'a hot, burning love.' But only very few have actually tasted the wealth of this love so indescribably abundant and fruitful. Those who have this love are not loath to bear the burden of great, heavy labor for my sake. It is difficult, too, to labor in such a way as not to lose the eternal wealth or the wealth already gained and won, and you shall labor so hard that you won't know whether you are coming or going. You have sacrificed yourself to me out of your own free will; for this reason I will weigh you down with an especially heavy burden to carry until you have performed all the hard labor that is still to be endured here and even after this life. Those who are unwilling to carry a heavy burden when they should be laboring will wail in purgatory: 'Woe is us that we did not carry the burden that was ours to bear in body and soul.' Their souls will long remain bound in the pain of purgatory, until they overcome there what they should have overcome here on Earth but refused to. But they who enjoy my mercy in this present time may gain much good for themselves and others in a very short time, something they could not gain in purgatory through many days of supplication and bitter pain. Had you not wept and labored on behalf of numerous people, they would have had to burn in purgatory for many years."

How the Lord placed his burden on her.

Chapter XXXIV.

It is to man's benefit to bear the yoke and the burden of the Lord from youth to old age. God's burden is to be discerned, as Dorothea revealed, through the hot, burning love; the mighty love; the wounded, debilitating love; through longing; burning desire; great devotion; abundance of tears; heavy internal labor; and any such gift as man will not receive merely because he wants or desires it. When he does receive it, however, he can neither do as he pleases nor put it aside whenever he wishes. Instead, he has to bear the burden put on him as long as the Lord, who bestowed it on him, wishes. And the Lord lays himself on whomever he burdens thus, pressing that person hard, as he did the blessed Dorothea for many years, to whom he said: "You cannot experience the effect of this burden in the same way year after year, nor perform an unvarying amount of labor in carrying it. You know very well that you have never been idle. But the longer you live, the heavier the load you have to carry will grow, for, as you well know, when I was hanging on the cross near death, I had to carry the heaviest burden of all.

"The people who become sanctified on earth are those on whom I lay my cross and whom I nail so tightly to it that they have to shoulder it and carry it along with the heavy personal burdens they are already carrying for as long as I desire. Such people are crucified in the real sense of the word, and when they die they will go to heaven without going to purgatory first. I have nailed you to the cross and have burdened you with a very heavy load. I have pursued you on Earth with excruciating internal labor and the tremendous effects I caused in you. Now pursue me in turn! You will do that whenever you love me passionately, desire me fiercely, and labor internally and externally so hard that in doing so you extend and expand all your strength as though you were rushing to ascend straight into heaven with these before-mentioned works to seize me greedily and with all your might. Whenever you have done so, you will have pursued me. However, you will not be able to accomplish this without my help."

How she was to practice self denial.

Chapter XXXV.

Our Lord Jesus Christ did not come into this world to work his own will but the will of his heavenly father who sent him. Through word and deed he taught us to break our own will and to withstand the wicked inclination toward sensuality which inclines human beings to fulfill their own desire, the desire to enrich themselves and follow their own senses, to avoid scorn, effort, and pain and to seek worldly honors, the comfort of the body, health and pleasantries. To resist these temptations forcefully -- that is self denial. Thus the Lord instructed the blessed Dorothea, saying: "Each single day you shall deny yourself many times, for as often as you avoid a sin for my sake, you deny yourself because nothing is yours except sin. Such self denial you practice all the more perfectly whenever you avoid committing one sin for my sake without simultaneously committing another. Take this as a lesson: If someone spoke evil of you or committed some other injustice against you, your nature would be stirred, bent on revenge if it were not mercifully kept in check. If you resisted such inclination by considering thus: 'I will neither take revenge nor defend myself but will leave these matters to God,' you would have practiced self-denial.

"The same is true whenever you break the strength of your own will for my sake -- when you would like to eat, drink, sleep, wander about idly, see a certain person, engage in conversation, look at his accommodations, hold his hand, accept a gift, and do other such things toward which you are inclined though they are neither utter necessities nor particularly useful. Whenever you refuse to give in to these inclinations, you have denied yourself. Such is also the case when you ignore your senses and your reason to follow my advice or holy writ. Whenever vainglory or vain comfort tempt you or when you are tempted to consider yourself someone special because of the mercies, virtues, or gifts I have bestowed upon you but you resist, ascribing none of these treasures to your own doing but to me, you will once more have denied yourself. And when you have thus denied yourself often in the course of a single day, busy yourself in the performance of virtuous deeds. Turning in hot desire to me, you will slay yourself through self-denial to die to sin and live for me. This you shall do until you are totally renewed in spirit and have become so insignificant in your own eyes that you are neither ashamed nor afraid of doing good. More, you shall be so simple-minded and child-like that you will not even consider doing well and refraining from sinning as your own accomplishments. Rather, you will credit them to me because it will seem to you as though I myself had committed each good deed."

How she was wounded in spirit.
Chapter XXXVI.

To increase her suffering and her understanding, the Lord Jesus Christ wrote the deep wounds of his bitter torments into her heart and soul with his own blood. In them she steadfastly read his pain and love and was awakened to heartfelt compassion and fired in grateful love to him. The Lord pierced and wounded her heart, flesh, soul, blood, and all inner and outer strength, as he himself revealed to her. Her wounds were spiritual in nature; nevertheless, they not only hurt her spiritually but physically as well. They were filled with bitter pain. They swelled up, they burned with heat, they turned cold, they twitched and bled in a spiritual way exactly as bodily injuries do. They caused even greater bitterness through their pain than do bodily wounds because, due to their internal nature, they were more severe and fierce, and she endured a greater number of them simultaneously than she had ever suffered physically.

Then the Lord said to her: "You endure far greater bitter suffering in your spiritual wounds than you ever did in bodily injuries. In fact, your internal suffering is so extensive that it spills over into your external senses, which I have pierced and wounded spiritually. As a result, your external senses now convey what hurts even more and suffering works even more forcefully in your internal spiritual wounds. Of this you have often become aware yourself when you were tormented so severely that you could scarcely breathe at the time such injury occurred. A person illuminated with my light can read and discern in your countenance when your spiritual wounds thus spill over into your body, for then the before-mentioned pains work their effects more severely on you, torment you more fiercely, and blanch your face visibly. More than enough and whenever I wish, I pierce and wound your soul and flesh. I have never allowed your body to heal as long as something evil remained therein. From your earliest youth I have chased and wounded you daily in body and in spirit until I had renewed your old flesh and had torn your old heart from it."

Here is to be noted how severely the blessed Dorothea was tormented in body and soul. The spiritual wounds generally brought on total physical exhaustion, lingering despondency of soul, and a burning desire for God and eternal life. Often she was drawn up to God so strongly that she had no control whatsoever over her physical senses and could scarcely breathe. In this state she was illuminated, burdened so heavily with internal labor, and visited with such divine mercy that she vigorously rejoiced in the good and piteously bemoaned evil. In that state she could neither have committed evil nor left good undone for anything in the world.

How her life was grievous and miserable.

Chapter XXXVII.

After many hardships and sufferings, the Lord still did not lead her to lasting rest but left her spirit in torment and anxiety. Her spirit was troubled at the thought of neglecting what was to be done or doing what was to be left undone, of performing the lesser rather than the greater task, of failing to do the good and in so doing prove incapable of living a holy life. To be with the Lord, her spirit was vigilant and labored in great desire with all its power for many an hour. It worked so manfully and mightily that she broke into a sweat, wept, and sighed deeply, groaning like a person mortally ill. In the course of a single day she often vacillated between consolation and suffering, sadness and joy and vice versa. Consequently, her life was so wretched that not only her spirit full of anxiety and love longed for heaven but her body, too, was so overwrought and exhausted that it desired to be parted from her spirit to rest in the ground.

Such a quarrel ensued between spirit and flesh that the spirit wished to go to heaven and the body into the earth. The flesh wished to rest while the spirit wished to labor. Concerning the misery of her life, the Lord said to her: "Even though you linger in illness because of great love and exertion like a deathly ill person scarcely able to survive from one day to the next, you nevertheless must keep on living. You shall live a holy life, prepared for death each day as though you were to die that very day. Ask your confessor this: 'Dear son, how long will this miserable life last? I feel that every three or four hours a day I am being plunged from one deadly illness into another, just like a moribund person falls from one disease into another within a few hours."

How she was and still is a great martyr.

Chapter XXXVIII.

Because of these sufferings described above, one may very well consider her a martyr. The Lord himself witnessed to that when he, twenty days before her death, spoke to her thus: "My beloved daughter, what will you now tell your two sons B and P about your life? You are a great martyr, tormented through and through with spiritual exercises, self-castigations, disciplines, and torments. But you can't possibly relate them all. For even if someone had been with you from the days of your youth and had recognized the varieties of your endless sufferings, he would have to write all day long every single day." As the Lord said this, she was illuminated in such a way that she could behold from beginning to end how these many torments and sufferings had passed through her body and soul and how she had been injured and martyred by them. And then the Lord continued: "Because you have endured such cruel martyrdom on Earth, you, even while you are still living on Earth, may behold the bliss and honor my martyrs enjoy with me through my esteem in eternal life. And your sons B and P shall bury you as benefits a martyr and shall esteem and honor you as such. Now thank me profusely and rejoice in the comfort of knowing that you may gain here what you will enjoy eternally. You can see and feel very clearly how I am drawing you to me. My dear mother and my beloved saints draw you as well so that you may come to us joyfully and honorably. Amen."

May the Father and the Son and the Holy Spirit help us all attain such blessedness. Amen.

Here begin the chapters of the third book
of the life of the blessed mother Dorothea, anchoress at Marienwerder.

144

benefit of fire and yet remained unharmed by the fierce cold.

How she, through devotion, vows, and the Lord's revelation
was compelled to move into an anchoress's cell.

Chapter I.

After much suffering, the blessed Dorothea for many years enjoyed gentle comforts through which she tasted God's sweetness and listened to his voice. However, in order to hear the Lord clearly and in peace quietly set apart from the world, to wake and serve him all the more completely, she had desired to live in an anchoress's cell for a long time, long before coming to Marienwerder, where the Lord in his prescience had designated a place for her. When she had been with her confessor for more than a year and it pleased the Lord to satisfy her desire for a cell, which he had kindled in her much earlier, he compelled her openly through his revelations to move into a cell and to ask her confessors P and B to aid her in this quest since it would be the best thing for her as well as for them. But her two confessors and spiritual sons did not immediately accommodate her in this matter: They delayed their decision to discern more clearly the will of our Lord concerning her enclosure, to test and observe her determination and suitability for life in a cell and, with God's help, find appropriate means for securing permission from their spiritual father, the lord bishop, and his chapter to build such a cell at the church of Marienwerder, for at that time hermitages within churches or attached to them were uncommon in Prussia and not seen there. They would have granted her request more rapidly had they not feared to be accused of carelessness.

During this delay she often complained to God about not being permitted to stay in the church with him through the night. She was allowed to stay there all day long but at night was turned out of doors. She wept often upon having to leave the church, saying: "My most beloved Lord, gladly I would stay with you through the night without food or drink, for it is a bitter pain to me to leave you." But the Lord comforted her many times and said: "When you come to live in your cell, you shall be with me always. Then you will have me at your beck and call, day and night, whether you are sitting up or lying down. Before you move into your cell, you will not have much leisure except when you are enraptured. But when you move into you cell, I will remove much of your misery. Hurry up, then! I want to reveal much to you there. You shall cleave to me tightly then and live a holy life and mark carefully all my works and my voice to learn to differentiate among my gifts. And you shall leave to others the singing and reading and whatever else they wish to do in my praise and honor. You, on the other hand, shall focus your full attention on me and mark the works I will perform through you and for your sake. Now beg me fervently with weeping eyes to help you be enclosed soon so that you may enjoy peace and be grateful to me. All things that need to be done in this world will be taken care of very well without your involvement." Furthermore, the Lord said: "Weep and beg me humbly to provide you with a dwelling where you may praise me appropriately, become pleasing unto me, and conclude your life."

How it can be determined whether a person is suitable
for enclosure in a cell.

Chapter II.

Jesus Christ Our lord who had cast himself into the form of total humility showed his bride Dorothea how sweet and delightful it is to be totally subservient to others in all things and to subordinate one's will entirely. And after having urged her for a long time to move into a cell, he said: "You shall speak to your B and P like this: 'Even though I would like nothing more than being in a cell, it shall not happen according to my will. I commend my soul to you and put my will into your governance. I do not want to retain any will of my own; instead,

I want to act according to your will and will never abrogate obedience to you.'"
When her confessors B and P had secured permission to build a cell and it was
finally completed, the Lord enlightened her about the special disposition a person
wishing to inhabit a cell has to possess.

Among the many necessary characteristics, three are vitally important:
The first is that sincere love impel people to such a life. This love must be so
overpowering that they weep and cry to the Lord to compel them toward it and
help them attain it, insisting that God never grant them a moment's rest until they
have achieved their goal.

The second is a pure, clean state of mind, which involves five qualities:
1. They must do this out of true love and desire for God and life in a cell and
with God's help must live it pure in spirit.
2. They must move into the cell neither on account of other people's advice or
command nor for the sake of temporal comfort, aid, or fame, to escape problems,
or to gain leisure or help for themselves or others. No! Pure in spirit through
God shall they be enclosed, driven only by God's love and his counsel.
3. They must be firmly committed and constant in their desire to do so, never
wavering or worrying 'how will I be able to forego this thing or that comfort?
How will I be able to break away from the world and the kind of life I am living?
People will gossip about me, no matter what I do.' Such concerns and worries
they have to overcome before they can be admitted to a hermit's cell.
4. They must trust God explicitly, absolutely certain that God can and will help
them do without, suffer, do and endure everything appropriate to their state.
5. They must possess a child-like respect for God concerning life in a cell. Those
who have these five characteristics have sufficient sustenance for life in the cell,
said the Lord.

This sustenance consists of burning love, hot desire, unassailable hope,
absolute trust, and a pure respect for God. God will satisfy every physical and
spiritual need of those who have these qualities. And these same blessings he
bestowed upon his bride Dorothea for sustenance.

A third point belonging to the first two items mentioned above is that individuals experiencing delays in their efforts of moving into a cell suffer from severe languishing love. "Languishing love," said the Lord, "occurs when human beings because of the extent of love, feel such tremendous yearning to be with God, to serve him steadfastly and to be rid of all worldly troubles that they find it impossible to perform bodily work to earn their living." When the Lord revealed this to Dorothea, she recognized many people in her cell, both men and women, who were very fragile and in great peril in terms of salvation.

The rules for living as an anchoress.

Chapter III.

The Lord provided Dorothea with a rule she was to observe in her cell and said: "You shall have a glass window that can be opened and closed according to your physical needs. A crucifix shall be suspended from it so that everyone who comes to you will be reminded that your cell is the home of the saints, for it is a good sign when I stand at the door. Once you have moved into your cell, you shall not extend your hand to anyone, touch anyone's hand, or accept any gift without your confessor's permission. You must confess having done any such thing as many times as you did so without leave. Also, you shall not desire to speak with people nor expect temporal goods from them but trust entirely in me. I will send you everything you need if you put your trust entirely in me. And if there were not a single human being to comfort you, I would maintain you in your cell as well as I will keep you in eternal life. You shall not acquire anything on earth, for the spiritual wealth you already possess is mine, not yours. Earthly goods are the property of creatures and are lent to you only to satisfy your absolute necessities."

From that time on, she dared not say any longer "this or that is mine" or "wrap my corpse into that cloth when I am dead." For the Lord desired her to be rid and free of all things and to leave it up to other people to feed her or bury her body naked or clothed. Moreover, the Lord said: "You shall live chastely in your cell, busy day and night to please no one but me. You shall live as a wife who has a strict, harsh husband because of whom she never dares to leave their house. And I will bring you such comforts that you will have no desire to leave your cell. On the contrary, you will delight in staying there.

"Among the many benefits I will provide for you I will grant you to receive me in the sacrament as often as your confessor. Should he be ill or absent, he is to delegate the task of giving you the sacrament to someone else." As the Lord said this, she thought: "On the blessed Christmas Day my confessor will celebrate three masses and will receive the sacrament of Our Lord three times. Will this be appropriate for me, too?" But the Lord answered: "No, you must be content to receive me just once daily.

"You shall put yourself entirely into your confessor's care, just as you have given yourself entirely into mine. If he wishes to speak to you, speak to him, and when he wants to give me to you, receive me with love. Tell him that whenever he celebrates mass in front of your cell no one is to be present but his assistant so you can be alone with me. Thank me for thus being separated from all other people. And if he should ask 'why do you want to receive the Lord in the sacrament so often, that is daily, which after all, is highly unusual for anyone who is not a priest,' answer him thus: 'You know full well that I cannot prepare myself. Rather, the Lord prepares a place for himself in me and creates a raging, impatient love and desire for him . And what good there is in me he brings about. He desires himself passionately in me and receives himself greedily in me. I, on the other hand, as you know full well and can see with your own eyes, am so poor and wretched a creature as may scarcely be found elsewhere.'"

How she was prepared for the day of her enclosure.

Chapter IV.

Finally the time came when her desire to be locked into a cell was fulfilled, the second day of the month of May in the year of Our Lord 1393. With God's help Dorothea had prepared herself worthily for this day. She was wounded by love: her heart was riddled by the arrows of love and so abundantly filled with divine sweetness that she could not have turned around or opened her mouth to speak while this abundance lasted, no matter what she might have gained by doing so. After that she was set ablaze in body and soul by the fire of divine love, eager to thank God. All the veins of her body were stretched as tightly as the strings of a musical instrument. Her beloved Lord caused such a multitude of tremendous effects of mercy in her that they cannot be described. He celebrated a great feast in her soul with indescribably joyous jubilation. He gave spiritual birth to himself in her soul and said: "You shall be fruitful through me."

At another time he demonstrated his glory to her; then that of many saints. Then he brought eternal life next to her. Sometimes, because of her deep union with God and through pure contemplation, all creatures disappeared from her consciousness. On those occasions she beheld the Lord and had him to herself, who in perfect quiet and without words spoke sweetly to her soul saying: "Now you shall behold my true glory as though I were saying to you, 'behold, everything is prepared. Come, my beloved. Come, my dear sister. From now on you will suffer no more bitterness but enjoy nothing but pleasure with me.'"

Many other lovely benefits the Lord bestowed on her that day. Together with his dear mother he most graciously showed himself to her, telling her that he wanted to be her dearly beloved and that she was to love him even more than his dearest mother. She burned so hotly in love that she could not have endured it had the Lord not sustained her by special means. For now it became apparent why the Lord wished to remove Dorothea from the world. The Lord did this, as he later revealed to her, because he wanted to give her his heartbreaking love, which is unknown to most people.

As the Lord brought about all these works of grace in her throughout the preceding night and far into the before-mentioned day-- it fell on a Friday-- many people in attendance at the church were moved to tears by her devotion and exemplary piety. They longed to enjoy the blessings of her merit. They wished her well and begged her to pray for them. She, in turn, still weeping, thanked them kindly, as the Lord had commanded her. Not long after that Dorothea received the praiseworthy body of Our Lord with great love, desire, and devotion. When he came to her with such noble comfort and jubilation, she was ecstatic and incapable of expressing her feelings in any way but to say: "I feel as though I had been in eternal life." Finally her two confessors and spiritual sons B & P-- one a master of holy writ, the other a master of canon law-- came to her. Leading her between them through a multitude of people, they escorted her down a long path to her cell, there to live at last as she wished, removed from human companionship after already having separated herself much earlier from her earthly friends in both body and spirit.

And not only had Dorothea withdrawn from her friends: she also had removed her love, desire, and spirit from the entire world and all perishable things to surrender her entire being to the Lord and cleave only to him. She was not at all ashamed of him whom she would have liked to hide from everyone. That is to say, his merciful deeds in her she would have liked to keep secret so that her saintly life would not be apparent to others. But since she could not do so very easily, she chose to be enclosed to keep her life a secret more easily and better obey the Lord's will and wait on him. She entered her cell well prepared, collected and calm in spirit and unconcerned about external matters. Her only worry was to hold on to the Lord, whose presence she felt, and to bring him into the cell with her. As she came to the Lord by stepping into the cell and was locked and walled in, the Lord granted her such abundant comfort in himself that she was too overwhelmed with happiness to imagine wanting anything else.

How the Lord instructed her to answer those inquiring
about her well-being.
Chapter V.

The Lord said to Dorothea now enclosed in her cell: "If anyone should ask you whether you enjoy sitting here, answer like this: 'How could I when I know a better place? I would not even be satisfied to dwell in the palace of a great, mighty king if I knew of a better place. But even though I don't enjoy sitting here all by myself, I myself did choose to stay here in keen anticipation of the love of my adored Lord Jesus Christ whose his sweet voice will sound in my ears saying: 'Come, my chosen turtle dove, my beloved, my sister. You shall enjoy happiness and sweetness!' In truth, I trust him entirely to speak these passionate words and therefore desire nothing else. But I know I cannot earn such bliss through my own efforts but that he will bestow it on me out of his own boundless grace.'"

Furthermore, the Lord said: "Should someone to ask you: 'Are you not afraid here?' you shall answer for the sake of my everlasting praise: 'How could I be afraid or annoyed in this place when I have never stayed in the homes of friends who felt a stronger, truer friendship toward me than those here? Nor have I ever been in any place where there reigned such peace as here. Here no one disturbs the peace or sows contention; all who are here live together in harmony and peace.' Furthermore, if someone should ask how you are, you may reply: 'I am very well, for all the days I have been here have been as praiseworthy, merciful, and joyful as the feast of Whitsuntide.'"

It happened after the blessed Dorothea's enclosure that her mother was told of her daughter's having been walled into a cell at the church of Marienwerder. Upon hearing this, Agatha was distressed, wept, and with streaming eyes said to those who had told her: "Dear God, what horrible sin has she committed to let herself be locked away like that? It is said that only very great sinners are thus locked up." As she had spoken much of it and had wept about it frequently, Dorothea, upon being informed of it truthfully, worried that God the Lord may hold such talk and weeping against her mother and therefore prayed for her. But the Lord said to her: "Should you ever hear your mother say that you have done a bad thing by moving into this cell, tell her this: 'My most beloved Lord Jesus Christ has given me a better name than my own mother. For by making me the bride of a mortal creature, she gave me the name of a mortal among other perishable beings. But my Lord has given me a far nobler name, for among his special friends I am called the bride of the eternal bridegroom.'"

Her complete trust

Chapter VI.

The Lord often praised her complete trust. Once he said to her: "The unwavering, absolute trust you showed toward me even before you moved into your cell has always pleased me. You did well never to worry about things that would make you speak or think like this: 'How or when shall I move into a cell? Who will serve me; who will send me what I need or bring me some water to drink?' You may confidently say to your confessor: 'Even if not a single person knew me, I would still trust the Lord implicitly that he would not let me be destroyed or remain uncomforted. So how could I not have such trust in God here among people? Even if my hermitage were in a wild forest or a desert, I would still trust that he would not let me come to harm.

'This confidence is neither presumption nor a challenge but the complete, sincere trust based in the perfect love I feel for the Lord. You need not be amazed that I trust him so much for even though I have dealt with you only for a short time, I trust equally that you, for the sake of my beloved Lord, would not abandon me even if you were to come to grief, pain, or suffer other harm because of such loyalty. You may boldly praise the Lord that you never had dealings with a human being who has trusted the Lord as completely as I do, placing in him all my confidence and hope, desiring comfort from no one but him.'" Moreover, the Lord said: "Tell your confessor that he may state truthfully that you show perfect trust by not worrying in the least about temporal matters. Once you entrusted your body and soul to me, the strength of your trust was such that you never considered what you must have or maybe allowed to have for maintaining your body. There are many people who do entrust their souls to me but never their bodies." The Lord went on to say: "You will have food aplenty while you are living in your cell: burning love, hot desire, unshakable hope, complete faith, and chaste fear of God. As long as you hold fast to these five virtues, you will never lack sustenance."

How those seeking the Lord through this anchoress
will not remain without grace.

Chapter VII.

The Lord who lets nothing good remain without reward revealed that he
would be merciful and reward all those who had performed a good deed for the
sake of the blessed Dorothea or who would seek him through her. He urged her
to pray to him to do so, saying: "Ask me humbly that those who come to you will
mend their ways and reap the benefits for doing so. If the canons of this cathedral
in Pomesania are to be blessed with you, you must keep them in your thoughts
constantly and expend much energy on their behalf. But you have not come here
solely for the sake of the canons now living, but also for those who have died and
those who are still to come. Neither did you come only for the canons but also
for all those who gave alms to the Pomesanian church and all those whose bodies
are buried here because they hoped to benefit from all the good that would take
place here in this place, that is this church."

As the Lord spoke, many of the living and the dead who had given alms
to the church appeared to her and begged to receive this grace. When the Lord
allowed her to observe the great desire for grace on the part of so many people,
she was terrified because she did not know how to fulfill their hopes. But the
Lord spoke to her most kindly: "Ask me on their behalf and pray that all those
who come to you mend their ways!" On another occasion the Lord said: "All
those who long to come to you or keep you in mind and by doing so seek me
through you shall enjoy great advancement and honor through me. You, on the
other hand, must take nothing and desire nothing from anyone. I am rich enough
to send you whatever you are meant to have, but whoever does something for you
for my sake or seeks me through you will not have done so in vain."

How the Lord visited her cell with his dear mother and many saints.

Chapter VIII.

Although generally speaking the almighty God is everywhere in his being, presence and might, through his grace he is nevertheless encountered more readily in certain places, as, for example, in his saints, and in still others through special demonstrations of his influence, which accomplish and make manifest the results of his merciful presence. In such a manner he was present in the cell of the blessed Dorothea to whom he showed himself most merciful. He often pointed this out to her: "Here in this ship, that is your contemplative life here in this cell, many saints are with you and many great lords. But I am the greatest lord here among the rest, your Lord God, who accompanied you as you stepped into this cell for I knew very well that you would not be able to stay here without me.

"And here also is my adored mother whom I made your mother the moment you desired to move into this cell. Many angels are present as well to serve me and protect you. And many other great saints of the new and old covenant have come here from eternal life--patriarchs, prophets, apostles, and others. For where I am, many saints are present as well, and wherever I bestow the miraculous effects of my grace, great holiness dwells. The longer you remain here, the more the holiness of this place will increase and the more saints will be present. For all this is part of the total contemplative life you have now entered. Furthermore, you yourself have great saintliness within you: your perfect love; your unquestioning, unwavering hope; your firm, holy faith and strong, holy desire for me. Moreover, your soul is faithful and devoted to me, your conscience clean, your confession honest, your conduct saintly, and your heart spotless and well prepared for me.

"Accordingly, you will conduct and show yourself chastely among those who are with you. Also, you must show yourself intimate and accommodating toward no one but me and whomever you know as my true friend. Now behold how great a peace and honor those enjoy who are here with you and what great respect is accorded them." According to Our Lord's command she then observed and recognized how each of them was honored, served, and revered far beyond the demands of status and degree of sanctity. Frequently Dorothea also experienced a variety of visions and physical manifestations of the Lord who at times appeared in the various physical stages of his life, from the first, second, third, and fourth year up to the thirtieth year of his life, so that she was surrounded by a group of well-favored human beings in the very shape and countenance of Our Lord when he lived on Earth. From time to time Our Lord filled her cell with his majesty so she could discern him everywhere through the eyes of the soul and knew not which way to turn her back so as not to show disrespect or display rudeness toward the Lord. She experienced this same dilemma whenever the Lord showed her that her cell was crowded with saints.

How Dorothea was punished by Mary and her child for
having conversed without asking their permission.

Chapter IX.

Mary, the mother of God, appeared to her graciously, sometimes alone, sometimes in the company of other saints, and often with her dear child, fondling, bathing, warming, diapering, feeding, carrying it, or playing with it. One morning, more than three weeks after Christmas, after graciously having shown herself and the infant to Dorothea daily since Christmas, she appeared with a stern countenance, diapered her child, and acted as though she was about to leave again immediately. Severely, though still kindly, mother and infant were punishing Dorothea for having conversed with someone without first having asked their permission.

Dorothea acknowledged her misconduct but did not dare apologize. Instead, she wept and asked for forgiveness. When she had implored them for a long time with tears streaming from her eyes, greatly worried that Mary might leave with the child at any moment or drive her from her cell, the mother of mercy seated herself facing Dorothea and spoke to her comfortingly: "Do not fear too much that we might leave you. As long as you live my child and I will never abandon you, for you could not remain here by yourself without us. If we were to leave you, though, you would have cause to be painfully embarrassed for having treated your host and hostess so shamefully that they chose to abandon you without intention of ever returning, leaving you alone in the house." Then the most gracious Jesus said to her: "Weep copiously and say, 'Oh, my most beloved mother, deign to abide with me, you and your child, and never leave me.'" When Dorothea had done so, the mother of mercy spoke to her still sternly, still punishing her by saying: "We have taken you in at this place and I sit here with you so that you may observe me and my labors and learn to serve my child as you see me do. And as you watch how I care for him and keep him, you are to do the same. You can see very well that I don't gossip or spend time with others. On the contrary: all my desire is to delight in my child."

Later, after she had confessed her sins, the Lord allowed her to partake of the sacrament. He came to her most mercifully with many kindnesses, and among other things, gave her much good advice: "How could you turn from me and my mother toward other creatures when you can hear my voice, my admonitions, and advice day and night without interruption? How could you talk to people without my permission? You are allowed to speak only to your two sons B and P in saintly, spiritual conversations in all due respect of me. I have drawn you to me, away from the world. Do you now want to draw the world to you and speak to all sorts of people?" After this punishment the Lord instructed her to travel the narrow paths that lead to eternal life. They were so narrow that she trembled traversing them as though she were balancing on a narrow plank, at first not daring to put one foot in front of the other. Later, this became easier.

How the Lord forced her to eat and instructed her
on proper comportment at table.
Chapter X.

Just as the Lord appeared often to his disciples and instructed them, encouraged them, and urged them to eat, he often appeared to his elected bride

Dorothea whom he admonished to eat at mealtime, at times even forcing her to do so. At table he often whispered sweetly to her; sometimes he comforted her pleasantly and taught her what to think about at table or what foods to eat. Occasionally, when she stopped eating even though she needed more food, the Lord said to her: "You need to be as concerned about eating too little as you are worried about eating too much food." Sometimes, when he wished to be especially gracious to her after dinner or wanted to indicate the impropriety of wasting too much time at table, he forced her to eat rapidly, like a man about to set out on a journey who hurries to avoid missing his traveling companions.

More, to reduce preoccupation with the desires of the flesh, the Lord taught her a valuable lesson. He said: "Those who want to serve me and own me entirely shall never eat foods or quantities of food that render them listless or sluggish in serving and praising me. Rather, they must eat in moderation and not worry unnecessarily about being impeded in their service to me on account of their modest consumption of victuals, for I will satisfy and strengthen them. My true followers have always shunned and avoided luxurious food in favor of simple fare. You may partake of food, though not much or often, even though I could very well maintain you without food for the body if I so desired.

"But I don't want to do that, for if I did, people would consider you a saint. But that is precisely what I want to keep from you, the delusion of sanctity. If you do possess any sanctity at all, you are to take it with you into life everlasting. While I was living on Earth, I could have maintained myself very well without food, but I did not want to do that but ate the same food as my disciples and those who followed me. And you must eat from time to time to strengthen your head. For this reason you must eat frequently, painful as it may be for you. Now say to your confessor: 'I am ill and ailing because of love. I have no desire to keep on living. Nothing tastes good to me, neither delicious food or drink nor worldly pleasures. There are many people so ill that they may not live even one more day; even to them food and drink taste much better than to me, and they still have a much stronger desire to live and to enjoy the world than I do.'"

How she was to pray before, during, and after dinner.

Chapter XI.

The Lord said: "Kneel down and pray devoutly in preparation for your meals. Consider my bitter torment and say:

'He who on the cross has suffered death

And shed his blood so red

May he bless my food and bread.

He who owns both Earth and heaven

May he bless this food and drink.

I beg you, dear Lord Jesus Christ, let me receive this food in this hour in such a way that I will not commit any sin. Praised be the Father, honored be the Son, and blessed be the Holy Spirit. Help me, dear Lord, to drink and suck from the five wounds you have sustained because of me in such a way that living water will flow from me on judgment day.'"

Furthermore, the Lord said: "When you sit at table ready to partake of food, say this: 'Lord Jesus Christ, may you be praised and honored forever for sending me this meal, food and drink, to nourish my body. Help me, dear Lord, to eat this food with all due respect, to return it to you in perfect condition when I enter heaven. Help me, sweet Jesus Christ, to pray to you on behalf of all who have worked to produce this food and those who sent it to me.'"

The Lord continued: "When you sit at table, thank me for my praiseworthy incarnation. Remember my holy infancy; remember me as a child and play with me in your heart. Consider the spotless Christian life I lived on Earth and the praiseworthy supper I ate with my disciples when I blessed the bread and turned it into my holy body and the wine into my rose-red blood, giving myself as their sustenance. Remember also that I graciously shed my precious blood for you! Then recall the bitter death I suffered for you. Sweat, hunger, and thirst for food to learn to hunger and thirst for me. After dinner say this: 'He who was spit upon and cursed by the Jews, be praised, honored, and blessed. Lord Jesus Christ, you became a human being for my sake and died on the cross. You have fed my body; feed my spirit as well so that your incarnation and death will be my final sustenance. I beg you, merciful Lord, for all the things you want me to beg for: Give your peace to blessed Christendom, your grace to the living, your mercy to the dead, and eternal life to us all. My God and dearly beloved Lord, feed and refresh all those who have fed me. Amen.'"

How she ate moderately once a day
and often experienced intense spiritual joy at mealtime.
Chapter XII.

For many years she ate no more than once a day and very little at that, and always penitential fare or a dish prepared with milk, never meat. It so happened that once she was ailing severely because of love. The Lord said to her: "If someone asks you whether you crave meat, answer like this:'I crave my Lord, eternal life, and everything that profits my soul. I desire these things so fiercely that I don't know what is good for my body.'" The Lord said this and much more. He continued: "Stay seated here until I feed you with my heavenly mercy. Your hopes, desires, trust, and abundant tears shall be spiritual comfort and pleasant nourishment to you. My holy, abundant consolations shall aid and strengthen you."

While she was at table, it often happened that she was drawn so highly from external things into the contemplation of divine things that she, upon coming to, knew neither how much nor where she had eaten, only that she felt well fed spiritually and physically. The Lord often confirmed this, telling her more than once: "Now you have eaten, yet you don't know whether you ate with me or I with you, whether you ate here or in eternal life. Nevertheless, your soul even in ecstasy was fully aware of the pleasure and joy she experienced. No one may experience such favor without being thoroughly disciplined in a variety of spiritual exercises."

Here is to be noted that when the Lord commanded her "ask me to stay with you and eat with you," which he told her often, he treated her graciously at table, as a bridegroom would his beloved bride. In true, chaste love he encouraged her to eat, showing her what to take, cutting her food for her and serving her most attentively. He whispered sweetly to her and prepared a great feast in her soul. Especially in the last years of her life it happened frequently that her physical sustenance vanished the moment her body received it so she could not tell whether she had eaten and never felt any distress or sluggishness because of it.

How she spent an extreme winter in her cell without benefit of fire
and yet remained unharmed by the fierce cold.

Chapter XIII.

The fire which is God ignited the blessed Dorothea so hotly that it burned not only in her soul but also spilled from the soul into her entire body, warming her at one time more than another. For this reason Dorothea even as a small child needed very little clothing and could tolerate the discomfort of severe cold quite easily. In fact, for many years her body was often so hot that even in the coldest winter she sweated profusely and had to cool herself on cold stones and fan herself as though it were hot summertime. On freezing cold days she often sat in the church of Marienwerder from morning until after vespers without feeling the cold at all. Even though two of the winters she spent in Marienwerder were so severe that the ink froze in her secretary B's quill, she was cold only twice.

During the first winter the following happened: One day she wanted to finish a prayer at vespers that she normally recited in the morning, for that day she had been unable to complete it then because the Lord had kept her in ecstasy and contemplation of secrets for a long time. Suddenly she started trembling with cold and considered going home. But the Lord told her, "a person without love is poor indeed," and set her soul afire and commanded her to pray. At once she was ignited in body and soul. She prayed and recognized her poverty. The Lord treated her so kindly that she would have liked to stay there overnight with him had it been proper for her to do so.

The other attack of cold occurred on the eve of St. Gregory [March 12] after she had lived in her cell throughout the winter without feeling the least discomfort. That day, however, as the sun rose, she started to shiver. Her clothes could not warm her. In her heart she still felt a little warmth; nevertheless, she was so cold that she thought she could not endure it for long. Then the Lord spoke to her in her prayer: "You must not think that you were never cold all this winter because of your constitution or the garments that have clothed and covered you. On the contrary. You may now recognize clearly that all winter long I have produced warmth and heat in you, just as I now make you cold." The moment the Lord said this, heat flared from her heart, traveling up and down the front and back of her body and along the sides, driving away the cold.

Here is to be noted that during the last winter of her life on Earth she generally felt a warming flame covering her entire body, her front, back, and sides. This flame travelled up and down and warmed her as pleasantly and cozily as though she were seated between the four doors of a well-stoked stove. At times she felt this same flame rising and then returning to its source, reigniting itself on the spiritual fire, and then go out again, rise up, and return. This the flame repeated until Dorothea was so fired up that body and soul became heated. Often she was so heated by the fire of love that she sweated until her breath rose like steam from a boiling kettle. Then her clothes got soaking wet from her sweat and steaming breath. Her body was often so hot that she could not tolerate the touch of her hand on her bare skin. Here is to know that although the last winter of her life was so extremely long and severe that many people froze to death and water and beer often froze solid in her cell, Dorothea never needed a fire nor anything warmed by fire other than her food. The Lord said to her: "Should anyone ask whether you are cold, say this: 'Even if I never were warmed by the fire and heat of my own body, the heat with which the Lord warms me would still make me comfortable, and I have faith that even if I were never to enjoy a fire, he would nevertheless protect me from the cold as though I were sitting in a warm, cozy place.'"

How the Lord admonished her to pray for many things.

Chapter XIIII.

It happened often that people stood by Dorothea's cell, observing her with weeping eyes because they felt sorry for her or because they had not entrusted themselves into God's care as completely as she had. God ordered her to pray for them so they would mend their ways according to her example, forsake evil, and turn entirely to him. The Lord went on to say: "You shall pray for all those who wish to be included in your prayers." Further, he commanded her to pray for all who had ever done anything for her, for the unification of the Church, for the pope, the cardinals, the archbishops and bishops, the rulers of the country, all spiritual people, the sick, and those in the throes of death. She was to pray for the benefit of sermons to their listeners and the improvement of many other ills.

And the Lord ordered her to ask him to grant many other blessings as well: "You must not be idle but do much good. There are many on Earth who are needy and poor who well deserve many good things to be done for them." In response to Our Lord's behest and because of her own love for others Dorothea was greatly concerned and labored continuously to prevent sins from being committed and to ask the Lord to mercifully forgive those already committed. Once, when she was much occupied and felt greatly weighed down with these concerns, the Lord commanded her to say to her confessor B: "I am so worried about people's sins that I don't know what to say, and I am especially concerned about the citizens of Marienwerder. It seems to me that I am to be the guardian of this town."

The abundance of tears through which she earned forgiveness of sins.

Chapter XV.

The Lord commanded Dorothea to weep copiously for many people, to pray for them, and to sprinkle the parched earth with her tears so he might take pity on them and send a beneficial rain. In spirit she traversed the nations of the world, according to the Lord's command who illuminated and fired her, and she witnessed many serious afflictions with heartfelt compassion and bemoaned them piteously with gentle, abundant tears. As she did so, the world appeared well-watered, as though water were still standing in the furrows as it does after a heavy rain. Only here and there dryness still prevailed.

About this, the Lord told her: "Observe how parched the ground still is in these places. Weep much and douse it, for I don't ignite you in love just for your own sake. Others, too, are to benefit from your state. And should your confessor ask you why you cry so such, tell him 'this is the Lord's work, not mine. It is his gift. If he did not give it to me and did not bring it about in me, I would no more be able to weep than you are. If you knew how abundant and varied my tears are, you would declare them gifts from eternal life, for such great spiritual wealth does not originate in the nature of any earthly creature.'"

Here is to know that she used to weep gently day and night. Now her tears were bitter, now sweet. They flowed from her eyes as constantly as from a well. She shed them out of sincere love, not through weakness of character or natural inclination, not out of innate compassion for her friends or because she could not enjoy physical pleasures. She did not weep for fear of hell or purgatory or for having committed some punishable offense but out of sincere love, which above all brings about true, heartfelt contrition. She cried heartily until the Lord took pity on her and said: "Rejoice all the days of your life, for I have forgiven you all your trespasses, your sins, and their punishment."

When she heard that, she was so joyful that she did not know what to do. Then the Lord told her: "When Mary Magdalene came into my grace and was forgiven all sin and punishment, she started experiencing true happiness, and my glory was with her from then on." The Lord continued: "But hot tears are useful and necessary not only to cleanse the soul but also for keeping her clean. For the cleansed soul easily becomes spotted again by the dust of insignificant sins, even if no great sin, deadly or venial, has been committed. These sins are so tiny that an illuminated person can see them and yet is incapable of describing them, as I have frequently demonstrated to you by letting you see the small sins that danced on the surface of your soul as tiny dust motes dancing on a sunbeam. So it is necessary for a human being to cry hotly once a day to wash them from the soul. For even if such tiny sins are not removed by hot tears or searing love at the time of death, the soul's progress after death will be impeded and will be unable to enter eternal life at once without mediation."

Her praiseworthy aspirations.

Chapter XVI.

The blessed Dorothea conceived the holy, burning desire to die toward all created beings and to attain the serene virtue of a purified soul who has reached the level of perfection she is meant to achieve in this present life. As she gained various degrees of perfection, her passion was roused all the more so that in good faith she dared to demand the praiseworthy body of Our Lord first weekly, then daily to enjoy the Lord who is the highest good and eternal life. And she not only experienced burning holy desire but also debilitating love, which often caused her to languish in fierce, burning love for God, eternal life, and the holy sacrament. She became ill and was often not in control of her body. This passion was the work of the Lord who drew her up to him and taught her to protect herself from mistaking as feeble or frivolous the pursuit of benefits which in reality are vital for the soul's salvation. For that eternal highest good she was to develop a fierce, hot, sublime desire. This kind of desire she felt so intensely that she could not describe it. She was far greedier to enjoy the above-mentioned blessing than a greedy person is for worldly possessions and could neither satisfy nor control her passion. Therefore, she often had to languish for love of God, his holy body, and eternal life. When she was thus ailing and languishing in illness, the Lord said to her: "You don't know just how ill you are, though you are aware of being unable to walk, sit, or stand. You can neither eat nor drink, even if you would like to. Moreover, your love and desire prevent you from assessing your condition accurately--whether you are sick or healthy."

Here is to be noted that Dorothea's holy desire was hot and strong, ailing, glowing, flaming, and rapturous. At times it flared way up, then even higher, and at other times higher still. It flared up whenever Dorothea, deep in contemplation and inspired by love, imagined heaven as so delightful that she had a horror of remembering earthly things. It flared even higher when she, united with the Lord, forgot all creatures and had nothing in mind but him. Her desire flamed up to its highest level when she in joyful, delightful union embraced the Lord tightly, glowing with passion and feeling eternal life approaching her as she rushed toward him. The Lord often complimented her on her blessed, powerful desire, which flared up but never died down, rising rapidly like a fiery spark from a pile of glowing embers. Once he stated: "You never feel better and I am never more comfortable than when flaming desire, flying with burning speed from your heart into your head moves you so forcefully that you can hear it with your ears and recognize it with your other senses internally as well as externally. Your desire then rises rapidly and penetrates heaven. There it fetches the treasures of eternal life and brings them to you. This, in turn, inflames your fiery desire even more so that you covet the eternal goods of heaven even more keenly than before. Thus it happens that by ascending and descending the mountain one desire produces another." Here is to be noted that the Lord often illuminated her so thoroughly that she actually saw everything the Lord told her. In this manner she saw how her desire entered the heaven, fetched precious goods, and returned with them to her.

Why the holy body of Our Lord was kept in a reliquary facing her cell.
Chapter XVII.

Dorothea's tremendous languishing passion and spiritual hunger for the praiseworthy body of Our Lord Jesus Christ grew especially fierce during the last fourteen years of her life, for she generally anticipated the holy feast days on which she was allowed to partake of holy communion in great pain and wretchedness. Then, when the feast day arrived, she was frequently so overwhelmed with happiness that she could not sleep for joy and said: "How blessed I am to be alive this day." Her desire and hunger, however, increased even more during the two years preceding her enclosure as she awaited the third day in great spiritual anguish for having to wait even that long. Therefore she said: "On the day on which I don't receive the holy body of Our Lord my soul is despondent unto death." Later, when she lived in the cell, she received the sacrament daily through special dispensation of the merciful Lord Jesus Christ. Even so, she was miserable during the hours preceding high mass, in the course of which she generally received the sacrament.

After having suffered such anguish for a long time because of her overwhelming hunger and need to receive the body of Our Lord in the morning, her confessor B came early to give her the sacrament at that time. But shortly thereafter she could not await that time either without severe pain. Her desire, hunger, and love grew so much that until the time came she filled God's ears daily with weeping, wailing, sighing, and screaming. Thereupon her confessor decided to succor her with the delectable feast of the body of Our Lord for which she yearned so fiercely during the mass which at Marienwerder cathedral was generally celebrated around midnight.

It happened daily for about twenty weeks before her death that her confessor thus served her at night. To be able to do this without attracting attention, he, with the permission of the bishop of the diocese and the prior, locked the host into an appropriate reliquary where chalices and other mass utensils were kept under lock and key. This reliquary was attached to a pew facing Dorothea's cell. That this locking up of the host in the pew and this nightly communion were pleasing to God the most beloved Lord made obvious to Dorothea in word and deed. He told her: "You have overcome me to such a degree that I do not wish to be separated from you in spirit or the sacrament. I want to work my purpose in you abundantly both day and night. You have now so overwhelmed me with your copious tears and wailing that I have become your closest neighbor. You used to shed bitter tears for me in this pew before you became enclosed, not realizing then what would be locked in it for your sake, that is to serve your need. I am here. I serve you and wait until you are prepared and want me. Your confessor B shall rejoice to be a mediator between me and your soul. He shall thank me greatly for it. But now it is your turn to give thanks by saying: 'Lord Jesus Christ, I thank you greatly for allowing yourself to be locked up in this way for my sake.'"

The Lord spoke as though his voice were coming directly from that pew through the window of Dorothea's cell and from there into her ears. This was seldom the case, for generally the voice of the Lord sounded in the internal ears of the soul without audible sound in her bodily ears. This and other testimonials the Lord provided, who also manifested his presence in the pew during the night of Good Friday by showing himself as clearly in the sacrament as if a priest were holding the praiseworthy body of Our Lord in his hand. And he consoled her, promising her that she would indeed receive him in the sacrament that very day, for she did not believe that her confessor B would give her the Lord since it was not customary to give the body of the Lord to anyone that day but the very ill. For this reason she had also assumed that her confessor had not left the sacrament in the reliquary as he normally did.

Her true joys and dalliances with God.

Chapter XVIII.

Dorothea enjoyed the profound, true joy which originates in the creator, not the creature, in whom carnal and worldly, that is natural joy, originates. The joy that is located in and issues from a pure heart she experienced on Earth, at one time more intensely than another, until she entered the joy of the Lord. Her joy increased and multiplied through God's comforting visitations, the taste of his sweetness, the fulfillment of her desires, his answering her prayers, and his revelations of friendship and secrets on Earth and in heaven. Her joy also increased when she felt herself transformed and improved: from a good, virtuous being into a more virtuous one still-- when she became spiritually inebriated, and when the Lord granted her a profound union with him, whispered sweetly to her, drew her to him, saluted her internally, or dallied merrily with her. He pleased her in so many ways by comforting her that it would be too time consuming to enumerate them all. Many times she was so joyful that she could not suppress laughter, merry words, gestures, or other displays of pleasure. Because of the intensity of her joy she often thought that she felt as well as if she were in eternal life. The joys she experienced through the Holy Spirit the Lord had often indicated in these words: they would be inexpressibly beautiful and easier to feel than to describe.

In the midst of such joys she uttered a wealth of tender endearments to caress her most beloved Lord of which she could later repeat only a few. Some of those were: "My most beloved Lord, my most beloved father, my most desired Lord, my god Jesus Christ, my creator, my protector, my guardian, my redeemer, my preserver, my comfort, my healer, pardoner of my sins, my benefactor, giver of mercy and virtue, my judge, my friend, my most beloved brother and bridegroom." She called the Lord by many other honorable names and added an appropriate epithet to each of them, such as: "Most merciful, intimate, merciful father, most faithful friend, most beloved, most honorable, most chaste, most beautiful, most wealthy, most praiseworthy bridegroom; most fair, most patient, most gentle judge. Oh, my beloved praiseworthy elected; most highly exalted one! White and red! My most beloved Lord Jesus Christ. Oh Lord, my God, there is nothing better than you, nothing greater than you, nothing more honorable or mighty, beautiful or gracious than you, my God, my Lord." In this state of love and immeasurable bliss she could formulate many other graceful expressions she could neither conceive nor express at any other time.

Her gratitude.

Chapter XIX.

According to the teachings of St. Bernard, a person who does not receive a gift with proper gratitude commits blasphemy against the spirit of mercy and by doing so deserves to have it taken away and is unworthy of receiving any other gift or good deed. For this reason, Dorothea, the chosen bride of God, busied herself to be grateful to God, the giver of grace, who generally reminded her of his gifts by saying: "Give thanks to me for my many gifts and my grace, so that the grace I have bestowed upon you may not be barren. For if I give my mercy to someone to prove my grace but that person is not grateful, my grace will elude him and avail him nothing." This and other admonitions of the Lord she took to heart so conscientiously that she completely lost all awareness of self on account of her great desire and effort to be appropriately grateful to God and to return to God with great love the many merciful deeds he had bestowed in her with such lavish affection. In her expressions of gratitude she generally observed six things: First, she considered all the good things that had happened both to her alone and in common with others, adding them all together. Then, upon recognizing and pondering them, she credited them to God's pure mercy rather than her own merits. Furthermore, she busied herself to praise the Lord faithfully with heart, mouth, and works; that is, whatever she could do in God's honor internally in her thoughts and externally in word and deed she did to the best of her abilities. Whenever possible, she also begged others to thank God for the many good deeds he had done for her.

In the fourth instance, whenever she realized how little thanks she could give for such great mercy, she was deeply ashamed and covered her face, not daring to lift her eyes because of the embarrassment she suffered over the insignificance of her gratitude compared to the magnitude of God's gifts, so much more profuse and dignified than she could ever appreciate. Therefore she said: "How could I ever give thanks to God for all he has done for me?" When she labored heavily to show her gratitude, the Lord often responded: "How you could thank me for all the things I do for you? You could not even thank me appropriately for everything you receive through your confessor B. The entire world could not thank me sufficiently for all my blessings."

In the fifth instance she often humiliated herself abjectly and considered herself impoverished for being so limited in showing her gratitude to God for his merciful deeds. She considered herself undeserving of his gifts and was terrified that because of the paucity of her gratitude they might even do her soul harm. In the sixth instance she performed the very best deeds she could think of to show her gratitude. At the same time she subjected herself entirely to God's will. She retained no authority over her person. She sacrificed herself completely to the Lord with the intense desire that he might inspire proper, sincere gratitude in her and would deign to thank himself for his inexpressibly great mercy and grace.

Our kind, merciful Father fulfilled her desire and produced such gratitude in her. He also provided her with excellent new and unusual expressions of gratitude. They were sweet and of such variety that she could not have conceived, formulated, or pronounced them without God's special effect. He also ordered her to teach others to say "Lord Jesus Christ, if I could praise you, love you, and honor you, appreciate you, and bless you as much as do your dear mother Mary and all the saints who are in eternal life, I still could not praise, love, honor, appreciate, or bless you completely. Therefore, dear Lord Jesus Christ, praise yourself, love yourself, honor yourself, appreciate yourself, and bless yourself. Thank yourself, my Lord God, my most beloved Lord, speak your own praise and honor!"

Her sincere, deep humility.

Chapter XX.

One of the true marks of Dorothea's saintliness was her deep humility, which gave rise to her intense desire to be subservient instead of being anybody's master. She desired to be despised rather than honored, to be considered a wicked, miserable sinner rather than a blessed or humble woman. In truth, even though aided by grace she stood high on the mountain of virtue by accomplishing difficult feats of virtue and received from God such wealth of gifts of mercy as to provoke amazement, she considered herself wicked, the most wretched among sinners, not only unworthy to receive any gifts from God but to accept any comfort or service from her fellow men. And she was amazed that anyone would want to seek her out, serve her, or even speak to her. Her humility was exemplary and had increased notably from the time of her youth until her death, especially in three respects:

The first was careful observance of her own insufficiencies, weaknesses, and defects. Therefore, when the Lord allowed her to see other people's sins and to pray for them, she never forgot her own. More, she considered her own far more severe and herself less worthy and more wretched than those whose sins she actually witnessed. And because of this she was very much afraid and diminished in her own eyes. So she often did not dare raise her eyes to the Lord who instructed her to speak to her confessor B: "I have good cause to weep, for after everything the Lord shows me to contemplate, I find nothing as distasteful to me as myself. It is strange; I find something to weep about in myself. Equally strange, I always find something in me that should not be there and find myself lacking in something good I should possess."

The second way in which her humility increased was in the obedience she showed toward others all the days of her life. For before her marriage she was obedient to her parents, during her marriage she obeyed her husband; then, during and after her marriage, she was obedient to her confessors. About this the Lord said to her: "Because you humbly followed my advice and were obedient to your superiors, I have clearly illuminated you so strongly that you could see and contemplate other people as though they were transparent. Because of this grace you must be more submissive than ever before and must give yourself entirely into the authority of your B and P. Behave so as to be worthy of their fellowship that you may sit with them, speak to them, pray on their behalf, or beg for something for their sake and say to them: 'I am such a wretched sinner that I do not deserve to come to you. And if you should refuse to let me approach you because of my unworthiness, I would not hold it against you.'"

The third thing to increase her humility was her pure intuition through which she recognized the goodness of her creator, the saints, and other human beings superior to herself. But confronted with the ultimate good, how could she consider herself anything but a speck of dirt, the lowest of the low? And thus she grew in humility, the effects of which were far greater at some times than others, even in the course of a single day. This the Lord and his mercy produced in her: The more gifts she received and the more mercies the Lord showered upon her, the more she humbled herself.

The obliteration of her own thoughts and words did not originate in a false, affected, or hypocritical humility but in true humility, the guardian of virtue and the foundation of that spiritual fortress without which her praiseworthy, honorable, holy life could not have endured. For without true humility, whatever the grace of holiness accumulates, the wind of vanity would scatter. Furthermore, it is to be realized that the words of humility she spoke or the Lord instructed her to speak arose from the true foundation of sincere humility. For the Lord lent strength to his words so that her humility was as profound as her words indicated. Nor did the Lord permit her to remain on a given level of humility but propelled her on and on, pressuring her relentlessly, speaking to her in many ways to humiliate her like this: "Weep profusely over your inability to achieve total humility."

How the soul, which can be kept spotless only
through great exertion, is to be trained diligently for spiritual life.
Chapter XXI.

"The human soul is to be trained with the greatest diligence," the Lord told Dorothea. "For just as a devoted mother busies herself to make sure her child is at all times clean, pleasing, and healthy to be presentable to its father, so people shall strive to present their souls to me, God, clean, pleasing, and healthy so I will desire to be with such a soul at all times. The soul in turn will yearn and cry for me and preserve sound health to feel my presence at all times. But the soul of the person enamored of the flesh is neither trained properly, nor responsive. That soul sickens and coarsens, unable to lift herself.

"But when the flesh is mortified through exercises and disciplines, the soul becomes agile, adroit, and inspired to rise to her creator. And to become entirely righteous and train the soul so well that she will become ample and great, a person must practice self denial, abandon himself, the world, and everything in it and ignore injustice and dishonor done to him. Doing this kills all sensuality for the world and all malice in order to live for God alone. You shall not let a single day pass without removing something harmful from your soul and without improving the soul in some way. For anyone incapable of finding something to remove and to improve her in some way is blind. Such removal is accomplished through sincere repentance; improvement takes place in the progress of life. Furthermore, you shall embolden your soul toward increasing her own well being by looking about vigilantly to check whether anyone is undermining, destroying, or breaking up her dwelling; whether anyone wants to harm or murder her by serving or offering a poisoned or otherwise harmful meal or drink. Encourage your soul to attack any brigand manfully and cast him out courageously.

"To assist you in the proper upbringing of the soul, you shall have servants who will help you keep the house of the soul, namely the three divine and the four angelic virtues. Your inner and outer senses shall be obedient to them, and your soul shall have such power over these virtues that she can employ them as guards and protectors at whatever place she may have need of them. When that happens, the house of the soul is well protected. From the house of the soul a bright, unobstructed, clear path shall lead to eternal life. I will be your soul's food. The Holy Spirit will be her cupbearer. But the soul thus trained and cleansed is kept at this state of purification only with great difficulty because she is spotted more easily than a coarse soul, just as a tiny black stain is more notable on a snowy white cloth than a huge blotch on a blue cloth or one not particularly clean. And you yourself found out just how hard this is and how easily your purified soul became stained again."

Dorothea said: "When I, in word or deed offended God my beloved Lord after my soul had been cleansed and healed of her wounds, I regretted it at once and was tormented by the wounds of my sins. I wept and cried for the Lord, the physician of my soul, to forgive my sins and heal my wounds. Restlessly I searched for my confessor. I could not have returned to my hostelry without confessing first, no matter whether it was morning or night. For I was terrified of the Lord, worried that he might kill me or turn away from me. I could not find rest or peace until I had gained his assurance of my sins having been forgiven. Through the grace of my most beloved Lord I became aware of the stench of even the smallest sin spotting my soul as quickly as one feels the dust mote that by accident flies into one's eye. This is to protect the soul from becoming stained."

She continued: "My most beloved Lord God amply demonstrated to me just how fragile the soul is and how easily she slips away from him and turns to other creatures unless he carefully prevents it. In a clear vision he also showed me that all my energies engaged in works pleasing to God were extended and strained to the utmost and, tied to them like a bundle, were all my intentions, discernments, and contemplations in powerful, perfect love and hot passion. They were drawn arrow-straight, without any crookedness, toward God the Lord. This happened with great jubilation in a clear, pure vision when all creatures had departed my consciousness. This vision and this union, during which nothing bent from God or turned away from him, on account of his special grace lasted perhaps for three hours. During this time I realized that something like this could not last long or happen often, for generally love, desire, and internal and external labor bend or turn away from God. Therefore, the Lord spoke to me: 'Keep your soul with devout love, and wash her with gentle tears and with confession. The soul I have won through heavy labor is a dear treasure. Accordingly, I insist that she be well protected so as not to be ruined. You will never be able to cleanse her too often, guard her too vigilantly, or elevate her too far, even if you had never sinned a day in your life, had always taken the right path, and had always protected your soul meticulously. Even then you could never have cleansed your soul enough. Improve yourself, my beloved. My dear sister, as you can see for yourself, the more virtuously you behave, the dearer you are to me.'"

How her soul after such praiseworthy disciplines became worthy of praise
and was greatly illuminated and cherished by God.

Chapter XXII.

Later the Lord said: "Souls disciplined in the manner discussed in the
previous chapter are good, blessed, happy, fruitful, praiseworthy, and holy. They
will enjoy much happiness and honor in eternal life. In that they resemble my
holy angels. I, my dear mother, and all the saints now experience joy with them
and through them. There are many holy angels and people serving them who are
commanded to serve them." When the Lord had spoken thus, Dorothea, clearly
illuminated in spirit, saw how the Lord Jesus, his dearly beloved mother, and a
great throng of saints gathered around her soul, so blessedly brought up in
accordance with the teachings of the Lord and thus brought to such a great,
praiseworthy state of perfection. She did not claim these things concerning her
soul because of frivolity or desire for fame but in response to Our Lord's
command, the source and shaper of her sanctity. He awakened and quickened her
spirit, which then discerned not only its own wounds and scars caused by sin and
the temptations confronting it, but also recognized these same conditions in many
other people. She also recognized clearly that the Lord loved her far more than
she loved him. She was greatly distressed about this and berated herself
unsparingly for loving the Lord so little in return. It also irritated all the powers
of her soul, her senses, and her soul's helpmates that she was incapable of loving
her dear lover more forcefully, more ardently, more passionately and completely.
Therefore, her blessed soul counted herself for nothing and was deeply ashamed;
her heart was deeply saddened to realize that the love with which he loved her
was infinitely greater than her own with which she loved him in return.

Her illumination and hot desire.

Chapter XXIII.

Among the many praiseworthy and precious gifts and mercies the Lord
graciously bestowed upon her were two very important ones, pure illumination of

her intellect and the burning flame of love and desire for God. The first enabled her to discern many things, some of which have been discussed already. She recognized the highest good, which is God, as immeasurably great and mysterious, even to those holy angels called the "burning" angels or cherubim. No matter how receptive and comprehending of its nature, still neither they nor any saint can grasp or contain the highest good in its entirety so that no part of it remains excluded. Often it appeared so immeasurably great and limitless to Dorothea that all creatures disappeared from her consciousness in contemplation of it. The Lord said to her: "Now your soul has grown wings. Her eyes have been opened. She flies way up high and gazes into the eternal clear sun without averting her eyes, just like the eagle looks straight at the clear corporeal sun. Your soul yearns to find sustenance and bliss in eternal life and constantly desires to learn from me how to fly higher still and be assured once and for all of being with me and from then on never again to be parted from me. For this reason your soul stays with me as closely as possible."

Dorothea also discerned how to make herself receptive for the Lord and his holy body and how matters stood between her soul and God, whether or not she had angered him with her sins, and how to avoid injury to her soul. Many other things in heaven and on earth she recognized as well. To enumerate them all would be too much and beyond my capability.

The hot flame of her love and desire made her soul light and swift. Shouting joyously, she swiftly ran to meet the Lord and received him lovingly when he came to her in the sacrament or through the Holy Spirit. In her love and desire, she ascended to the Lord in contemplation and ecstasy. About this the Lord said: "Your soul is alive and emboldened by me to stand by the door at all times, looking for me and to me. Now your soul quickly departs to meet me halfway. Your soul embraces and kisses me. Now your soul is meeting me, embracing me, and kissing me as quickly as I formerly have done these things to her. Now I open my hall, now my secret room, the bridegroom's chamber, which your soul may enter without fear. Sometimes our union happens swiftly and lasts longer at one time than another." His other gifts the Lord increased so much in his bride Dorothea that in the end her heart broke from love and intense desire.

How she became rich and was to grow richer still,

and how others were to profit from her wealth.

Chapter XXIV.

Jesus Christ, the richest bridegroom of all, after having made his elected bride Dorothea rich in spiritual possessions, said to her: "No pauper may enter eternal life without first having grown rich in the Christian faith. Look at me. I am much richer than you. Look how many precious goods I own. And still, I have many more of which you know nothing. You have not yet sampled all my goods; yet I will let you taste them all. From now on you and yours never again need to worry about temporal goods for you shall own all my wealth in common with me." After this Dorothea was enraptured to contemplate divine treasures of which she saw and recognized so many that she could not even describe the thousandth part. Frequently the Lord also opened the eyes of her soul when she was not enraptured, and through them she saw how all the space around her was filled with spiritual goods, spread out much farther than she could survey.

The Lord intended her to increase more and more in spiritual riches. But when she was filled to overflowing with abundant grace, certain to have enough to last forever, she sat quietly at rest without laboring. Then the Lord punished her and said: "When you feel enriched through the presence of my Holy Spirit or ill through my mercies, you sit idly and behave as if you had come home already. But since you know very well that you cannot enter without me, why do you sit here without yearning and exertion to get there? Implore me without ceasing to help you and draw me to you with all your might! You shall never become too satisfied to desire imperishable treasures but shall always suffer great restlessness and impatient yearning for them since even perishable goods cannot be attained at leisure without tremendous effort and exertion. But you shall be so filled with eternal, imperishable wealth that you will have no hankering after temporal, perishable goods."

After this lesson Dorothea experienced such intense longing for eternal goods that she could not comprehend what the Lord revealed to her at the time. Her desire for eternal things grew and increased through many kinds of visions of heaven and revelations through which much delight and many new good things became known to her. They in turn kindled her yearning to be spiritually rich all the more strongly. Through her praiseworthy labor and desire she attained a large treasure and became so rich that she could share it with many others to help them. The Lord witnessed to her about this by saying: "I have rained the abundance of my grace on you like a dew from heaven so that for your sake grace may be visited upon your friends to share it with you. Now you shall contemplate my property more clearly, grow richer on account of it, administer it more effectively, and govern it more decisively than before. For a wise bridegroom does not right away commit all his property to his bride. Rather, upon first leading her home, he assigns her a part of his wealth. Only if she manages that well and governs it faithfully, does he commit all of it to her care. You now have power over all my goods. I am your bridegroom: rich, gracious, and handsome. All my brides on Earth shall have part in my property and shall enjoy a wealth of grace and beauty with me. You, however, are to weep copiously that there are so few of you on Earth who wish to be my brides and abandon temporal, perishable goods for my sake." Later the Lord demonstrated the abundance of his wealth, grace, and beauty to her and said: "My bride, I have made you rich, as I enriched my elected after my ascension to heaven by sending them my Holy Spirit." Furthermore, it is to be known that the Lord gave his elected bride Dorothea many other indications of her wealth and her control over his possessions too numerous to be recorded. Let those reading this be patient until they have read the entire book.

How her soul was brought to perfection by the Lord and so grew rich.

Chapter XXV.

No one may quickly arrive at the highest level of perfection. Instead, a person must traverse and ascend through various degrees of virtue before arriving at the ultimate degree of perfection. In this manner the Lord brought his elected bride Dorothea to perfection, as he has revealed. When he had set her afire with his love and she had performed and suffered so many spiritual exercises, disciplines, and self-castigations to become receptive to God, the Lord sent her his Holy Spirit, invisibly with his hot, burning love so that she was illuminated and could understand what she was to do and could perform the heavy labors of virtue more joyfully. At that time she was still married and because of her responsibilities to her husband, servants, and the world, could not entirely cleave unto God and abandon everything. For this reason the Lord sent her the Holy Spirit who was to console her and correct her whenever she offended God.

Though she repented and improved, her human weakness and worldly wisdom nevertheless prevented her taking the Holy Spirit's punishments and instructions entirely to heart. Therefore, God sent her the Holy Spirit to teach her the kind of divine wisdom the world considers a foolishness: to abandon the wisdom of the world altogether. When she had learned the wisdom of the saints and had increased in spirituality, Our Lord sent her his Holy Spirit to awaken the taste for spiritual wealth in her and quicken her soul by bringing her spiritual delight and divine sweetness, which gladdened her unspeakably.

Through such spiritual delights the Holy Spirit drew her so forcefully that many times she abandoned or lost all zest for bodily delights in favor of the burning desire with which she had been ignited and which now enabled her to taste spiritual and divine sweetness continuously. Her desire never deceived her: she was always comforted by the Holy Spirit who was sent to her frequently, bringing precious gifts through which she became rich in the Lord. As a result, all bodily desires became bitter and all spiritual, holy things most delectable to her. It annoyed her to be alive, and she yearned for death to be with God whom alone she desired and who later more than before sent his Holy Spirit to her both day and night, often for two, three, four, five or six hours at a time, sometimes seven, eight, or even nine times.

And this happened through many degrees of his love, great mercies, and abundant gifts through which the Lord enriched Dorothea and brought her to the perfection he had ordained for her in his eternal providence. Through the missions of the Holy Ghost, said the Lord, Dorothea's soul became a sound lord and ruler with whom he dealt for many years before granting her total dominion of Dorothea's body and all things which had become subject to her and over which the soul held dominion in this world. The Lord mentioned five gifts in particular, of which he said this: "Among others, I have granted you five gifts which are most precious. These are your pure illumination, your clear discernment, your deep humility, your inordinate desire to be poor, and your strong desire to be despised in this world. These are not bestowed on you by this world but come from above, from my pure grace. No human being may pass them to another."

How she was adorned and endowed.

Chapter XXVI.

To become the bride of the eternal king, Dorothea's soul was first adorned, then courted and endowed, and finally wedded to Jesus Christ, the son of the eternal king, who finally led her into his kingdom and into the bridal chamber. Her praiseworthy adornment consisted of the cleanness of her conscience, her perfect love to God and fellow human beings--which is called her bridal gown-- and a variety of virtues decked in an array of colors. That she was indeed well adorned the Lord indicated when he told her: "I have adorned you well and in many ways, for my brides, even in the clothes they wear on Earth, are to display a variety of colors and styles because this variety of garments and hues signals the abundance of grace, virtue, love, comfort and good deeds the Lord provides, such as the exhilarating love, the inebriating love, the inseparable love, the overflowing love, ecstasy, joy of heart, profound humility, and other such virtues." Of these Dorothea owned many on account of the great perfection that adorned her.

After her adornment, the handsome bridegroom courted her through many messengers and courtiers he sent to her. These courtiers and messengers were the Holy Spirit himself and the Holy Spirit's admonitions and advice as well as his drawing her to the Lord; his ecstasy, his illumination, and his comfort. Concerning these, the Lord said to her: "I am in the habit of wooing by brides for a long time. I send an honorable messenger to my bride, your soul, who is the Holy Spirit. He illuminates her, comforts and enriches her. This messenger is so honorable that from his reputation alone she can easily discern that I will come to her with great riches. Customarily I also give the Holy Spirit to my brides as a bridal gift. This gift I have also bestowed on your soul, who laments fiercely and longs for me." From this we realize that the Lord gave her the Holy Ghost as a bridal gift and with it a taste of his sweetness.

How she was espoused to Jesus, her heavenly bridegroom.

Chapter XXVII.

Not only was she espoused in faith and mercy, as others commonly are, but in a special manner as well. It happened often that the Lord Jesus, the most beloved bridegroom, wanted to indicate his desire for their espousal through his merciful visitation of his bride Dorothea. On these occasions he sent her gifts of grace in such abundance that she could not even relate the thousandth part of what she had received. Nor could any tongue have described the laudable, sumptuous visitations the Lord bestowed on her, of which there were many. I merely want to relate a little of what she had to say about one of them.

At that time Dorothea was clearly illuminated by God and highly favored, her body having been made transparent to her sight like a clear crystal. She examined soul and body with her inner eye. Her soul, her flesh, her bones were all melting because of her intense desire which, spilling from her soul, flowed into her body and bones. She wondered about herself and her condition, speculating whether she would now simply cease to be, for she thought it impossible to bear the sheer magnitude of God's abundance of grace and overwhelming passion.

The Lord had created a great festivity in her soul. Joy and jubilation were without measure, her rejoicing without end. Her soul was like the daughter of a great and mighty king, exquisitely dressed and endowed abundantly, just as a bride appropriately adorned with gold, silver, and precious stones who sits in a comfortable, richly furnished hall with her ladies, waiting and looking eagerly for her noble, praiseworthy, well-born bridegroom to come through the door of the hall in the company of his friends. Her face was turned to the door in greedy, passionate anticipation of her bridegroom; nothing could deflect her gaze. At the same time, she constantly inspected herself to make sure that nothing could be found on her person to cause her bridegroom's eyes the least displeasure. Whenever she spied even the tiniest dust mote of a minute transgression, she or one of her handmaidens washed it off immediately. The maidens who were with her served her as attentively as they would the daughter of a great king. They served her with great diligence and decorum to prepare her fittingly for being espoused to such an honorable, noble bridegroom.

All the while sweet, mild tears flowed from the eyes of the bride. Of them the Lord said: "These tears your soul has scooped from the rivers of eternal life and brought them with her into this life. But to bring the rivers of eternity to Earth, a person must first perform heavy labors, and such a person is blessed indeed who here on this Earth is prepared and made capable to do so. As for me, in you I have prepared the kind of dwelling I desire. You cannot prepare such a place without me, for I have decorated it with virtues, strewn its floors with my grace, and furnished it with my mercy and passion."

The bride, having wept in wounded love and having waited long for the arrival of her bridegroom, finally espied him in the distance. The most beautiful-- not only above all human beings, but also more beautiful than the holy angels; the most honorable; the most noble; and the most praiseworthy ever to appear on Earth, he arrived with a huge, mighty host. This army was excellently equipped and made up of handsome, well-born men especially selected to accompany the bridegroom. The bridegroom himself appeared ever more gracious, handsome, and joyful as he drew near, well-mannered and polite.

As the blessed bride Dorothea was busily examining the bridegroom and his retinue, she realized as truth that the groom was nobler, more honorable, more exquisite in manner, and more beautiful than any one of those with him, even though she had never before seen such handsome, rich, noble, and gracious men, all of them clothed in purple gowns. And when they arrived at the door, the bridegroom in their midst, to lead him with all due decorum to the marriage ceremony, they all removed their birettas and respectfully bowed their heads to the bride. And when at last the bridegroom stood in the door, his face glowed as purely and brightly as the noonday sun.

And the Lord spoke graciously: "I will not enter any dwelling, unless it is spotless, bright, and well-lighted. The hall of my dwelling shall be strewn with roses and lilies, that is with love and purity, and with all sorts of flowers, that is with an abundance of virtues. Yet my bride shall be more profusely adorned still, for I will lead the bride I take as my wife into the wine cellar of my sweet love, that is into the paradise of passion and desire, and into my secret chamber. There I shall show her the secrets of my heart I don't want to reveal to anyone else." As the bridegroom said this, the bride became flushed with searing love and examined herself closely to make sure that there was nothing amiss to annoy the eyes of her bridegroom. But she found herself very well prepared by her adored bridegroom Jesus and worthily adorned for her nuptials with him. The marriage ceremony between Jesus and Dorothea mercifully always took place at the time Dorothea received the holy, gracious sacrament of the true body of Our Lord Jesus Christ.

How after their nuptials Dorothea was showered with gifts.

Chapter XXVIII.

Whenever he came to her, the praiseworthy bridegroom told Dorothea much more pleasantly than anyone can repeat: "From now on I will come to you more graciously than ever before. Here on earth I want to sustain you with many comforts until I bring you into my kingdom and into my house. We will melt together into one ball to be united and alone with one another." As the Lord said this, the fire of divine love melted Dorothea's soul to resemble the liquid ore used for casting bells, flowing with God into one mass. And Dorothea's soul felt clearly how she was united with God and totally immersed in him. Her soul was so softened by inexpressibly radiant joy and divine passion that she was convinced not to be able to bear it for long.

Then the Lord spoke to her: "Any soul here on Earth who accepts me as fully and opens herself to me as sweetly as you do now can be sure of eternal life where she will enjoy great power and live in great joy and honor. And you may certainly say of yourself 'I myself am a heaven and carry eternal life within me.' For in truth you are a heaven because I will not be contained except in a heavenly place, and I, who is life eternal, dwell within you. As you sit here, so full of joy and divine sweetness, you are convinced that you contain all of me, for you assume I can neither be anywhere else except within you nor have anything to do with anyone else but you, even though I am a great, unlimited, immeasurable good. I am very rich and mighty, and to those whom I wish to give something of my wealth, I give myself. I deny myself to no one who greatly yearns for me. On the contrary, I give myself to them according to the strength of their longing. I especially enjoy coming to those who fiercely desire me from the bottom of their hearts, who wish for my speedy arrival from the depth of their desire, who suffer bitter torment when my coming is delayed but who nevertheless anticipate it eagerly even though my tarrying causes them severe distress. But I have no desire to come to those who are indifferent to me. I also refuse to enter any dwelling not carefully prepared for me." These words were exceedingly sweet to his chosen bride Dorothea.

How Dorothea's soul became the beloved bride of Christ
whom he led into his wine cellar.

Chapter XXIX.

It happened on another day after the marriage ceremony described here and after her confessor had recorded it that the Lord said to her: "Speak as follows to your confessor B:

I did not intend to say as much about my praiseworthy bridegroom and our honorable espousal as I did. Moreover, we cannot take any credit for what I did say and what you have written down, but must credit it all to the Lord who has accomplished this and has revealed it for his own honor. It is he who also said: "I delight in adorning my brides sumptuously and have the means to do it. Those to whom I want to give myself quickly I want to instruct myself and clothe them in my personal property. Those I want to make pleasing to me and prepare them so they become as I desire them. No one else can accomplish this. I, the bridegroom, delight in a clean, beautiful, chaste bride. If she is also well adorned, the bridegroom takes great pleasure in her, even if she did nothing but love him with all her heart and sat in his hall adorning it with her presence. The bridegroom's spirit is further delighted when he finds that he has a bride of keen vision who rigorously guards and observes herself before her bridegroom's arrival to make sure she will be spotless when he comes."

Furthermore, the Lord stated:

Worthy of praise is the bride who has elected as her bridegroom the most beloved, most powerful, most beautiful, noble, and honorable man. For only then does she have no need to fear that some other bride may have a bridegroom even greater, more powerful and wise, beautiful, noble, or honorable than her own.

Then the Lord went on to say: "But now you must say something about yourself." As he said this, the bride's soul, that is Dorothea's soul, was elevated far above herself. She saw herself in a heavenly palace, spacious and well-appointed. From it God's heavenly friends led her into a beautiful chamber to her lord bridegroom who received her with joyful countenance and treated her with kindness and deference. She was respectfully received by all present and seated at the head of the table where she was fed with the delightful abundance of divine desire. As she was served a variety of sweet, delectable, and tasty libations at her bridegroom's table, a great crowd of saints entered the king's, her bridegroom's chamber, followed by another, so as one group came out, another entered. They all saluted and received the bride, that is Dorothea's soul, with great respect but without much talk. Another group departed for at that time no one was permitted to converse with her. Then the bride, according to the bridegroom's promise, was led into the wine cellar, where she was given drink according to his will and desire to make her spiritually drunk. Then two of the bridegroom's noble, well-born chamberlains took her between them and merrily escorted her from the king's chamber, through an antechamber where she saw many saints inebriated by the liquor of divine sweetness. She asked to stay and speak to them, but her request was denied. Instead, she was led away by the bridegroom's aforementioned chamberlains and released from her ecstasy. When she came to, she found herself spiritually intoxicated and so full of divine sweetness that she realized how truly well fed and plied with drink she was, which, however, she would not have divulged had the Lord not ordered her to do so.

How she was to comport herself in his absence,
and how he showered her with gifts.

Chapter XXX.

The blessed Dorothea was often comforted by her bridegroom's consolations. He instructed her by saying: "You shall conduct yourself like a bride whose wedding gown and wedding preparations are now completed and who now, clothed in her bridal gown, sits and eagerly awaits the arrival of her bridegroom, free of reservations but filled with an all-consuming desire for the bridegroom to come right away and take her home at last." As the Lord said this, the bride Dorothea, to put herself into that ultimate state of preparedness appropriate for a bride about to follow her bridegroom wherever he desired, examined herself to see whether anything she should have might still be lacking in her. But she found herself ready and would have preferred to go with him at once rather than wait any longer. He spoke to her: "On Earth my brides each day experience excruciatingly hard labor and hot desire for me as they court me and entice me to come to them. They must also feel an overwhelming desire for me to grant them my grace abundantly here, prepare their palace with great care, and send the treasures I have bestowed on them in this life ahead of them into eternal life. Through these preparations they will realize that I am about to come to them in person, and when they have accumulated as much treasure as they need to be ready, they must refrain from doing anything but sit and wait for me in burning desire and vigilant anticipation.

At another time the Lord came to Dorothea with his dear mother and many saints and spoke to her most pleasantly: "At times I come to you in spirit, at others in the sacrament to prepare you and shape you as I want you to be. And whenever you do not guard yourself carefully from uttering idle words, from thinking foolish or incorrect thoughts, and from shirking good works, I punish you severely, for it is proper for my brides to keep themselves clean and flawless at all times through vigilant self-discipline. Furthermore, I have showered you, my bride, and all your servants--the forces of your soul and your virtues, with gifts. They have each received so much that they can't possibly wish for anything else. Notice: Your soul cannot desire more while the fullness and extent of such merciful grace remain present and constant." In addition the Lord said: "You have eternal life within you-- that is me. You are a heaven unto yourself. I bring you many gifts and keep you like a rich bridegroom keeps his bride: in such a state that she cannot possibly complain about him. And how could you possibly complain about me when I take you to me so often in ecstasy, allow you to come to, and then join you?"

How Christ led her to the marriage feast and whispered to her.

Chapter XXXI.

When the blessed Dorothea found herself among the elected brides of whom Matthew speaks in his gospel when he says that "those who were ready went to the wedding with him," she took great care to be found in readiness. For this purpose she prepared herself with her bridegroom's help by amassing great virtue through her holy life, praiseworthy speech, clear conscience, searching, burning love, and proper opinions. And through flaming, leaping desire she amassed much precious treasure and enticed the Lord Jesus, her bridegroom, to come to her. And he visited her often with his mercies and at times of grace led her to the feast. Generally this happened when she was in ecstasy. Then, bathed in the light of truth, her soul was led to the summit of his holy mountain, into his heavenly dwelling, into his treasury, into his private inner chamber. There she beheld the king in all his glory with inexpressibly great delight. There she tasted the delectable food prepared there for holy souls. Blessed are they who there can satisfy all their want. There she was crowned like the bride of a king, sumptuously adorned, highly honored and paid homage to. There she pleasantly and intimately conversed with the bridegroom. There she saw and heard divine matters not appropriate to be discussed. But she also was allowed to see and hear a number of secrets she was allowed to relate.

At times when her heavenly bridegroom led her into his heavenly chamber where they could be alone together, she could hear the sweet whispering the Lord conducted with her soul. Here it is worth knowing that at times the bridegroom whispered to the bride; at other times the bride whispered to the bridegroom. The former kind of whispering occurs when the Lord converses so secretly with the soul that what is being said can't be expressed in words and takes place when God draws the soul into herself to rid her of all external influences. In this state the Lord sweetly speaks to the soul and the soul hears his sweet speech without literally hearing what is being said. If the soul actually does hear it, she will be unable to remember or repeat it.

This is one kind of whispering. The other is that in which the bride engages her bridegroom, who is God, when her burning desire for him is so overwhelming that the soul is totally withdrawn into herself and so completely removed from all creation by the Lord that nothing remains in the soul's memory but God her bridegroom. The height of this desire is inexpressible; therefore, it is called a whispering. But this desire also has a booming voice, for there is no voice more delightful to God than overwhelming passion for him. As they were whispering, God said to Dorothea: "You will never know entirely what I do to your soul. Our intimate whisperings cannot be related to others because whenever I want to reveal a secret to your soul that is to remain a secret, I first intoxicate your soul. That way your soul can neither remember nor repeat what I whisper. At times the soul hears my whispers clearly but still cannot deal with them rationally."

Signs that prove that she was led to the marriage feast
with her bridegroom.

Chapter XXXII.

Just as Moses descended the mountain on which the Lord had spoken to him as one friend to another with shining countenance, Dorothea brought back many signs of her experiences when the Lord released her from her ecstasy after having led her to the feast and into his private chamber. At times her face was merry, rosy, and attractive, especially when she emerged from her ecstasy still drunk from their carousing and full of joy and exultation. However, if she returned from the ecstasy of divine feasting only mildly inebriated and in a slight state of drunkenness, she displayed different signs, as for example, an unseemly desire to return to that which she had just tasted and seen. On such occasions she wept piteously, shedding floods of tears, unable to derive comfort from anyone. When she was in this condition, anything people did for her in word and deed to console her was more a torment than a balm to her. She would sit there, desolate, crying miserably; she would scream and sigh until her merciful bridegroom took pity on her and led her once more to his heavenly feast or released her of this tremendous, impetuous passion raging within her through some other kindness or mercy.

Dorothea was asked by her confessor how she could determine that she had been enraptured and her visions during her ecstasy were neither dreams nor delusions. She answered by saying: "I dare not say what I have seen or heard unless after my rapture the Lord should let me do otherwise. I am afire with love and desire for God, my most beloved Lord, and my fellow beings and yearn to return to the miraculous comfort I experience during my ecstasies. Generally, even after I come to, such inordinate, hot desire to return to such bliss remains with me that I would rather die than live just so I could remain without ceasing in those joys, comforts, and pleasures. More, in all my revelations and raptures I am always ignited with love for God and all creation and moved to adoration and affection. I am made to rejoice in just how poor I really am; that I am to be despised and that I am to confess all my sins often in sincere contrition. At such times I also despise sins more than ever; they are disgusting to me. I am also fortified to endure adversity patiently. My body becomes laden and weighed down, but my spirit is strengthened. After such rapture it desires more ardently to commit good deeds and to praise more enthusiastically than before, to die for the sake of faith and justice and to struggle mightily to attain the three divine and the four angelic virtues."

Dorothea was granted yet another sign to prove that she had not fallen victim to deception, for she was assured of the genuine nature of her illuminations by being so filled with joy and divine passion during ecstasy and even afterwards that her soul was softened to the point of melting. Such illumination, joy, exultation, and delicious taste of divine sweetness in a state of such abject humility and negation of her very being she could not have attained from the deceitful spirit. Furthermore, the Lord frequently assured her that he himself would keep her safe from that evil.

The path of life that led from her soul to eternal bliss.

Chapter XXXIII.

The Lord said that from the house of the soul, which is constructed of many virtues, the path of life will lead directly to eternity in such a manner that the soul, upon looking up, can see it. This road must have three properties: it must be elevated, level, and spacious. It must have a certain elevation so not just anyone can simply step on it and wear it out with his feet. Its height each person determines through humility in good fortune and patience in adversity, in disdaining delights and wishing to suffer misfortunes. And when spiritual matters are precious in such a person's eyes and physical, temporal things scorned as trash, the elevation of the road leading to eternal life will be such that it touches heaven and transcends all other paths. The road must be level, not rough or uneven, so that there is nothing there on which to bump one's feet. This smoothness results when worldly delights become distasteful and bitter while the heavenly, spiritual goods become delicious and flavorful. And when a person recognizes that divine goods are coming to him from heaven, the road will level out. In the third place the road must be wide enough to enable the soul to travel it in the company of a great number of companions rather than having to journey in solitude. In this manner the soul can and will travel that much more safely. The width of the road is determined by the pure, sincere love for one's friends as well as one's enemies, self-denial, renunciation of personal willfulness, flight from vainglory, and the desire to be annihilated and despised.

The Lord went on to say: "Once the road is well prepared, the soul must daily send a variety of the fruits of virtue to eternal life by way of it, for this road must never be left empty. And as the soul sends up this good fruit, the bridegroom in return sends even better goods back to her, as when he sends her the Holy Spirit, his dear mother, and many of his saints. He gives himself to the soul as food and drink and sends her many other goods to nurture and improve the fruit she wishes to send up to heaven."

When the Lord had thus demonstrated the many virtues one needs to prepare the path to eternal life, he also showed her the beautiful bright path constructed by her own virtues, which led from the house of her soul into eternal life and brought her many goods from there. Dorothea also saw and felt how the Lord drew her forcefully to him and to life everlasting. In the company of his most honorable mother and many of his saints he met her frequently on this road from the house of her soul to eternal life. Frequently she observed angels and many saints coming down to her on this road and witnessed the bliss and honor they enjoyed in eternal glory. More, by looking down the length of the path, she saw the gates of eternal life standing open in readiness for her. There was no impediment keeping her from entering eternal life save death, for which she found herself prepared through God's grace. And she experienced an overwhelming desire to enter eternity and to exert all her energies to bring it about.

How after years of yearning she was promised eternal life.
Chapter XXXIV.

After Dorothea had felt searching, flaming, great desire for life everlasting not only many years before her death but also before the exchange of her old heart for a new one, God solemnly promised her eternal life when he appeared to her, treating her so graciously as if he longed to behold her face: "When you first started exerting yourself to gain my holy body and to long for it with weeping, I did not immediately satisfy your craving but waited to see whether you would prevail and not slacken and tire of your endless labors. When you persisted in your efforts and desire until you could no longer exist without me, I saw to it that you could receive me every day. In this very same way I will fulfill your craving for eternal life, which you have felt for many years now and for which you yearn and have labored hard with pious weeping. But I want to wait until I can see that you cannot be discouraged by the long wait or the hard labor; until all your strength will be exhausted and you will be incapable of carrying the burden of your scalding, flaming, yearning desire into eternal life; until your heart will break on account of this overwhelming exertion. At that time, my dear daughter, I will transport you to my eternal joys. Therefore, be not discouraged; you will enjoy me in that inexpressibly great bliss that never ends." After this, the Lord often reiterated how her longing for him and eternal life would grow with each day until she would no longer be able to go on living and that her two confessors B & P could very well say and write that her entire life had been nothing but an unappeased hunger for eternal life.

How God assured her of eternal life and sanctity.

Chapter XXXV.

The many great and perfect virtues, blessings, and mercies the Lord bestowed upon Dorothea were evidence of her sanctity, as were the words of his eternal truth which assured her of the reality of eternal life and her presence in it. Of the many occasions when he spoke of this, consider these five: Once he told her: "You shall rejoice with me here and in eternity. You will enjoy eternal life with me and great honor. All your pain will be turned into bliss, and you will have dominion over all I own." At another time he said: "you can rely on me fully; you can be certain of eternal life." At the third time he said this: "You shall suffer great pains for the sake of eternal life until I come to you and say, 'Come, my chosen one. From now on you will suffer no more pain or sadness but enjoy eternal bliss. Wait patiently; I will give you as much of my treasure as you are capable of receiving.'" Another time he appeared to her in the company of a large train of saints and behaved as though he was about to lead her soul into eternal life immediately, saying: "You shall rejoice greatly that no one except you and I will be able to touch your soul. Behold my might, how high, how wide, how deep it is. You have conceived me in all my greatness. Your soul, my bride, shall contemplate me. I will unite with your soul in such profound love so deeply that after your present life people shall know it and speak of it everywhere. Now tell your two confessors B & P: 'My most beloved lord in his mercy has ordered me to inspect the precious goods my soul shall own in eternal life. Furthermore, the Lord has revealed to me that my soul shall journey into eternal life, there to enjoy limitless bliss, honor, and dominion immeasurably greater than I can put into words.'" On yet another occasion the Lord spoke to her and pleased her soul greatly by saying: "When you come into eternal life, you will be a great saint. And because you, for my sake, refused the adornment of your body, your soul shall enjoy exquisite adornment eternally."

It would be wrong to assume that Dorothea spoke these words to draw attention to herself. She spoke them in great humility, for the more the Lord praised and comforted her, the more she humbled, debased, and annihilated herself. This the Lord worked in her by endowing her with profound humility as he granted her his abundance of precious gifts. He commanded her to speak these words so they would be recorded as eternal praise to him and as a model of improvement for all Christians.

Her desire to die.

Chapter XXXVI.

When the blessed Dorothea had experienced fierce yearning for eternal life for a long time and eternal life indeed had been promised and prepared for her, she felt a keen desire to die to be with Christ Jesus, her dearly beloved bridegroom. Her desire to die was such that it annoyed her to continue living. To indicate something of her desire to her confessor, the Lord commanded her to say this to him: "You have never spoken to anyone as well prepared for death as I am. You may trust me when I say that if someone wanted to kill me in whatever way he wished, I would gladly suffer it for the love of my dear Lord so I could join him that much sooner, for I would rather be with him than live in this place. I have often mentioned the anxiety of spirit that grows out of my love's desire to be with Christ. It also happens more and more often that I am ill and suffer more from this intense love than I ever suffered from bodily illness throughout my life."

Dorothea's prediction about her own death
and various others that came true eventually.

Chapter XXXVII.

Often after having suffered such excruciating desire to die and be in eternal life she lost her coloring, turning pale and yellow in her great longing for Our Lord, who often comforted her by saying that she would die soon and had not long to live. This happened frequently during the last year of her life, during which she also predicted her own death as imminent. Whenever she mentioned this to her confessor, he begged her repeatedly to tell him the exact hour of her death because he would have liked to be with her. She, however, replied: "Why can't you be satisfied knowing what the Lord has revealed and demonstrated to me--that the remaining time is short and I will die soon?" But since her confessor kept insisting, she often said: "If the Lord commands me, I will tell you."

But many days passed between this conversation and the day of Dorothea's death. During that time the Lord sometimes appeared with a large retinue and ministered to her with his many precious comforts. These she revealed to her confessors B & P. From the nature of these consolations they should have realized that death was swiftly approaching her door. Her confessors, however, fervently wished her to go on living; so they did not take these matters to heart as indications of her impending death. They were encouraged in their thinking since she had already predicted her immediate death for more than six months, so they expected it to be delayed for some time yet. They also entertained hopes that through God's mild mercies, at least one of them would know the hour of her death. Why Our Lord did not want them to know only he, to whom all hidden things are revealed, can know.

The Lord also commanded her to say this: "When your two confessors B & P will take in hand what they have written about you to set it straight, they will come to love heaven and will develop a great longing for eternal life where these recorded words originated. And I, too, will become more desirable to them because I allowed them to hear all this through and about you. After your death, your confessor B shall kneel and thank me with uplifted hands and eyes raised to heaven by saying: 'My beloved Lord Jesus Christ, I thank you sincerely for mercifully having helped me to proclaim your praise and honor in this woman. May you be praised and honored for all eternity.' He shall also rejoice in me and thank me profusely for having granted him the privilege of having accomplished my praise and honor through his ministrations to you. You, on the other hand, must weep profusely and implore me: 'Jesus Christ, my beloved Lord, help him to bring your laudable praise and honor invested in me to a worthy conclusion and take my soul to you for you see only too well that you are all my hope and desire.'"

Moreover, the Lord stated that Dorothea was to tell her confessor what he was to preach publicly after her death to make people take notice, improve, and thank him profusely. And Dorothea saw spiritually how after her death people through this sermon of God's honor would become as devout as they had ever been in church. And through God's grace this is indeed what happened, as will be related here later. The Lord went on to say: "When you die, there will be great rejoicing on Earth and in heaven. The saints in heaven will delight in having you among them. On Earth, many of those who know you will rejoice, for they will entertain great hopes about your having come into eternal life." Another time the Lord said: "You shall die because those in eternal life await you longingly." As the Lord said this, Dorothea beheld the heavens opened to her; Mary, the queen of heaven, preciously adorned, and many saints greatly honored and beautiful beyond measure, were waiting for her in joyous anticipation, behaving as though they had great need of her. Visions of this kind she enjoyed frequently, and through them she was drawn forcefully toward eternal life.

The five processions preceding her death through which
the Lord enticed her to join him.

Chapter XXXVIII.

To increase her desire for eternal life, Our Lord Jesus Christ, his dear mother, and many saints appeared to her many times to draw and entice her. Shortly before her death, however, he appeared to her more splendidly and magnificently than ever before in five grand processions spread over five consecutive days. During these the Lord poured his precious treasures into her soul as abundantly as if it were raining from heaven. In the course of the first procession she was filled with joy and sweetness and wounded by heartbreaking love, and the Lord and his saints treated her so graciously during this procession as if he wished to take her soul with him into eternal life at that very moment. Because of this, Dorothea was greatly comforted and hoped her heart would break immediately through the impact of this heartbreaking love.

In the course of the second procession he did the same, and letting her see her prepared path to eternal life, said to her: "As long as you are still alive, you shall be severely wounded. I shall demonstrate the joys of heaven to which I am drawing you: the more you desire them, the more abundantly you shall receive them. Turn away from all creation and in love turn entirely to me; abandon yourself totally and submerge yourself in the depth of my divinity. You may enjoy my presence anywhere: the more you cleave unto me and spurn the creature comforts of earthly existence, the more highly you will be elevated in my majesty."

In the third procession the Lord appeared to weigh her down with the severe pressure his work exerted on her. He said: "I am visiting you together with my father and the Holy Spirit, with my beloved mother and a great number of my saints. We are coming straight from eternal life because I want to provide you with a reminder of the holy trinity." As the Lord Jesus spoke, a beautiful, well-appointed path leading from heaven into her cell appeared to her. Those who were traversing it up and down enjoyed such intense, ineffable joy that she not only could not express it but could not even fully comprehend it. She was convinced that the entire heavenly host had come to her in its joyfulness-- all the prophets, apostles, martyrs, confessors, virgins, and saintly widows.

On the day before the fourth procession was to take place the Lord caused much spiritual wealth to rain and flow into her heart, which was raised up high in anticipation of him. He said: "Receive my grace into your heart, which is lifted to me into heaven. I will place my most precious treasures in it so that when you die it will contain nothing of this Earth but only that which I have put there. Your soul, my bride, shall overflow with my grace until the day of her birth, the day you will deliver her into eternal life." As the Lord spoke thus, he appeared to her with a large retinue of his saints with such friendly demeanor as though he would at once take her soul with him from earthly life to eternity. Immediately after these great joys he granted her his heartbreaking love. As she felt the fierce, bitter pains of a woman in labor, the Lord said: "When you suffer the pains of a woman on the verge of giving birth to a child, the hour when you shall enjoy the bliss of eternal life is near. You endured great labor and pain when you gave birth to both bodily and spiritual fruit. However, you will endure the fiercest exertions and the most excruciating pains yet to deliver the noblest fruit of all as you give birth to your soul into eternal life. Don't let that oppress you too much, though, for I had to labor with all my might when I had to deliver the whole world once more into eternal life. For this reason you will have to bear the pressure I exert on you until I come and say: 'Come, my friend. You shall never again suffer pain but enjoy nothing but bliss.'"

On the day of the fifth procession she was overwhelmed by the heartbreaking love and was wounded severely. And the Lord instructed her to speak to her two confessors like this: "Even if all the powers of your bodies and souls could and did write diligently for may days, they could still not record what the Lord has accomplished in me lately and this very day. Take note! Through God's illumination it is clear to me that I will die because of my great longing and will see the Lord take my soul into his hands and into his authority. Therefore, give thanks to my beloved Lord who now has so often come to me with his adored mother and a large retinue of his saints. I now hope to die soon."

The heartbreaking love, which was the cause of her death.

Chapter XXXIX.

The heartbreaking love grew so tremendously in this same woman Dorothea that it finally broke her heart, for this love strengthened the life of grace to such a degree in her that it overpowered and extinguished the life of the creature and guided her soul into the life of divine glory, just as the Lord had prophesied. Actually, Dorothea had already experienced the workings and effects of this kind of love for many years before its name was revealed to her for the first time just four weeks before her death. In fact, by that time she already had a far more extensive experience with it and understanding of it than she could communicate to others.

She had felt it especially in five kinds of manifestations or effects:

1. She felt how through this love she became inflamed more ardently in both body and soul than through any other. In this condition she exuded a powerful spiritual flame far stronger than any real fire fanned by a severe wind.

2. She recognized that this love instigated a turbulent, insatiable desire to love God with all her might and to possess him fully.

3. She clearly discerned the ardent fire ignited by this love which set her body and soul ablaze and her own passionate, immodest, insatiable desire to love and possess God as consequences of this particular kind of love rather than any other. Her soul became greedy to reach God as quickly as possible, like a person driven by fiery passion who is not ashamed of running through a crowd of people to be embraced by the beloved in front of perfect strangers. She said to her confessor B: "My desire to love God is so immodest that I am afraid it might be inappropriate here as well as in eternity. My dearest Lord has commanded me to say that he has given me such a severe, heartbreaking love that I neither know what to do nor how to behave, for no matter what I do, nothing satisfies my cravings."

4. She felt herself filled with immeasurable sweetness and insatiable inebriation. Because of this she would have liked to die at once without caring

about the nature of her death, just as long as she were really being killed, even if she were being cut into tiny little pieces. She felt such hot frenzy that she would have gladly prayed for such a death or would have purchased it had doing so been seemly behavior.

5. She felt the impact of this love in a strong, powerful pull through which her soul was drawn forcefully toward eternal life and felt clearly how much she loved the Lord and how the Lord loved her more exuberantly still. Because of these experiences she developed an unquenchable thirst to love God and an unsatisfied hunger to be united with God and enjoy him. In her greed to love God she gladly would have spent the strength of heart of a thousand people without a moment's hesitation to fulfill her desire. Consequently, the vast power of this love caused her heart to beat and tremble wildly. It pulled and drained the strength of her heart so often and so fiercely that her heart would have broken had the Lord not prevented it. But he prevented the shattering of her heart only until the time he had appointed as her time of death, now through profuse sweating and weeping, now through rapture, at other times through conversation with her soul or by inspiring her to love certain persons he brought to her attention. From time to time the Lord placed other things between himself and Dorothea to relax the tension of her heart and so prevented her heart from breaking in response to this great love. He did this for the reasons he told her: "Even when I grant you my heartbreaking love you shall nevertheless remain among the living, though this is only possible through my protection." Another time he said: "With the depth of the love I have for you I force you to love me as much as you can. If I wanted to, I could and would love you with such ardor that your heart would break at once." This he revealed as if to say "you must not presume that this heartbreaking love originates in you without my special influence."

Her spiritual hunger for the sacrament of the body of Our Lord
and how she received it for the last time.

Chapter XL.

Daily the desire for Our Lord burned in this blessed friend of God,[38] to receive him in spirit and in the sacrament, and whenever she had received him, her desire for eternal life flared up immeasurably. To offer her soul untainted to God, she washed and bathed her soul daily in hot tears of contrition. In truth, her regret over her sins; her desire brought on by hot, burning love; and her hunger and thirst for Our Lord Jesus and his praiseworthy body caused her to weep bitter tears daily, sigh continuously, moan longingly, and grieve piteously. She did this with such abandon that she filled the ears of her gracious lover Jesus and those of her confessor and so inclined them to fulfill her desires mercifully. Jesus, the most gracious lord, rushed to her quickly in the sacrament; her confessor B out of compassion for her plight, hurried to come to her aid as soon as possible.

Even though her burning desire and agony for Our Lord were severe every day, they were much more so on the last day of her life. That day shortly after midnight as mass was about to start and she had confessed her sins, she sobbed and wept, yearning fiercely for the soul's nourishment to satisfy her spiritual hunger. Finally, because of her ravenous craving she could not tolerate waiting any longer. Contrary to her habit, she pushed her head through the window of her cell so that her confessor B would be able to absolve her even more speedily, confer her penance even more rapidly, and then give her the sacrament without further delay, which he did for he well understood what she meant and asked. How devoutly, tenderly, ruefully, passionately, greedily, and affectionately she received the Lord I can't possibly convey; it all was boundless. As soon as she received the praiseworthy sacrament she quieted down, enjoyed great comfort and calm, and her soul, now in ecstasy, was deeply united with God. Later she came

---

[38] Johannes uses the term *gotisfrundynne*, the feminine form of the term often applied to the Rhineland mystics in the circle of Meister Eckhart.

to, full of joy on account of divine pleasures and spent the day in her customary praiseworthy manner without physical weakness or illness. Here is to be noted that she had never before forced her head through that window or the grating of her cell. Her doing so was a clear sign of her extreme, passionate, uncontrollable need.

How her confessor B spoke to her for the last time;

how on the last day of her life her craving for

the holy sacrament of Our Lord Jesus

compelled her to ask for it a second time.

Chapter XLI.

Now that the hour of her natural death was near, the fire of divine love started to burn more fiercely and the heartbreaking love started to assault her heart more violently with searing passion, the love which the Lord had prophesied would break her heart though she would die with her mind intact. In truth, she was wounded in soul, heart, and her entire body by the rays and arrows of love. For even though these wounds were spiritual in nature, they produced violent, bitter physical pains throughout her body. The Lord had an inexpressibly bitter effect on her. She felt severely oppressed and suffered greater, more bitter pains and pangs than she had endured while giving birth to her children. There was nothing miraculous about this, however. After all, as the Lord had predicted many times, she now was to deliver her soul into eternal life with more severe and bitter pains than when she bore her children into this transitory life.

Through divine illumination, the honorable servant and bride of God now discerned that the hour stood at her door when the Lord in the company of his adored mother and many saints was to come to fetch her as he had promised. She had implored him many times before then to protect her at her death and not to permit robbers to despoil her of the wealth she was to receive through his grace. The Lord had assured her that she was not to worry, for he himself would be with her together with his dear mother and many saints and would take her soul from her mouth to lead her into life everlasting.

At this hour she sent for her confessor B to attend her. When he arrived, she made three noteworthy statements to him. The first: "I feel excruciating pain because the Lord has wounded my heart and limbs through and through with the rays and arrows of his love, which he shot without ceasing into my heart, arms, back and shoulders, and all about my heart. I move about like a woman about to give birth and can find neither rest nor leisure sitting, walking, standing up or lying down." She spoke as if to indicate to him "the time has now come of which I told you earlier, the time when I am to deliver my soul into eternal life."

Her other statement to B was this: "If you were illuminated by divine light to behold the joy of the saints in life everlasting, your heart would be torn apart by desire and longing. I see heaven near and opened wide, and the delight of the saints is revealed to me. The path to heaven lies before me, straight and unobstructed. Nothing but death itself keeps me from entering." Her confessor, upon hearing this, replied: "Dear mother, pray for me that I may behold the bliss of the saints after this life. It is because I am not worthy that I cannot see what you see." Who would not yearn to enter heaven upon beholding the joy of heaven? He too would say with St. Peter: "Lord, here it is good living."

When she had spoken to her confessor for about two hours, flaming desire and spiritual hunger for the soul's sustenance and the living bread overpowered her. So Dorothea who throughout their conversation had been standing by the iron grate of her cell now moved right against it and knelt down. Sighing deeply, she voiced her need to God and said to her confessor: "Please give me my adored Lord, that is the sacrament of Our Lord, for through love of him I cannot do without him any longer." As she said this, she appeared small and frail. Her mouth was so dry that her tongue stuck to the roof of her mouth. Her confessor recognized this hunger and weakness as the same spiritual need she had suffered many times previously. He kindly encouraged her to drink something refreshing since she had already received the Lord that day and he, therefore, could not bring her the sacrament again.

But Dorothea replied: "I can't bear to partake of food and drink" and did not stop begging him to give her the body of Our Lord. Finally her confessor said: "Dear mother, since I have already given it to you today, I dare not do so again. You must wait until after midnight. As soon as the hymn *Te Deum laudamus* starts, I will bring you the precious sacrament." He commented on the unusual nature of her request, reiterating what the Lord himself had told her when she moved into her cell, that she was to be content to receive the sacrament once each day. Dorothea, greedy for God, responded, sighing deeply: "I don't know how I will be able to wait that long" as if to say: "Waiting that long is impossible for me--too bitter, too hard." Her confessor did not discern the immediacy of death in her words because several times before this she had also hungered to enjoy the sacrament a second time. Never before, however, had she actually asked to receive it again.

How her confessor B found her dead after mass,

and how her death had been prophesied exactly as it did happen.

Chapter XLII.

After having spoken these words, Dorothea seated herself and discussed a few practical matters with her confessor. She told him nothing of her impending death. When he said that it was now time for him to leave, she acted as if she would have liked him to remain with her a little longer, although she did not say so. He bade her good night, bowed toward her, asked to be included in her prayers, and then left to take part in the compline services about to begin. Looking back over his shoulder, he noticed her longing glance following him as if to say: "If you, dearest son and father, knew what I know, you would stay with me a little longer." Indeed, he would have gladly remained with her had he only known death to be so close that it would claim her within three hours after his departure.

Right after midnight, during the hymn *Te Deum laudamus* her confessor B returned, just as he had promised, to give her the body of Our Lord Jesus

Christ. He found her dead though at first he did not realize that she had departed for a more blessed saintly existence. Since her cell was so quiet, he assumed she was in rapture, as he had encountered her many times before. So he returned to the choir. After mass he went back once more, listening, peering into her cell, finally lighting up her cell to give her the wholesome nourishment, anticipating her passionate desire for it which he had witnessed so many times before. As he kept listening and glancing about without observing the slightest sign of life, however, he sadly realized at last that she indeed was dead from heartbreaking love, just as the Lord had revealed to her earlier when, long before her death, he commanded her to say to her confessor B: "I have often heard from my most beloved Lord and have been promised that I shall die in sound mind. Should it happen that I die with my mind in disarray, which God does not want to happen, you need to be very worried that this happened because I did not thank my beloved Lord sufficiently nor was appropriately grateful, or that some secret evil lodged within me. Should it happen, though, that I die suddenly without anyone being aware of it, know that I did so as a result of great love and extreme desire and that the Lord brought it about miraculously. If that should be the case, you shall rejoice in God."

Now, you readers and listeners of this book, mark how the Lord has predicted her death for more than six months before it actually took place and that she should die with all her mental faculties intact. In fact, he had already predicted all this four years before her death. To make sure she understood all of this clearly, he had often made this prediction elsewhere in his revelations and in a variety of ways. In one instance he said this: "You shall die just as I have revealed to you. You will not die from any physical infirmity but from debilitating love and in full possession of all your senses." In many other revelations the Lord Jesus Christ said in addition to all this written here that her heart would break of love and longing when she died.

At this point it is worthwhile to know that as she was dying, the spotless, humble Dorothea positioned herself on her cot differently from the way she ever had before by placing her head toward sunset and her feet toward sunrise, the way the dead are placed in their graves. She had closed her eyes, her right hand cradling her right cheek. Her left arm was extended to her belt, her hand dangling from her cot. She was lying on her right side as if she were sleeping peacefully, dressed in her gown and veil, the habit in which she wished to be buried, with her body and feet covered modestly. From all this one can deduce that she expected to die upon retiring for the night, especially since as long as she had inhabited her cell she had never positioned herself in this manner but had always lain with her head at sunrise and her feet pointing to the sunset. Furthermore, it is well to know that no mortal creature witnessed her death, just the Lord in the company of many saints had promised her so often. It is also to be presumed that through God's special dispensation she did not receive extreme unction since she was to die free of physical illness and the sacrament of extreme unction is to be administered to the physically afflicted rather than those who are physically sound, even as they journey to death.

Her praiseworthy funeral.

Chapter XLIII.

Johannes, the honorable father and lord, bishop of Pomesania, appeared as soon as he heard of her death to attend her burial. He gave alms aplenty to the poor and organized a great celebration in her honor. He ordered masses for her soul for two full consecutive days and celebrated the funeral rites in person. With all due solemnity and the dignity due a great treasure, he returned Dorothea's body to the earth in the same chapel where the bishops are laid to rest. These ceremonies were attended by the canons, many priests, clerics, devout lay people both ignorant and learned, men and women in great number who all devoutly and dutifully surrounded the bier bearing her body, that vessel of so many mighty and holy works. There was much grieving and lamenting among all present, but especially among her spiritual children.

During her funeral mass her confessor B preached about her strict life, which she had conducted in complete virtue. Until that moment much of it was unknown to those present, especially her wounds, spiritual exercises, self-mutilations, revelations, the exchange of hearts, and the numberless other great mercies and good deeds the Lord had bestowed on her. As they heard all this, they were amazed by such great sanctity kept secret while she lived. Many of them wept copiously on account of not having known anything about it. Through God's grace there were many among them who from then on improved their lives and declared that never before in their lives had they been so moved and able to weep so much. She was committed to the earth with all appropriate respect and honor during the vigil of Sts. Peter and Paul [June 29]. Before that, during the night of the feast of the two holy martyrs St. John and St. Paul [June 26], she had been found dead in her cell in the year of Our Lord one thousand three-hundred and ninety-four.

How God venerated her and how we are to thank him.

Chapter XLIV.

Dorothea's burial followed God's plan. He makes the poor wealthy if he so desires, elevates the destitute and despised according to his will, and raises the humble. Look up! She has been elevated to eternal glory who here debased herself and fled the glory of this world. There the Lord of eternal glory has granted her eternal rest for the temporal labors she performed here--life in exchange for death, the realm of the heavenly father for this misery, delight in place of sadness, eternal freedom in exchange for the prison of her cell, dominion for service, unlimited treasure for poverty, the mountain of joy and fulfillment of all her desires in place of the vale of tears and need-- all this accompanied by such immeasurable wealth that no human mind may comprehend it. For these reasons all true Christians must rejoice with me and praise and honor the Lord of eternal glory for having taken the praiseworthy martyr Dorothea where she will never have to endure any suffering whatsoever but enjoy nothing but pure, everlasting delight.

We must also praise and honor the Lord and thank him profusely that he in our time would visit such profound grace on his elected bride Dorothea as is described in this book, and for having given her to us as a helper, intercessor, and peacemaker between him and us. Now let us all pray together devoutly: "Lord Jesus Christ, we thank you as best we can for having sent us your wholesome fruit Dorothea. May we be able to praise you fittingly and thank you for all you have done for us through her and will do in the future. We would gladly do this at all times. Unfortunately, though, we are incapable of doing so and would not be deserving of your grace even if the entire heavenly host thanked you with us. Therefore, so our thanks be pleasing to the heavenly father, Our Lord, we beg our most merciful Lord Jesus, his only begotten son, to make himself and all his accomplishments our sacrifice to his heavenly father as an acceptable offer of thanks. May the Father, the Son, and the Holy Spirit assist us in accomplishing this. Amen."

Here begins the fourth book.

The blessed Dorothea experienced many beautiful revelations, many great intimations of the effects of Our Lord's grace, and an even greater love for God and her fellow man, of which is to be written for the first time in the fourth book. After that the honorable, praiseworthy sacrament of Our Lord's body will be discussed.

Divine love has thirty-seven degrees and names. To speak, write, hear and read of love is delightful and merry and tastes delicious to all those who possess true love. The blessed anchoress Dorothea, the great, true lover of God, proved this very well. She very much liked to speak and hear others speak of the abundance of divine love, and to hear it preached or read. Of this love she differentiated thirty-seven names or degrees which the Lord had taught her to speak about and had taught her to express toward him.

1. The first degree and name of this love is the incomparable, immeasurable love, for we are to love God above all things in such a manner as not to esteem anything more dearly, more highly, or equal to him, nor love it as much. One should rather put aside and do without all creatures before doing without God. This is the fundamental condition for loving God without which no love can exist. Dorothea fulfilled not only this condition but also the second condition basic to the perfection of love: not to love any creature except through God and for God's sake to avoid being preoccupied with winning or protecting perishable things. This kind of love overwhelmed her so completely that it was painful to her to concern herself with earthly things. Accordingly, she was

tormented by wearing and possessing expensive clothes, as has been recorded earlier in the first book.

2. Dorothea's name for the second kind of love is long-lasting love because this love is not satisfied to love God for a week or a year or only in prosperity. To the contrary: this love wants to love God to the same degree, in prosperity and adversity, whether things go according to her will or not.

3. The third name of love, or better, the third kind of love to be discussed now and later is called broad love because God's love not only wants to love exclusively and forever but also reaches one's friends and one's enemies to love them too.

4. After this comes the wide, inclusive love which is not satisfied loving God and one's fellow man at all times but beyond them wishes to love to perfection everything worthy of being loved, as, for example, God, who is Lord over us; that which is next to us, such as our fellow creatures; things beneath us, such as our bodies. Everything that is part of these above-mentioned four things this love wants to love appropriately and for this reason it is wide love.

5. The fifth kind of love is called limitless love because this love not only wants to love God and all human beings now alive but all those who have lived or will be alive in the future. All those this love wants to love with God at all times -- eternally and without end. For true love does not want to end but eternally seeks to love God and all he desires to be loved.

6. The sixth consisting of both broad and wide love is active love because in spirit this love sees everything far and wide and in contemplation explores the ailments and needs of mankind. This love is busy bringing aid to those in need through prayer, words or works because it is merciful and full of pity.

7. The seventh is called constant or unending love for true love is not idle but active and busy, practicing the labors of love unceasingly. As long as it exists, true love never ceases, just as fire burns while it lasts.

8. The eighth love is the deep-rooted love which has sunk deeply into the soul of the person who has practiced the labor of love often and for a long time.

9. After this, love grows strong, capable of not only loving and succoring friends but enemies too. Strong, courageous love endures natural death for God's sake and kills off beastly existence and all worldly and fleshly desires. This love also performs many other great, difficult tasks, such as inspiring people to wound themselves in a variety of ways and to impose discomfort on themselves through vigils, fasts, and prayer, and to endure poverty, scorn, destruction, cursing and wicked deeds not just patiently but joyfully. For these reasons, this love is appropriately called strong and courageous.

10. The tenth love is called firm, uncompromising love because it is rooted so firmly and deeply that no opposition can hinder its works. It is capable of bearing and enduring anything: praise and condemnation or cursing, good or bad reputation, wealth and poverty, health and disease, preferment and neglect, friendship and enmity, life and death. Firm love does not permit itself to become separated from God's love by hatred, fear, disgrace, bribes, or anything else. For this reason it is aptly named firm, uncompromising love.

11. The eleventh love is the hot, burning love, so named because any person in this state of love is set ablaze by the fire of divine love and on account of this inflammation will sweat and weep; will be illuminated and capable of performing great deeds, able to suffer for God's sake. This love originates in the one preceding it when people exert themselves in the labors of love for such a long time that they become hot and hotter until they ignite.

12. The twelfth love is the steaming love which originates in the burning love, for when people burn often, they become inflamed through and through. Their strength is disrupted and softened like something made pliable through fire. Then a hot breath issues from the heart through the mouth until the entire body emits a vapor much like a boiling kettle. Such people shed many burning tears too.

13. The thirteenth kind is humbly-desirous love. What this love desires it desires for the self and others and makes people beg and weep. This love does not seek individual comfort but is inclined to search vigorously for the common

good. For this reason this kind of love is not without desire. However humble, love desires good, virtuous, and holy things; and the greater especially the hot, burning and the steaming love are, the greater the desire they produce will be, for desire springs especially from these two.

14. Desire, in turn, increases at the same rate as does the heat of love, ultimately turning into passionately desirous love, which is love number fourteen and on account of which human beings come to desire great things for themselves and others. Steeped in this kind of love, Dorothea desired so fiercely to enter eternal life that she became terrified. Her head drooped, and through this consuming hot desire tears gushed from her eyes.

15. The fifteenth love is the high-flaming love because, if one has experienced hot desire for a long time, it becomes a flame that rises way up high and does not rest until it has grasped the ultimate, the highest desirable good, which is God. How high and how far Dorothea was drawn through this kind of love and how her soul, rid of all creation, was united only with God, may be too lengthy and complicated for the readers to hear. Therefore I leave this and the many other praiseworthy effects of this and other types of love unrecorded here. I have written much about them in my Latin work.[39] Those who are interested may follow up on them there.

16. The sixteenth love is the mighty love, which overwhelms the soul far beyond her nature by drawing her high above herself in ecstatic rapture. It is also called "mighty" because in its desire and effect it becomes powerful enough to compel the almighty God to descend from his highest throne and fulfill a person's most ardent desire.

17. The seventeenth is called wounded love, not because love herself is wounded but because she wounds a person's heart and soul with the arrows, rays, or spears of love. When the soul is thus captured, ruled, and overpowered by the

---

[39] Johannes is referring to the third work in his so-called trilogy, the *Septililium venerabilis dominae Dorotheae Montoviensis*, which forms the basis of Book IV of *Leben*. See notes 2 and 27 for more details.

passion of her lover Jesus that she can't control her own desire for him, she can't help but signal the heat of this passion in various ways. That the heart is wounded through and through with love and longs desperately for the Lord is made evident through sighs, profuse sweating brought on by hot, burning love, and hours of copious moaning and weeping. Sometimes all that weeping produces paroxysms of sobs and violent choking.

18. The eighteenth love is called restless love for making people wounded by love restless. Their being so severely wounded makes them run this way and that, in search of him whom their souls love wherever and whenever the opportunity to do so presents itself. But while love is incapable of harnessing passion and keeps on searching everywhere for the object of her desire, the Lord does not allow himself to be encountered that readily. Consequently, the soul becomes restless from this state of affairs.

19. The nineteenth is called impatient love, the product of the long, unsuccessful search for the beloved. The result of searching without finding is that love becomes dissatisfied or displeased with everything she encounters, convinced that everything not furthering the fulfillment of her desire is utterly useless. Clearly, after the long impatient wait for the most beloved and highest good, love lapses into praiseworthy impatience.

20. The twentieth is the irrational, riotous love, which is present whenever a person because of exuberant, fierce passion for the Lord weeps inconsolably, neither listens to advice nor follows reason, and does not accept any comfort from anyone but considers what people offer as consolation as its very opposite. Worse, any such consolation appears contemptible or cumbersome because the yearning for God is so intense that the lover of God refuses all things in favor of him who is the heart's desire. Therefore, such a person also pays no heed to the acquisition or preservation of temporal things. The world, not surprisingly, regards such people as fools and idiots.

21. The twenty-first is the sweet love that sweetly loves the Lord without turning bitter toward those who hate or attack her, for this love is filled with

divine sweetness by him who first lets himself be pursued with many tears, cryings, and moanings but at last makes himself available to be tasted in all his sweetness.

22. The twenty-second love is greedy love. In her greed this love wishes to do everything to live a holy life, to love and enjoy the Lord totally, for she has tasted and enjoyed his sweetness through his sweet love and knows how pleasurable it is to be with him. Once awakened and directed toward God, this love grows ever more eager: the more she tastes his sweetness and his grace, the more her greed increases. This resembles criminal greed, which grows in proportion to the wealth it amasses. In the same fashion people become greedier for God: the more they enjoy him the more they long for him.

23. The twenty-third is insatiable love. Our beloved Lord, after having removed himself from a person to let himself be pursued greedily with many tears, long vigils, devout prayer, and many virtuous deeds and exercises -- all performed in hot desire, at last allows himself to be found, grasped, and tasted once more. But not for long. On the contrary: as his seekers believe to hold him, they find that he has extricated himself yet again to arouse still more fervent desire, greed, and hunger for him in the soul and thus inspire a still more diligent search. This is to make sure that when he is found once more, his lovers will hold on to him still more tightly and keep him even more carefully than before. Even so, he does not tarry long, removing himself again as before. This pattern of allowing himself to be found only to remove himself again God continues until he has raised the soul to a level of insatiable hunger and desire. Consequently, the soul unceasingly searches for her lover for nourishment and satisfaction. But here on Earth the soul can never be totally satisfied, for our dear Lord does not allow himself to be grasped and tasted to satisfy the soul but to awaken hunger and appetite for him.

24. The twenty-fourth is the languishing, debilitating love. This love languishes for God because of the effusively fierce longing and insatiable desire the soul feels for God. The soul desires no satisfaction from any creature or anything but God, and whatever the soul receives as medicine or nourishment

merely increases her torment. This saps a person's strength; he becomes so weak that he loses control over his body. The soul, ailing in love may say: "Tell my body that I languish for love."

25. The twenty-fifth love, inebriated love, so intoxicates a person's spirit that this drunkenness spills over into the body. The face becomes ruddy and the heart merry, unmindful of worldly possessions, reputation, or life. A person thus inebriated stumbles like a drunk and would happily die for God's sake. As the Lord revealed to his servant Dorothea whom he frequently intoxicated, this drunkenness has its origins in two kinds of drink. The first libation the Lord gives to the soul is sweet and gentle to make her tipsy. He keeps plying the soul with it until she is drunk. It is while she is in this state that the soul first experiences rapture. Now, while in rapture, God offers her the other drink, called the strong drink. At first he pours just a little sip. But then he serves more and more of it to bring about a different kind of spiritual inebriation, which the Lord calls insufficient drunkenness.

Of both types of drunkenness the Lord has revealed much to Dorothea, yet he provided much more actual experience by letting her feel their effects on her or recognize them in other ways. Whenever she had languished long in insatiable desire and hunger for him, her strength had been consumed, and she had tormented herself, he came at last to make her hunger no longer. Then he gave himself generously and graciously gave her to drink of his sweetness until he had make her drunk. At times he kept her in this state of spiritual inebriation for a month, sometimes for a quarter for a year or more, sometimes less.

26. The twenty-sixth is called rich because this love enriches the soul with the great, precious treasures the Lord bestows on her during spiritual drunkenness. Sometimes a soul in that condition ascends far only to descend more inebriated still, laden with gifts. This love pays no heed to worldly goods but considers them trash. Rather, she is careful to garner spiritual wealth and seeks to suffer poverty, scorn, and torment for the sake of him whom she loves and who is the true and the highest treasure of all. Clearly, this love is rich.

27. The twenty-seventh is called exhilarating love. The soul in possession of true spiritual wealth through sincere contrition and penitence has rid her conscience of all punishable offenses, determined to suffer for God's sake anything he may send or impose on her, be it damage, dishonor, scorn, or any other kind of suffering. Such a soul may very well hope and trust that the Lord will not abandon her but keep and protect her from sin, gracing her with his merciful presence. From this unwavering trust and love for God the soul derives much comfort and joy in God to gladden her greatly. It is easy to understand why those in possession of true love generally love everyone.

28. The twenty-eighth is the gushing love. Because of the wealth described earlier, the soul sometimes is filled with such great abundance that sweetness floods the soul, forcing her to expand. Finally, though, love spills over, first into the heart, then, when the heart is overflowing, too, into the entire body. Thus soul and body are gladdened and filled with spreading sweetness.

29. The twenty-ninth is called the overflowing love. Emanating from the soul flooded with spiritual wealth, joys, and sweetness -- so fragrant to the soul as they gladden, nourish, and fill her to overflowing -- the sweetness of this love not only flows into the body but also pours out on others, causing the soul to love them with great sweetness as well. Through this kind of love all inner senses feel and experience great happiness and joy, full of spiritual wealth, each to the degree appropriate to its nature. On account of this abundance of divine sweetness, people believe heaven and Earth to be flowing into one another, certain that all mankind is filled with love and without blemish.

30. The thirtieth is called the wise or sensible love and is closely related to the kinds of love described so far. For if people were not wise, they might exhaust themselves by laboring foolishly in their fasts, vigils, self-castigations, and spiritual exercises and lose their reason. Therefore wise love is a separate kind of love, mistress over the others and their protection and guardian.

31. The thirtieth-first, invincible love, is commonly called by that name when the internal powers are so great and so strongly endowed that they become

insuperable.   What will not yield to sensible strength fortified by wise love? What temporal wealth will not be vanquished by passionate strength filled with spiritual wealth and desire through overflowing love?   And what might raging strength tempered by inebriated love and fortified by powerful and mighty love not overcome?

32. The thirty-second love is the inexhaustible love which arises directly from invincible love.   God's sweetness lends her such strength that she can perform any task and endure anything for his sake.

33. The thirty-third is the inseparable love which unites the soul with God so intimately and powerfully to make her one spirit with him.   Through this love the soul considers it easier and less difficult to separate herself from the body than from her bridegroom, Our Lord.

34. The thirty-fourth is the love that can never be lost.   Because of her great strength, she cleaves so strongly unto God as to become inseparable from him and thus is able and willing to endure hunger, thirst, cold, heat, poverty, riches, ostracism, envy, hatred. This love declares: "I have found him who loves my soul.   I will not leave him until he brings me into his kingdom."

35. The thirty-fifth is the undying love. The kinds of love described so far cause the soul to die to the love of the world, the flesh, the evil spirit, sins and vices.   Then, through the effects of this love, the soul, like Christ, who is her life and for whom alone she lives, rises from death with him and with him becomes immortal, for how could the soul die inseparably united to God her life by refusing to be apart from him?

36. The thirty-sixth is a bold, daring love that surpasses the thirty- five degrees of love described so far.   Because of its extent it has often been called the inexpressible love by the master of the great lover Dorothea.   This phase of love transforms human beings in ways that make them immortal, immune to suffering, and all-powerful.   Upon suffering violence or injustice, they behave as though they can neither feel nor recognize that it is unjust.   They show themselves friends to all people.   Like St. Paul they make themselves accessible to enemies and

friends alike to win them all equally. The fire of this love also prevents them from observing appropriate behavior in every situation. They place themselves like a wall before their brothers and in a sense even dare to defy God when they do like St. Paul, who asked to be separated from Christ for the sake of his brothers, or like Moses who, ravished by this love, asked the Lord to "forgive this people its trespasses or eradicate my name from the book in which you have written it." Obviously, then, this love brings it about that a man dares do and suffer what is far beyond him. For this reason this love is also called exuberant love.

37. The thirty-seventh and final degree of love is the heartbreaking love, so named for its effect. The love of God from the first to this thirty-seventh degree has so increased in strength as to overwhelm the body. This love has acquired the searing heat necessary to devour the body's naturally accumulated fluids. This love destroys the heart's resilience by pulling and stretching it until it bursts. This love ignites and fans the fire of grace until it rages fiercely enough to kill man's natural life and transport the soul into the life of everlasting glory. May the Lord help bring us to that end through the love of him who has revealed these degrees and names of love and who has taught his elected bride Dorothea, his passionate lover, to demonstrate them in her works and words. May she also deign to purchase for us the boon never to be separated either from God or his love. Amen.

The second part of the fourth book is about
the mission of the Holy Spirit.

Why the Holy Spirit was sent so frequently to the blessed Dorothea;
what messengers to send to the Holy Ghost;
the condition a person must achieve
to receive the Holy Spirit often.

Chapter I.

The Holy Ghost was often sent to the blessed Dorothea because of Jesus Christ's grace and mercy, who spoke to her thus: "I will often send you the Holy Ghost, day or night, whether you are lying down or sitting up, so he may prepare you for me and mortify your flesh and make you spiritual.... No one can mortify the flesh as those to whom I send my Holy Spirit for he is truly the slayer of the flesh and the reviver of the spirit. I send him to you so he may see how you are, gladden your heart, and help you pass the time. For how else could you remain free of vexation if the comforter, my Holy Spirit, were not with you?" From these words one may gather how graciously the Lord treated his maiden Dorothea to whom he so often sent the Holy Spirit as a comfort.

The Lord also taught her which messengers to send after the Holy Ghost to enjoy his aid more frequently still: "There are two types of people who, accordingly, send two different kinds of messengers to the Holy Spirit. The first are the holy and blessed; they send five messengers: hot, burning love; inexhaustible love; hot, steaming love; and a praiseworthy, passionate desire. The hot, steaming love must be so powerful as to make seekers of the Holy Spirit shed copious tears and sweat profusely. On account of the intense heat of divine love, thick steam will issue from the mouth as from a boiling kettle, and all physical strength will be stretched and tightened from their labors like the strings of a musical instrument. There are many messengers no one can employ who is not well prepared. But those who can shall desire nothing but me.

"Those who cannot command these worthy messengers have others to send to the Holy Spirit, namely stricter, more numerous fasts, more frequent prayer, more generous almsgiving, more strident self-castigations and genuflections, and more devout preparation for prayer; and if they are priests, a far more careful preparation for mass than they commonly observe. Beyond these preparations they shall yearn for the Holy Spirit day and night and constantly implore me, their God, to send him. For I will send the Holy Spirit after mass if they keep themselves in readiness for him, and they shall enjoy him in a way they never felt or tasted before." Through these words the Lord indicates how those to whom he wishes to send the Holy Spirit often are to prepare themselves. They are to experience a tremendous increase and elevation in their spiritual life. For this reason the Lord also insisted that they shall not be encumbered by external matters. They shall be dead to sin and the world, cleaving unto the Lord, begging for eternal life.

Here are recorded seven ways in which the mission
of the Holy Spirit was first revealed to Dorothea.

Chapter II.

After the removal of her old heart the Lord taught Dorothea how to confess all her sins until she received assurance from the Holy Spirit that they were all forgiven. The Holy Spirit was sent to her often, and the first thing he taught her was to recognize his presence by revealing the seven ways of coming to her. First, she felt his presence in a hot love that set her afire. Another time she felt him through a great holy joy of divine rather than natural origin. In a third way she perceived his arrival in a gentle breeze full of delectable sweetness filling her body and soul, which often made her ecstatic. Fourthly she felt him in the erudite lessons he conducted to teach her the Christian way of life according to the commandments and utterances of the Lord. In the fifth instance he appeared with severe punishments when she had not done what he had taught her to do or had not left undone what he had taught her not to do. He took her to task on each of these, one after the other. In the sixth instance he was sent to her with dire warnings. If she had not totally done or left undone what the Lord had taught her to do or refrain from doing and had already been punished for her disobedience once or twice, he threatened her beyond measure and reprimanded her once again for trespasses he had already punished earlier, as has been described already in Book II. Whenever the Holy Spirit threatened her or punished her with such severity, she wept piteously for a long time, begging him to forgive her until she finally gained his pardon. In the seventh instance the Holy Ghost approached her with great commotion and fearsome noise, as if the whole building were about to collapse on her. At that time her external senses were closed and her inner senses opened. In that condition she would have been unable to get up, stand, or move about. In fact, she would have died then and there had the Lord not provided special assistance by reducing the abundance of the Holy Spirit's effect on her. In this manner she was passionately inflamed, illuminated, and wounded by the rays of love and enjoyed such profusion of spiritual wealth that she was incapable of expressing even the twentieth part of it.

How the Holy Spirit was sent to Dorothea in a variety of ways.

Chapter III.

Even though the Lord is singular in his nature, he is infinitely varied in his effects, which he has amply demonstrated through the manifold missions of the Holy Spirit whom he sent to the blessed Dorothea in such abundance of ways that I don't know whether anyone could account for them all or record them fully. For sometimes he sent him to her ten times daily, sometimes nine, on other days eight or seven times, but generally five or four or three times each day. Generally speaking, the Lord sent her the Holy Spirit once or twice daily for many years within the nine or ten years before her death. Often these missions occurred through the hot, burning or steaming love; the humbly desirous, passionately desirous, or mighty love; wounding, restless, impatient, or irrational, riotous love. At other times the Holy Spirit was sent to her with sweet love, gushing, greedy, or insatiable love; with inebriated love, overflowing love, or inexhaustible love. At still other times he appeared with still other kinds of love or in various degrees of a given type of love.

Here is to be known that any love attending God's mission of the Holy Spirit succeeded in her task. For whenever the Holy Spirit was sent to Dorothea with two, three, four, five, six, seven, eight, nine, ten or eleven kinds of love, as happened frequently, the degrees or kinds of love all accomplished their aim, at times all together, at times in combinations of two or three. Sometimes each worked individually, one after the other. But that was less common, for when they were sent together, they generally all worked together too. Here is also to be noted that the Holy Spirit not only was sent with the kinds of love mentioned and described above but also with great joy, appropriate gifts, clear illumination, deep humility, severe mortification of Dorothea's will and senses, with a passionate desire to be ignored or disclaimed as unworthy, and many other virtues.

The manner in which the Lord worked his merciful deeds in her is to be taken to heart even more. His missions of the Holy Spirit were so extraordinary and of such variety that the Lord made Dorothea consult with her two confessors B and P about them: "Ask them whether they have read or heard of any saint dwelling with me in heaven ever having experienced anything similar to what I make happen to you. Whoever will read about my merciful companionship with you, which they [B and P] have recorded, may certainly feel inspired toward self-improvement." This is not to be construed that the Lord meant to imply there had never been a saint to whom he sent the Holy Spirit as often as he did to her. Rather, God meant to suggest that he sent the Holy Ghost to her so often that they had not read the like about any other saint. And indeed they never had read this about any other saint even though it did happen. For this reason it astonished them all the more.

> How Dorothea, in the state of pure illumination,
>
> understood many secret things.
>
> Chapter IV.

The Holy Spirit inflamed and cleansed Dorothea of her sins. Through constant exercise of virtue he led her to the purification of her heart and inspired her receptiveness for divine illumination and discernment of secrets hidden from the sages of this world. Some of these are described here. It happened often that she could see into her own soul as she might see through a clear crystal or glass, to see all sins and stains in her soul, no matter how small. She often observed how even the tiniest sins and stains settled on her soul like dust motes dancing on a sunbeam without her being able to prevent it, no matter how hard she wept and shed hot tears. From time to time, when it pleased the Lord, she also saw all the sins she had ever committed and all the good deeds she had left undone, which caused her to weep copiously in abject humility. Such insights she often had into other people's sins as well, recognizing their desires and thoughts. Some of them learned details about these things from her -- what their words, desires, and thoughts were.

I say all this in God's praise and honor, for I know that she spoke to many people about sins they had committed many years earlier. And she has told me, too, what I thought and coveted long ago, even though I had never revealed anything to anyone in word or deed so that she could not possibly have heard anything about it. She also saw people designated for eternal life, though she did not identify them by name or in any other way because she was not permitted to do so. Also, she often saw people with her inner eyes whom she never saw with her external eyes. Thus she even saw much wealth in the hands of exalted spiritual personages far away and unknown to her personally. She frequently knew when someone had made a true or false confession, and many other such secrets too numerous to record she discerned in the light of God and her own illumination by the Holy Spirit. Now let us pray to the Holy Spirit, of whom we have utmost need, that we may journey in his illumination to the everlasting light. May he help us in this quest with Our heavenly Father and his only begotten Son, Jesus Christ Our Lord. Amen.

The third part of the fourth book treats of
the praiseworthy body of Our Lord Jesus Christ.

How Dorothea, hungry for God, felt a great need
to receive the praiseworthy sacrament
of the body of Our Lord.

Chapter I.

Through the life-giving perfume of the body of Our Lord the blessed
Dorothea from childhood until death felt an intense need to see and receive the
body of Our Lord Jesus Christ. No matter how often she saw it, she remained
eager to see it again, even if she had done so a hundred times already. Her
hunger to receive it often became so fierce that she could not sleep and could
scarcely await the day she was to receive the wholesome sustenance. Then, when
that day finally came, she sometimes could not sleep at all the night before
because of her great joy or extreme spiritual hunger. For this reason she kept
checking the window to see whether day was dawning. Often, because of this
great longing, she was so hungry, ill, exhausted, and weak that she had to stay in
bed. Sometimes she could not stand up, at other times she could not even pray,
and now and then she was convinced her heart would break if she did not receive
the body of Jesus Christ Our Lord.

How her great desire was a precious gift of God.

Chapter II.

Dorothea's fierce desire and spiritual hunger for the holy body of Our Lord was a special gift of God and pleasing to him, as was shown already by the example of Zachaus, who through his passionate desire compelled the Lord to come to him, as God himself pointed out by saying: "Zachaus, come down rapidly. Today I must stay in your house." In this same manner Dorothea, through her great love and desire, inclined the Lord toward her, inviting him to come to her, so that long before she died he arranged for her to receive him every day. To manifest her love and desire for him, he ordered her to say to her confessor B: "I have such love for the Lord that I would rather receive him spiritually in the sacrament than any worldly riches. If someone were to offer me all the wealth of the world while you offered me the body of my most beloved Lord, I had rather come to you, for the other's treasures would be worthless and contemptible to me. Now I thank the most gracious Lord for having granted me such great desire for him, for on this Earth he could not have given me a more precious gift. I could never have conceived such desire for him out of the strength of my own love, not ever.

"I am also to tell you this: When I tell you that I would like to receive my most beloved Lord, saying so is a small matter. But the internal torment I have to endure on account of my desire is such that I cannot explain it at all, for my heart and all my physical powers tend to labor so severely to receive the body of my most beloved Lord Jesus Christ and eternal life that I sweat as though I were immersed in a steaming hot bath. And the Lord has spoken to me thus: 'Before you receive me, you shall suffer fierce pain and hunger for me. And after having received me, you shall perform heavy labor and feel raging hunger for eternal life all that day. Those who do not exert themselves to consume and exhaust their strength before receiving me cannot experience the revival of the body that receiving me brings. And whoever does not hunger for me will not take much delight in me either, for how could anyone savor the pleasure of the meal and appreciate it sweetness without first having hungrily anticipated it? And how could anyone possibly be satisfied without taking delight in the food? Clearly, no one can anticipate my arrival joyfully without having yearned for me first.'"

The many lovely words the blessed Dorothea uttered
when the Lord came to her in the sacrament.

Chapter III.

Dorothea, fiercely desirous of the holy, praiseworthy body of Christ, received him with great honor. Her soul hurried toward him, and in spirit she loudly proclaimed many lovely endearments with which to receive the Lord. While running toward him in hot desire for him, she sometimes chanted expressions like these: "Jesus Christ, my most beloved creator," "Jesus, my most beloved redeemer;" "Jesus, my most beloved savior." At other times these: "Oh, you honorable, praiseworthy, eternal, blessed, sweet, almighty son of God!" Often this: "I thank you, most beloved Lord, that you have come to me so graciously and have given yourself to me to drink of your holy divine blood. Oh, Lord, my God, enlarge my soul now and illumine it." These and many other lovely phrases her soul used to chant with great love and desire and to recite them in a loud voice, repeating them often while she was hastening to meet the Lord and until she was deeply united with him. When this union had taken place, on the other hand, there was complete silence in her soul and complete peace. But before being united with he Lord, she was extremely restless, and her soul was often troubled about receiving the Lord properly, just as anyone about to be visited by esteemed guests would be much concerned about serving them well at all times and to honor them by paying them due respect as best he might.

How the Lord came to her in the sacrament with emotions
most pleasing to her.

Chapter IV.

The maid of God was seated in the shade of him whom she desired. His fruit was exceedingly sweet and refreshing to her spirit. This fruit she tasted in his merciful presence each time she received the body of Our Lord who came to her in many more forms than can be described. Hear first a few of the single ones followed by others combining the former.

1. With his appearance the Lord brought her great calm after the great restlessness and exertion she had felt before his arrival.

2. The Lord revitalized all the energies that had become worn and exhausted in her labors for him: he immediately restored them to make them as strong or even stronger than they had been before.

3. He brought her great sweetness in exchange for the bitterness of her body and great comfort to soothe the discomfort she had endured in her long wait for him. Even two hours or less seemed endless to her because she was weighed down heavily by raging spiritual hunger.

4. He came to her with abundant good health to drive out her ailments and with a joyous remedy to heal the wounds of her heart and soul. She often felt the strength of Our Lord surging through all her limbs, through body and soul, and how they were refreshed and gladdened by his power. Thus, what was troubled in her was gladdened, and what was bitter, sweetened. What had been wounded was healed spiritually and made so joyful as though her wounds had been anointed with an excellent healing ointment. Sometimes, when both body and soul were enjoying great sweetness and gladness, the Lord said to her: "Now you may well understand that I am all your strength , all your joy, and all your comfort. I am with you entirely. Now say: 'Lord, my God, you are all my strength, my salvation, and my blessedness.'"

5. After she had suffered extreme hunger and thirst of spirit, he brought her profound satisfaction to gratify her body and soul far better and far more joyously than if she had feasted at a sumptuous table. Here is to be noted that the gratification of the body resulted from the deluge of sweetness and passion which were poured into her soul in such abundance that they spilled over into her body.

6. The Lord came to her in the sixth manner, taking from her the crudeness and clumsiness of body and soul caused by taking food or drink even though she ate seldom and sparingly. He made her graceful, quick, and strong, able to comport herself well and perform heavy, virtuous labor energetically.

7. She noticed clearly his coming to her in the sacrament, killing and

driving out all her vices, that is, all inclination toward sin, to which man is prone through carnal weakness, for man is susceptible to sloth, vainglory, desire for temporal things, impatience, vengefulness. So, as God killed and drove out vice, he brought her much virtue -- obedient humility, adoration, devotion, the strength to perform good deeds, contempt of worldly goods, intense longing for spiritual and heavenly treasures, destruction of worldly renown, a desire for worldly disdain and painful suffering for God's sake and for the sake of justice; immense patience, trust, and hope. Through the wholesome nourishment of the heavenly bread she resisted temptation and accomplished the good. She suffered hard strokes and happily endured whatever the Lord visited upon her.

8. In this form the Lord came to her in a delicious taste and inexpressibly great sweetness of spirit and heart. This happened in a variety of ways, sometimes this way, then that, and on other occasions again different from those but ever more joyously, happily, and comfortingly. This variety was such that she could not differentiate or describe the many kinds of delicious tastes and sweetnesses. It happened frequently that she was overwhelmed when the Lord came to her with yet a new kind of sweetness or yet another delicious taste and amazed at the preciousness of Our Lord. The abundance of this sweetness often poured into all her limbs. Then her mouth was filled with a sweet nectar; her entire body was rejuvenated but burned so fiercely that she sweated as though she were sitting in a steaming hot bath. At times she was convinced she would melt through the intensity of love, joy, and desire, for the passion of the spirit often was so excessive that she thought herself incapable of carrying this burden any longer, even though these joys generally did not last long.

9. Here the Lord came to her with such abundant joy that all her limbs were set into motion and she could not keep them still because of her great bliss.

10. In this manner the Lord came to her with a great banquet in her soul. During this banquet she feasted on heavenly sweetness and ate the fattened calf, that is Our Lord Jesus Christ, who at the behest of the most gracious Father has been killed on the cross for the sake of the prodigal son to atone for our sins. In

the sacrament he was to her sweet beyond measure and more blissful than she was able to describe, and she experienced in it a joy equal to that experienced by all who gather for a banquet. It often happened that when she had received the Lord in the sacrament, she heard with the ears of the spirit the voices of those feasting together and the merriment of a company enjoying such happiness. Often when she found herself partaking of the indescribable merriment of such a spiritual banquet, the Lord said to her: "Now the fattened calf has been slaughtered and good friends have gathered. Now you may smell and taste and feel the great feast of the soul with all your inner and outer senses." Accordingly, she often experienced this banquet through her senses, exactly as the Lord, who is the Truth, had told her.

11. In this the Lord came to her with overflowing consolation and such abundance of wealth that her desires were stilled, satisfied, and killed immediately and she desired nothing more. At such times she forgot all external things and was drawn up high into contemplation of the godhead. From time to time, when she had received the sacrament, she was ravished, deeply immersed in God, and sweetly united with him. While she was thus united and drawn out of herself by God, she was amply served with the most precious potion her soul had ever tasted. Often she heard the angels' song, and in the course of such inexpressible delight, she was aware of the sweet whispering between God and her soul. She also felt the tenderness of the Lord's embraces of her soul and the sweetness of his kisses. At these times she also discerned many other tokens of true friendship between God and her soul. Then, when she was released from her rapture, she was so exhilarated with joy that the hymns sung in church seemed to her as joyous those she had heard sung in eternal life. She tended to remain enraptured for a long time, though longer at some times than others. While she inhabited her cell, it happened now and then that her beautiful face remained caught in the grate of the window after she had received the praiseworthy body or Our Lord. This happened because she was sometimes enraptured the instant she received the sacrament and so didn't even have time to assume a different position.

12. The twelfth way was the Lord coming to her in the form of total spiritual inebriation, for he not only fed her with the heavenly bread of his body but also gave her to drink of his precious blood as of an intoxicating liquor, saying: "Now weep copiously and sober up."

13. Here she felt the Lord remove the inebriation of her spirit if he came to her while she found herself in that state. Whenever that happened, she realized where she really was, for in the drunkenness of spirit she always imagined herself in a foreign country.

14. The fourteenth way came about through numerous kinds of love which the Lord brought with him. Sometimes he came with the hot, burning love, the steaming, wounded, languishing, inebriated, gushing, exhausting, insatiable, or heartbreaking love. Occasionally he also came with one, two, three, or four kinds of love simultaneously or with other kinds of love, the same in number as the ways in which God sent the Holy Spirit. And because one kind of love evokes different emotions and effects than another and two of them together different ones than one or three, or four, it is easy to see that this fourteenth way was most varied, causing as many differences in emotions and effects as the kinds of love the Lord chose to bring her. Each produced special effects in her. The hot, burning love, for example, set her afire to make her hot in body and soul, sometimes more so than at others, and forced her to weep, both privately and in front of others. Under the influence of this love she also sweated profusely. Like the hot, burning love the other kinds of love produced their effects with equal force each time the Lord brought them.

15. In this the Lord brought her an intense desire to die out of all creation, to be dead to everything, to live for God alone and to possess nothing but him and eternal things.

16. Here the Lord brought her an anxious concern for the well-being of other people: that they should not keep on sinning but free themselves from the sins they had committed in the past and live holy lives or at least develop certain virtues and never let go of them.

17. In this the Lord came with excruciating internal and external labor: that is with weeping, sweating, praying, kneeling as well as physical disciplines, self-castigations, and spiritual exercises.

18. In the eighteenth way he imposed heavy pressure. He weighed her down as if he had placed an excruciatingly heavy burden on her.

19. In the nineteenth way he came to her with an uncontrollable hunger and thirst for eternal life. Often her hunger was so strong that she was bedridden. With it the Lord also brought her a new burning desire far more exuberant and of an entirely different nature than any she had felt before. It made her dizzy, and often her heart remained pierced by this desire for three days, all because of this excessive longing and yearning for eternal life and the ultimate good. In this state of desperate yearning she often cried to the Lord, imploring him to take her to him. As she wept and wailed, the heavens were frequently opened to her and the saints, ablaze with hot, burning love, resembled glowing embers. This sight inspired even more severe yearning, setting her body and soul afire too. When she endured hard internal labor, hunger, thirst, and fierce desire for eternal life, the Lord often commented: "The more you suffer hunger, thirst, and yearn for me before receiving me, the more hunger, thirst, and desire you will feel for eternal life after having received me. This great desire and hunger for the sacrament of my true body and for eternal life you and your confessor B shall discuss and record frequently for such yearning and hunger are rare in this world."

20. Here the Lord came promising her eternal life, which she had craved so long and so intensely that she was ailing. With this promise he increased and fortified her trust and hope. After having done this many times, he finally assured her of eternal life and the bliss into which she would enter.

21. In the twenty-first way the Lord came to her far more amiably that at other times and revealed special secrets.

22. In the twenty-second way the Lord came whispering merrily into her ears. On such occasions it often happened that the body of Our Lord impressed itself into her soul immediately so that she could not tell whether it had ever

touched her mouth. But as it reached her soul, it immediately created such intense quiet that she entered a state of profound calm and peace.

23. In the twenty-third way her beloved Lord came to cool her after she had blazed fiercely for him in burning desire.

24. The Lord visited her with his dear mother and cheered her, drawing her with all his might when he and his mother returned to heaven. Often as they left her, the Lord demonstrated the bliss of the saints in eternal life to her and by doing so attracted her even more forcefully to himself and eternal life.

25. The Lord appeared in all his grandeur and omnipotence, that is, he demonstrated the quality of his power so convincingly in a variety of effects and benefits she could neither express nor comprehend. On these occasions his glory made her lose sight of everything else in heaven and on Earth for in his presence all creation fell into oblivion.

26. In the twenty-sixth way the Lord appeared in his divinity. When that happened she could neither taste nor feel the sacrament through the carnal senses all creatures possess. The instant the Lord brought a new delicious taste for her soul she was once again oblivious of all created things.

27. The Lord came to her with the Father and the Holy Spirit, and together the persons of the trinity produced one single effect in her. That was the time when all her inner and outer senses were given so much drink or even made drunk by the spillover of divine sweetness from the soul that she would have felt no horror of suffering any kind of pain, no matter how excruciating or severe, which cruel, fierce pain, torment, or even death might have inflicted on her.

28. In the twenty-eighth way the Lord rushed toward her with tremendous speed, saying: "Behold, I the true god and true man come running to you from my highest throne on a straight, level path. I have worked long and hard to prepare this road." Following the Lord's instructions, she described receiving the sacrament as receiving God's body unbroken, without any taste, smell, or semblance to real bread and its passing from her mouth to the bottom of her heart and soul as God's rushing to her. In this union the two met halfway, that is Lord

and soul rushed toward one another because of their great desire for one another. This the Lord explained through a parable: "I desire you and you desire me. I hasten toward you as speedily as a man rapidly traversing a smooth highway without stopping until I embrace your soul and your soul embraces me."

29. The twenty-ninth way took the form of a spiritual pregnancy during which the Lord gave birth to himself in her soul. Sometimes he enlarged her womb. Then she felt a lovely child moving about this way and that, kicking merrily as though it enjoyed great affection and delight.

30. In the thirtieth way the Lord granted her the power to deliver herself spiritually into eternal life, to give birth spiritually to Our Lord, or to give birth spiritually to other people or bring forth vital spiritual fruit on this Earth.

31. In the thirty-first way he came and made her extremely grateful, imploring, and extraordinarily affectionate toward him. At those times her gratitude was enormous, her prayers and dalliance with the Lord especially affectionate and loving.

32. In this way the Lord came and made her agile and spirited in body and soul. At such times she was often lifted above the ground and floated free of all physical encumbrances.

33. In the thirty-third the Lord came and made her body tremble like an aspen leaf. To relieve her, her most beloved Lord brought her sweet calm and peace. At other times he brought her heavy labor, exertion, inner strife, and restlessness, only to return, once more bringing her tremendous new delights to take away her sadness and tears. At still other times he came and made her weep so hard that the tears flowed without ceasing, as though one tear were chasing the other. Then her sobs and sighs were so uncontrollable and noisy that she was unable to hide her weeping even though she would have liked to conceal it.

34. Here the Lord came to seal her outer senses and open up her inner ones to make them sensitive to the Lord and spiritual treasures.

35. In the thirty-fifth way the Lord appeared wounded all over and dripping blood to tell Dorothea who at such times could not help but feel a

tremendous passion for eternal life: "I have not come to you as the tiny infant I was when I was born. I have come to you as an adult, as wretched as I was when I was hanging on the cross and my body was tormented through and through, destroyed and devoured."

36. The Lord visited her with an abundance of fruit that comforted and gladdened her spirit so lavishly and diversely that she not only found it impossible to describe it: she could not even grasp it in her mind.

37. In the thirty-seventh way the Lord arrived totally inaccessible to her, reminiscent of a closed door. This was the case whenever the Lord was present with some special grace, which she, however, neither quite recognized nor really felt.

How the Lord came to her somberly and made her despondent.

Chapter V.

The blessed Dorothea also discerned or felt many more complex ones originating from these single sensations, more of them than one could possibly record. So let it suffice to contemplate just five of the many she spoke of: Concerning the first of these, she said: "When the Lord came to me in the sacrament he was somber and stern with ailing love, desirous love, and great bitterness of body and soul. He impressed himself upon my soul like a sprig of myrrh, and indeed I felt him in this wise. More than that, he not only was somber but restive, disquieting body and soul. A great tempest was raging in them, and they suffered great restlessness, hunger and thirst for eternal life, which the Lord had awakened with his arrival. Needless to say, my soul was deeply troubled by all this and dared not meet him halfway to receive him." Nor did she dare caress him with graceful, affectionate speech or prepare the feast she customarily did for the most beloved guest Jesus Christ when his arrival was joyous. "When I had been sitting there for a long time, listening despondently to hear whether he would say something but he remained silent, my soul became disturbed and oppressed and began to cry out to the Lord with a loud voice to caress and beseech him.

My soul sought rest and peace but found them not.

"At last the Lord spoke to me: 'You want to be gratified constantly. So what hunger are you still willing to endure for me? It has been a long time now since you have really hungered for eternal life after receiving my worthy body.'" As the Lord spoke, her soul began to wail. "I responded through my soul: 'Most beloved Lord, at all times I would rather be satisfied through you than to hunger for you.' The Lord replied: 'Since yesterday when you received me in the sacrament, I have stayed with you in a singular manner, keeping you in a state of immense joy and satisfaction until you received me again just now. Therefore, hunger for me now!' As soon as the Lord said this, body and soul felt fierce hunger to enjoy peace in the Lord -- the body in its grave and the soul in heaven. They began to wage war against one another, desirous to be separated and were sore afraid. They were oppressed by the solemnity of Our Lord, who said: 'when your soul is troubled, all the powers that previously shared your pleasure are fully engaged.' Then as hunger, thirst, and my labors for God and eternal life tormented me even more painfully than before, the Lord said to me: 'Such torment I endured on Good Friday when I suffered martyrdom for you. Therefore, suffer the same for my sake and take to heart all I do for you. For I do all this for your own good, for the blessedness of your soul, to make certain of your being taken up into eternal life that much more readily.'"

How, after she had suffered severe pain,

the Lord came rushing toward her and set her afire.

Chapter VI.

"Another day," Dorothea said, "I was ignited by the Holy Spirit, which was sent to me often. I wept so hotly, imploring and caressing the Lord that I did not notice the Lord being elevated during mass. Now that the moment had come for me to receive him, the Lord commanded me to weep copiously, to fall on my face, and to pray to him for the sake of Christendom with all its shortcomings. As I was praying, the entire world appeared before me replete with all its problems and the many grievous sins in so many people. While I was praying as I had been commanded for the sake of others and my own, imploring him to prepare me properly for him, I was choked with tears and sadness and did not know how to comport myself to receive my beloved Lord.

"But as I did receive him, he came to me, the most beloved Lord, rushing toward me in his divinity with many kinds of love, giving pleasure, sweetness, and heaviness to body and soul. To my eyes he granted gentle tears; my soul, because of hot, burning love shouted many a loving, cheerful phrase as she rushed forth to meet him, something like 'a most praiseworthy, honored guest has arrived.' During these caresses my soul called the Lord by names such as these: 'My guardian, protector, keeper! My blessedness and confidant, savior, master, advisor, superior, benefactor.' Later the Lord said to me: 'Speak thus: Lord Jesus Christ, command all my strength and senses, external and internal, to serve you.' As I was burning, sweating, and weeping in the throes of searing hot, burning love, the Lord was most gracious to me. He stood over me, admonishing me always to labor still more, caress him more, and to keep on weeping with the same fire of love so that he would not need to inflame me further. In response to this admonition gentle tears fell from my eyes and rivers of sweat ran over my body. I was burning so fiercely that, sweating and weeping in severe hot, burning love I implored, caressed, and thanked him for more than six hours without ceasing. During these six hours, whenever I wanted to stop to get a little rest, the Lord urged me not to relent or stop, and to help me persevere, he sent me the Holy Spirit with his inexhaustible love."

How at the end of her sufferings the Lord brought her many gifts
and suffused the forces of her body and soul.

Chapter VII.

"One morning, as I came to after an intense rapture and got up, I felt immense pain and discomfort. It hurt me so much and made me so ill that I could not even open my mouth to pray. I started to faint because my heart was so hot and my body sweated so profusely from the heat. Spiritual hunger pained me so much that I lay down again, thinking 'since I cannot prepare myself for the praiseworthy body of Our Lord through prayer, I will have to forego him today.' However, as soon as I had bedded down, my beloved Lord called me: 'Rise quickly and prepare yourself to receive me in the sacrament.' I rose immediately, even though I was so ill that I was unable to stand up. So I supported myself with both hands as best I could to get down on my knees to pray. In the course of the prayer I recited in preparation for receiving him I gained such powerful longing for the Lord that I could scarcely wait for the sacrament, and even though the pain crucified me, I was filled with joy, knowing it had a spiritual, not a physical source.

"As I received the sacrament, the Lord came to me divinely, mightily, amply, joyfully and with his hot, burning love. This love brought me an abundance of burning tears. But though they welled from my eyes burning like flames, they did not burn me, injuring neither my eyes nor my cheeks. They were sweet and gentle, an excellent balm for my eyes. In truth, I felt how the Lord suffused all the powers of my body and soul with his joyful strength, restoring them internally and externally, comforting and gladdening every part of me. There was nothing in my body or my soul that was not touched and penetrated by this joyous, divine strength and sweetened to a far greater degree than it had previously been filled with bitterness. I also felt how during the visitation described here perfect health and strength were granted to me. I felt no more discomfort, ailment, or pain. As I marveled over this miraculous visitation, tremendous gratitude, ardent, prayerful adoration and delightful dalliance accompanied by many tears rose in me.

"All this the Lord had accomplished, who then said: 'Gratitude, prayer, and dalliance with such tears shall be your most convincing proof of my having brought about these good things in you. And when they have become so much a part of you to make you even more grateful, prayerful, and open to dallying with such hot, happy tears, there will be no more need for you to worry about being deceived by the evil, deceitful spirit. Moreover, just as I had oppressed all your inner and outer strength and visited you with severe hunger pangs and yearning for me, I now visit all your energies with comfort and joy. But those who do not hunger for me and are not tormented by any longing for me also can't be delighted by receiving me. You, on the other hand, to receive me, shall perform a tremendous amount of hard labor involving all your strength. Such labor is seldom seen on Earth and known only to very few human beings. Certainly there are many who wish to receive me, but very few of them are willing to take on the tremendous labor they would have to perform for my sake.'"

How the Lord Jesus Christ, Dorothea's heavenly bridegroom,

visited her with a great throng of saints

and filled her soul with many joys.

He suffused her, ignited and softened her,

and securely locked the palace of her soul

when she had received the holy, praiseworthy sacrament

of his body.

Chapter VIII.

On the Sunday following the octave of Christ's appearance [January 6], when Dorothea was cruelly tormented by spiritual hunger and had shed many tears, Mary, the mother of mercy, appeared to her, inclined toward her with maternal pity, and said: "You have helped me bathe my child. Therefore, I will prepare him now and bring him to you at once." When she, the mother of mercy, had said this, the Lord told Dorothea: "Say this to her: 'Oh, my most beloved mother, deign to come to me with your child without delay. You know well that I can't stand waiting any longer!'" When Dorothea had done as she was bidden, the Lord said: "I am now standing at your door and want to enter right away." When she heard this, she begged him with hot tears not to tarry. The Lord replied: "I hurry to you at the same speed as you rush to receive me, and whoever is famished with hunger for me will be fed abundantly." With these words the

Lord opened the eyes of his elected bride Dorothea so she could see how appropriately Jesus her bridegroom prepared himself to visit her in the company of his honorable mother and this heavenly courtiers. This honey-sweet vision ignited the bride Dorothea more passionately than ever before, and her spirit cried with a loud voice: "Lord Jesus Christ, son of the living God, my sweet blessed Lord, mercifully come to me!"

Upon hearing her pleading voice, the bridegroom endowed his bride Dorothea so richly with his treasures that she could describe neither the magnitude nor the quality of all this wealth. He prepared a sumptuous feast for her soul and granted her the overflowing love with all attendant properties, which are too extensive and varied to be enumerated. Dorothea's body and soul were filled with sweetness and were burning so fiercely with hot, burning love that there was no part of the bride's body that did not feel fiery heat. She was also so inundated and saturated by this divine sweetness that to her both heaven and Earth seemed to be flowing with milk and honey: more, the entire Earth appeared changed, as though all people were holy and full of spiritual wealth. Dorothea assumed this because of the abundance of spiritual wealth and sweetness in herself, just as the drunkard assumes that everyone else is drunk as well.

Dorothea, the blessed bride, felt the tremendous effects of her beloved Lord and bridegroom and of his merciful visitations at work in her, and the more she feasted on his heavenly sweetness the more the fire of divine love fanned the flames in her body and soul. Her bridegroom appeared to her in such magnificent estate that she trembled like an aspen leaf. She and all her servants, that is all her internal strength and senses, holy thoughts and virtues, were seated properly and introduced themselves politely to the bridegroom who said to her: "What better thing could you have done than to long for me passionately and to give yourself and sacrifice yourself entirely to me? Whoever desires passionately to possess me on Earth shall share my wealth and honor for eternity. Look up and take note: as my bride I have endowed you and your servants with plenty. The fattened calf, that is I, has been slaughtered, and a sumptuous feast is prepared." As the Lord spoke, the mass to be celebrated in the presence of the bride began, and she was totally overwhelmed by the intensity of her bridegroom's love. Softened by divine passion, she started to melt, convinced that she could not endure it any longer. But she pulled herself together and purely illuminated gazed upon her palace, that is her soul, which she found beautifully appointed. At the bottom was humility, true love at the top and all about, and the entire palace was adorned with various virtues throughout.

As she beheld herself in truth, beautifully adorned by her bridegroom, the Holy Spirit inspired her spirit to exclaim loudly: "You sweet wind from the east, perfume my palace with roses and lilies and all kinds of flowers!" Immediately the bridegroom wafted through her palace, that is her soul, with hot, burning love, deep humility, and numerous spiritual blessings, saying: "Much of the treasure I have given to my bride to adorn her palace is the same my saints enjoy in eternal life and is just as indescribable here as it is in eternity." When the bride Dorothea heard this, she fixed her gaze entirely on her bridegroom to contemplate him alone, whom she now saw nearby with a huge powerful well-equipped host, rushing toward her with great speed. Seeing this, hot, burning love and passionate desire made her cry out with a loud voice: "Oh my holy, all-powerful king, my rich and blessed king, come to me with your mercy." Without taking her eyes off her glorious bridegroom she continued this joyful, adoring shout until he entered her palace, that is her soul, through the sacrament of his praiseworthy body. He approached her comfortingly and revealed many secrets, filling her soul brimful with divine treasure, like a sack that is being stuffed until, stretched to the limit, it is chock full, unable to hold more without tearing.

As soon as the bridegroom had entered the palace of her soul, it was locked at once so that no one could leave or enter. And the bridegroom said: "You shall at all times do good deeds and live a holy life. The more you grasp of me, the more you shall enjoy my presence. You still don't understand clearly and fully just how great a treasure I am -- how merciful, just, wise, and great -- and how much grace I possess. But these qualities you can never comprehend fully until you come to your place in eternal life, where you will behold me clearly without end and will enjoy me passionately, never desiring to do anything but sing joyous, sweet hymns of praise to me."

The fifth way,

which is recorded in the XXVI. chapter of the third book

Chapter IX.

The Lord came to his elected bride Dorothea through the sacrament in so many other ways that it would be too much to record them all, though the hungry ones will not be satisfied with this. But here the XXVI. chapter of the third book can be shown or cited as the fifth way. The Lord also often instructed her how she was to prepare herself and how she was to thank him; how she was to plead with him to come to her and stay with her day and night, eat and drink with her, and never abandon her or leave her in misery, but take her with him into eternal life. Amen.

Here ends the life history of the blessed woman Dorothea,

anchoress at Marienwerder

in the episcopal see of Pomesania in the land of Prussia.

Bibliography

Barstow, Anne L. Introduction. *A Mirror for Simple Souls.* By Marguerite Porete. Trans. Charles Crawford. New York: Crossroads, 1990.

Bell, Rudolph M. *Holy Anorexia.* Chicago: U of Chicago P, 1985.

Benz, Ernst. *Die Vision--Erfahrungsformen und Bilderwelt.* Stuttgart: Klett, 1969.

Bogdanowicz, Ks. Stanislaw. *Dziela Sztuki Sakralnej Bazyliki Mariackiej W Gdansku.* Gdansk: Zbigniew Bryk, 1990.

Bowie, Fiona, and Oliver Davies, eds. *Beguine Spirituality: Mystical Writings of Mechthild von Magdeburg, Beatriejs of Nazareth, and Hadewijch of Brabant.* New York: Crossroads, 1989.

Bryant, Gwendolyn. "The French Heretic Beguine Marguerite Porete." *Medieval Women Writers.* Ed. Katharina Wilson. Athens: U of Georgia P, 1984. 204-26.

Bynum, Caroline Walker. "'...And Woman His Humanity': Female Imagery in the Religious Writing of the Later Middle Ages." *Gender and Religion.* Eds. Caroline Walker Bynum, Steven Harrell, and Pamela Richman. Boston: Beacon, 1986. 257-88.

---. *Fragmentation and Redemption.* New York: Zone, 1992.

---. *Jesus as Mother.* Berkeley: U of California P, 1982.

Cumming, William P., ed. *The Revelations of Saint Birgitta.* London: EETS, 1929.

Eimer, Brigitte. *Gotland unter dem deutschen Orden.* Innsbruck: Wagner, 1966.

Firtel, Hilde. *Dorothea von Montau: Eine deutsche Mystikerin.* Freiburg: Kanisius, 1968.

Funk, Philipp. "Zur Geschichte der Frömmigkeit und Mystik im Ordenslande Preußen." *Zeitschrift für die Geschichte und Altertumskunde Ermlands* 30 (1960): 1-37.

Grass, Günter. *Der Butt.* Darmstadt: Luchterhand, 1977.

Heise, Joh. *Die Bau-und Kunstdenkmäler der Provinz Westpreussen.* Vol. 11. Gdansk: Bertling, 1898.

Helm, Karl, and Walter Ziesemer. *Die Literatur des deutschen Ritterordens.* Gießen: Schmitz, 1951.

Hipler, Franz. "Christliche Lehre und Erziehung in Ermland und im preußischen Ordenstaate während des Mittelalters." *Zeitschrift für die Geschichte und Altertumskunde Ermlands* 6 (1877): 81-183.

---. "Johannes von Marienwerder, der Beichtvater der seligen Dorothea von Montau." 1864. *Zeitschrift für die Geschichte und Altertumskunde Ermlands* 29 (1956): 1-92.

Hollywood, Amy. *The Soul as Virgin Wife.* Notre Dame and London: U of Notre Dame P, 1995.

Horst, Ulrich P. "Beiträge zum Einfluss Taulers auf das Deutschordensland Preußen." *Johannes Tauler: Ein deutscher Mystiker.* Ed. E. Filthaut. Essen: Driewer, 1961. 408-21.

Johannes von Marienwerder. "Des leben der zeligen frawen Dorothee clewsenerynne in der thumkyrchen czu Marienwerdir des landes czu Prewszen." Ed. Max Toeppen. *Scriptores rerum Prussicarum.* Vol. 2. Eds. Theodor Hirsch, Max Toeppen, and Ernst Strehlke. 1863. Frankfurt/Main: Minerva, 1965.

Jorgensen, Johannes. *Saint Bridget of Sweden.* 2 Vols. Trans. Ingeborg Lund. London: Longman's, 1954.

Kieckhefer, Richard. *Unquiet Souls: Fourteenth-Century Saints and Their Religious Milieu.* Chicago: U of Chicago P, 1984.

Korioth, Dom. "*Vita Dorotheae* in moderner Sprache." *Zeitschrift für die Geschichte und Altertumskunde Ermlands* 10 (1893): 297-504.

McLaughlin, Eleanor. "The Heresy of the Free Spirit in Late-Medieval Mysticism." *Medievalia et Humanistica* 4 (1973): 37-54.

Meinhold, Peter. "Die Marienverehrung in der deutschen Mystik." *Saeculum* 27 (1976): 180-96.

Neel, Carol. "The Origin of the Beguines." *Sisters and Workers in the Middle Ages*. Eds. Judith M. Bennett, et al. Chicago: U of Chicago P, 1989. 240-60.

Newman, Barbara. *From Virile Woman to Woman Christ*. Philadelphia: U of Pennsylvania P, 1995.

Nieborowski, Paul. *Die selige Dorothea von Preußen*. Breslau: Ostdeutsche Verlagsanstalt, 1933.

Obrist, Barbara. "The Swedish Visionary and Saint Bridget." *Medieval Women Writers*. Ed. Katharina Wilson. Athens: U of Georgia P, 1984. 227-51.

Petroff, Elizabeth A. *Body and Soul*. New York: Oxford U P, 1994.

---, ed. *Medieval Women's Visionary Literature*. New York: Oxford U P, 1986.

Rossmann, Heribert. "Johannes Marienwerder O. T., ein ostdeutscher Theologe des späten Mittelalters." *Archive für Kirchengeschichte von Böhmen-Mähren-Schlesien* 3 (1973): 221-53.

Rühle, Siegfried. "Dorothea von Montau: Das Lebensbild einer Danziger Bürgerin des XIV. Jahrhunderts." *Altpreußische Forschungen* 2 (1925): 59-101.

Schleiff, A. "Die Bedeutung Johannes Marienwerders für Theologie und Frömmigkeit im Ordensland Preußen." *Zeitschrift für Kirchengeschichte* 60 (1941): 49-66.

Stachnik, Richard ed. *Die Akten des Kanonisationsprozesses Dorotheas von Montau von 1394-1521*. Köln: Böhlau, 1978.

---. "Die Geistliche Lehre Dorotheas." *Zeitschrift für Ostforschungen* 3 (1954): 589-96.

---. "Die Klosterchronik von St. Birgitten in Danzig." *Zeitschrift für die Geschichte und Altertumskunde Ermlands* 30 (1957): 63-119.

Stachnik, Richard, and Anneliese Triller, eds. *Dorothea von Montau: Eine preußische Heilige des 14. Jahrhunderts.* Münster: Selbstverlag des Historischen Vereins für Ermland, 1976.

Stammler, Wolfgang. "Studien zur Geschichte der Mystik in Norddeutschland." *Altdeutsche und Altniederländische Mystik.* Ed. Kurt Ruh. Darmstadt: Wissenschaftliche Buchgesellschaft, 1964. 386-436.

Stargardt, Ute. "The Beguines of Belgium, the Dominican Nuns of Germany, and Margery Kempe." *The Popular Literature of Medieval England.* Ed. Thomas J. Heffernan. Knoxville: U of Tennessee P, 1985. 277-313.

---. "Dorothea von Montau, the Language of Love, and Jacop Karweysze, 'goltsmyd.'" *The Ring of Words in Medieval Literature.* Eds. Ulrich Goebel and David Lee. Lewiston, N.Y.: Mellen, 1993. 305-321.

---. "Male Clerical Authority in the Spiritual (Auto)biographies of Medieval Holy Women." *Women as Protagonists and Poets in the German Middle Ages.* Ed. Albrecht Classen. Göppingen: Kümmerle, 1991. 209-38.

---. "The Political and Social Backgrounds of the Canonization of Dorothea von Montau." *Mystics Quarterly* 11 (1985): 107-22.

---. "Whose Life History is this Anyway? Johannes von Marienwerder's Narrative Strategies in the German *Vita* of Dorothea von Montau." *Michigan Academician* 27 (1995): 39-56.

Toeppen, Max, ed. "Aus den anderen Schriften Johann Marienwerders." *Scriptores rerum Prussicarum.* Vol. 2. 1863. Frankfurt/Main: Minerva, 1965.

Triller, Anneliese. "Der Kanonisationsprozess Dorotheas von Montau in Marienwerder 1394-1405 als Quelle altpreußischer Kulturgeschichte und Volkskunde." *Preußenland und Deutscher Orden.* Würzburg: Holzner, 1958. 309-43.

---. "Häresien in Altpreußen um 1390?" *Studien zur Geschichte des Preußenlandes.* Ed. Ernst Bahr. Marburg: Elwert, 1963. 397-404.

---. "Konrad von Wallenrodt, Hochmeister des Deutschen Ordens (1391-1393), im Spiegel der Quellen über Dorothea von Montau." *Zeitschrift für die Geschichte und Altertumskunde Ermlands* 34 (1970): 21-43.

Weinstein, Donald, and Rudolph M. Bell. *Saints and Society: The Two Worlds of Western Civilization, 1000-1700.* Chicago: U of Chicago P, 1982.

Wentzlaff-Eggebert, Friedrich Wilhelm. "Erscheinungsformen der *unio mystica* in der deutschen Literatur und Dichtung." *Belehrung und Verkündigung.* Ed. Manfred Dick und Gerhard Kaiser. Berlin: de Gryuter, 1975. 86-123.

Westpfahl, Hans. *Dorothea von Montau.* Meitingen: Kyrios, 1949.

---. Introduction. *Vita Dorotheae Montoviensis magistri Johannis Marienwerder.* Köln: Böhlau, 1964.

Wisniewski, Tadeusz. *Dom und Schloß zu Kwydzyn (Marienwerder).* Kwydzyn: Gesellschaft für Freunde der Stadt und Land Kwydzyn, 1994.

Index

STUDIES IN WOMEN AND RELIGION

DATE DUE

HIGHSMITH #45230

Printed
in USA